INSTANT REFERENCE

BRITISH HISTORY

TEACH YOURSELF®

For UK orders: please contact Bookpoint Ltd, 78 Milton Park, Abingdon, Oxon 0X14 4TD. Telephone: (44) 01235 400414, Fax: (44) 01235 400454. Lines are open 9.00–6.00, Monday to Saturday, with a 24-hour message answering service. E-mail address: orders@bookpoint.co.uk

For USA and Canada orders: please contact NTC/Contemporary Publishing, 4255 West Touhy Avenue, Lincolnwood, Illinois 60646-1975, USA. Telephone: (847) 679 5500, Fax: (847) 679 2494.

Long renowned as the authoritative source for self-guided learning – with more than 40 million copies sold worldwide – the *Teach Yourself* series includes over 200 titles in the fields of languages, crafts, hobbies, business, computing and education.

British Library Cataloguing in Publication Data
A catalogue record for this title is available from the British Library.

Library of Congress Catalog Card Number: On file

First published in UK 2000 by Hodder Headline Plc, 338 Euston Road, London NW1 3BH.

First published in US by NTC/Contemporary Publishing, 4255 West Touhy Avenue, Lincolnwood (Chicago), Illinois 60646-1975, USA.

The 'Teach Yourself' name and logo are registered trademarks of Hodder & Stoughton.

Copyright © 2000 Helicon Publishing Ltd

Picture credits: Hulton Getty Picture Library 5, 19, 60, 120, 142, 164, 174, 195; Lionheart Books 7, 39, 81, 85, 87, 115, 125, 150, 189, 198, 201; Fotomas Index 17, 26, 55, 62, 69, 76, 94, 99, 107, 112, 136, 146, 159, 176.

Text editors: Michael March and Bender Richardson White
Typeset by TechType, Abingdon, Oxon
Printed in Great Britain for Hodder & Stoughton Educational, a division of Hodder Headline Plc, 338 Euston Road, London NW1 3BH, by Cox & Wyman Ltd, Reading, Berkshire.

Impression number   10 9 8 7 6 5 4 3 2 1
Year   2006   2005   2004   2003   2002   2001   2000

Contents

Bold type in the text indicates a cross reference. A plural, or possessive, is given as the cross reference, i.e. is in bold type, even if the entry to which it refers is singular.

abdication crisis

The constitutional upheaval of 16 November to 10 December 1936, caused by the British king **Edward VIII's** decision to marry Wallis Simpson, an American divorcee. For the king, as the 'Supreme Governor' of the Church of England, to marry a divorced person was unacceptable, and on 10 December Edward abdicated and went to live in France. He was succeeded by his younger brother, the Duke of York, who became King **George VI**. Edward was made Duke of Windsor and married Mrs Simpson on 3 June 1937.

act of Parliament

A law that originates in **Parliament**. It is also called a statute. The body of English statute law includes all the acts passed by Parliament, from 1235 to the present. An act of Parliament may be public (general in its effect), local, or private. Unless an act is stated to be of a fixed duration, it remains on the statute book until it is repealed.

Before an act of Parliament becomes law, it is called a bill. Not all bills succeed in reaching the statute books. To do so, a bill must complete its passage through Parliament, as follows, and be formally approved by the Queen.

- *First reading.* The title of the bill is read out in the House of **Commons**. After this, the bill is officially published.

- *Second reading.* Members of the Commons debate the bill and vote on whether it should proceed to the next stage.

- *Committee stage.* A committee of members of Parliament looks at the bill in detail and makes amendments.

- *Report stage.* The bill goes back to the Commons, where further amendments may be made.

- *House of **Lords**.* The bill goes through several stages, as in the Commons.

- *Last amendments.* The House of Commons considers any amendments proposed by the Lords and makes any final changes.

- *Royal assent.* The Queen gives her formal assent, and the bill becomes an act of Parliament and enters the statute books.

Adams, Gerry (Gerard) (1948–)

Northern Ireland politician, president of **Sinn Féin** (the political wing of the **Irish Republican Army**) since 1978. He was elected to the House of Commons from Belfast West between 1983 and 1992 and from 1997, but did not take his seat.

In 1991, he began moving his party toward a strategy of peace talks and opened discussions with John **Hume**, the leader of the Social Democratic Labour Party. In August 1994 the IRA declared a ceasefire, thanks largely to Adams's efforts. This broke down in February 1996 but was resumed in July 1997. In 1998, Adams signed the 'Good Friday agreement', renouncing violence and allowing his party to be represented in a Northern Ireland assembly.

Afghan Wars

Wars waged by Britain against Afghanistan over Russian influence in Afghanistan and the threat to British India.

- *First Afghan War; 1838–42.* The British invaded Afghanistan to put a pro-British emir, Shashoja, on the throne. The Afghans rebelled, wiping out the British garrison at Kabul, and the previous emir was restored after Britain withdrew.

- *Second Afghan War; 1878–80.* The British invaded a second time when Emir Shir Ali received a Russian mission but would not accept a British one. Under the terms of the Treaty of Gandamak, in May 1879, Britain gained territory and the right to an envoy in Kabul. However, the murder of the envoy several months later led to British troops occupying Kabul and eventually to the defeat of the Afghans in 1880.

- *Third Afghan War; 1919.* When Afghan troops attacked British India, Britain sent an aeroplane to Kabul, the first ever seen there. This proved enough to secure peace, by the Treaty of Rawlpindi, which also guaranteed full independence for Afghanistan.

Agincourt, Battle of

A battle of the **Hundred Years' War** in which **Henry V** of England defeated the French on 25 October 1415. The French lost more than 6,000 troops compared with only 1,600 on the English side. Henry's victory, which owed much to the superiority of the English longbow, gained him control of France, and the French princess Catherine de Valois as his bride. The village of Agincourt (modern-day Azincourt) is south of Calais, in northern France.

Agricola, Gnaeus Julius (AD 37–93)

A Roman general who became governor of Britain from AD 78 to 85. He romanized the south of England and extended Roman rule to the Firth of Forth in Scotland. His fleet sailed round the north of Scotland, proving that Britain was an island. He was the first Roman to subdue Britain effectively, but was recalled to Rome by the emperor Domitian, who was jealous of his success.

agricultural revolution

Sweeping changes that took place in British agriculture between about 1750 and 1850 to meet the increased demand for food from a fast-growing population. The changes included the **enclosure** of open fields, the introduction of crop rotation, the use of winter feeds, such as turnips, for cattle, the development of inbreeding to produce improved livestock strains, and the use of machinery. Some of these changes took place before 1750, whereas farm mechanization did not occur till after 1859.

Recent research has shown these changes to be part of a much larger, ongoing developmental process, in which scientific and technological advances in the 20th century have further revolutionized agriculture.

Agricultural revolution: chronology

c. 1701	Jethro Tull develops the seed drill and the horse-drawn hoe.
1745	Robert Bakewell begins experiments to improve livestock.
1760s	Start of widespread enclosure of common fields and wasteland.
1783	First plough factory in England.
1785	Cast-iron ploughshare patented.
1793	Invention of the cotton gin.
1800	Early threshing machines developed.
1820s	First nitrates for fertilizer imported from South America.
1830	Reaping machines developed in Scotland.
1850s	Use of clay pipes for drainage well established.
1850s–90s	Major developments in transport and refrigeration technology alter the nature of agricultural markets with crops, dairy products, and wheat being shipped internationally.

Alamein, El, Battles of

Two major battles of **World War II** fought in the northwestern deserts of Egypt. Defeat for Germany in the second battle effectively ended its North Africa Campaign.

- *The first battle, 1–27 July 1942.* The British 8th Army under Auchinleck successfully held off attacks by German and Italian forces led by Rommel. Neither side could claim a victory.
- *The second battle, 24 October–4 November 1942.* Australian troops diverted Rommel's forces by attacking along the coast road, so that the 8th Army, now under **Montgomery's** command, could launch an attack farther south. A major tank battle followed, in which the Germans were heavily outnumbered. By 3 November Rommel had only 30 serviceable tanks in action and the next day he began his withdrawal.

Alfred the Great (*c.* 849–*c.* 901)
Anglo-Saxon king of Wessex who founded the first English navy and introduced a legal code, the 'Dooms' of Alfred. He also encouraged the translation of works from Latin (some he translated himself), and promoted the development of the **Anglo-Saxon Chronicle**.

Alfred was born at Wantage, Oxfordshire, the youngest son of Ethelwulf, king of the West Saxons. In 870 Alfred and his brother Ethelred fought many battles against the Danes, and in 871 Alfred succeeded Ethelred as king. By the Peace of Wedmore in 878 the Danish leader Guthrum agreed to withdraw from Wessex and from Mercia west of Watling Street. But a new landing in Kent encouraged a revolt of the East Anglian Danes, which was suppressed in 884–86. After the final foreign invasion was defeated in 892–96, Alfred strengthened the navy to prevent fresh incursions.

> ❝ Many Franks, Gauls, Pagans, Britons, Scots, and Armoricans, nobles and poor men alike, submitted voluntarily to his dominion; all of whom he ruled, loved, honoured and enriched as if they were his own people. ❞
>
> **Welsh monk Asser**, *Life of Alfred, c.* 900

Allenby, Edmund, 1st Viscount Allenby (1861–1936)
British **World War I** field marshal who captured Jerusalem from the Turks. He served in France before taking command of the British forces in the Middle East from 1917 to 1919. After taking Jerusalem, he drove the Turkish army through Syria before securing the armistice of Mudros in September 1918. He was made a viscount in 1919 and served as high commissioner in Egypt from 1919 till 1935.

American Revolution or American War of Independence

A revolt by the British North American colonies that resulted in the founding of the United States of America. The war lasted from 1775 till 1783.

Resentment by the colonists grew from 1765 after the imposition of taxation through the **Stamp Act** and the Townshend Act, which levied duties on imported goods, including tea.

The first real battle, at **Bunker Hill** in 1775, was a limited victory for the British, but they finally lost the war at Yorktown in 1781. The independence of the United States was recognized by Britain in 1783, although Canada remained a British territory.

> ❝It is inseparably essential to the freedom of a people, and the undoubted right of Englishmen, that no taxes be imposed on them but with their own consent given personally or by their representatives. ❞
>
> Letter to the British government from the nine colonies attending the Stamp Act Congress, 1765

Amritsar Massacre or Jallianwallah Bagh Massacre

The slaughter of Indian demonstrators by British troops at a Sikh religious shrine in the Punjab in 1919. The soldiers opened fire without warning on a crowd of some 10,000 who had gathered to protest at the arrest of two Indian National Congress leaders. Three hundred and seventy-nine were shot dead and 1,200 wounded.

Anderson, Elizabeth Garrett (1836–1917)

The first English woman to qualify in medicine. Refused entry to medical school, she studied privately and was licensed by the

Anderson *Elizabeth Garrett Anderson as a doctor, c. 1875.*

Society of Apothecaries in London in 1865. She was physician to the Marylebone Dispensary for Women and Children (later renamed the Elizabeth Garrett Anderson Hospital). In 1873 she became the first female member of the British Medical Association and was dean of the London School of Medicine for Women from 1883 to 1903.

Anglo-Dutch Wars

Three conflicts between Britain and the Netherlands between 1650 and 1674.

- *The first war (1652–54)* was sparked by the **Navigation Act** of 1651, which aimed to minimize the role of the Netherlands in maritime trade. It ended with the Dutch making heavy concessions.
- *The second war (1665–67)* was caused by a clash over British and Dutch colonial possessions in Africa and North America. A compromise was eventually reached.
- *The third war (1672–74)*, in which Britain was at first allied with France, ended with the Dutch recognizing New York as British.

Anglo-Irish Agreement or Hillsborough Agreement

Agreement reached in 1985 between the UK premier Margaret **Thatcher** and Irish premier Garret FitzGerald. It increased cooperation between police and security forces in Northern Ireland and the Republic of Ireland and gave the Irish Republic a greater voice in the conduct of Northern Ireland's affairs. It was rejected by Northern Ireland Unionists who saw it as a step towards renunciation of British sovereignty.

After further talks in 1993, the UK premier John Major and the Irish premier Albert Reynolds issued a joint statement declaring that the consent of the majority of the people of Northern Ireland would be required before there could be any constitutional change.

After the **Irish Republican Army** declared a permanent ceasefire in July 1997, multiparty peace talks on the future of Northern Ireland started in September 1997. This led in 1998 to elections to a Northern Ireland assembly, which included members of **Sinn Féin**, the political wing of the IRA.

Anglo-Saxon Chronicle

A history of England from the Roman invasion to the 11th century, consisting of a series of seven chronicles written in Old English by monks, begun in the 9th century (during the reign of King **Alfred**), and continuing until 1154.

❝ In this king's time there was nothing but disturbance and wickedness and robbery, for forthwith the powerful men who were traitors rose up against him. ❞

Anglo-Saxon Chronicle, referring to the reign of King Stephen

Anglo-Saxons

Germanic invaders of Britain between the 5th and 7th centuries. They included Angles, Saxons, and Jutes. The Angles and Saxons came from Schleswig-Holstein, and the Jutes were probably from the Rhineland. The invaders established conquest kingdoms in Britain, which were united in the early 9th century under the overlordship of **Wessex**.

The Norman invasion by William the Conqueror in 1066 put an end to Anglo-Saxon rule.

Anglo-Zulu War

A conflict between British forces in South Africa and the Zulu nation in 1878–79.

As the British extended their South African colonies northwards, they came into conflict with the Zulus under their king Cetshwayo. He was captured and defeated in 1879. Zululand became a British protectorate and in 1897 part of the British colony of Natal.

Anne (1665–1714)

Queen of Great Britain and Ireland from 1702 to 1704. She was the second daughter of James, Duke of York, who became James II, and his first wife, Anne Hyde. She had a Protestant upbringing, and in 1683 married Prince George of Denmark. Of their many children, only one survived infancy: William, Duke of Gloucester (1689–1700). Anne deserted her father for William of Orange, her brother-in-law, during the **Glorious Revolution** of 1688, but she later engaged in **Jacobite** intrigues.

She became queen on William's death in 1702 and, although her sympathies

Anne *The Great Seal of Queen Anne, after the Union of 1707.*

were Tory, she accepted a predominantly Whig government in 1704–10. Anne's family loyalty convinced her that her successor should be her father's son by his second wife (Mary of Modena), James Edward Stuart, known as the Old Pretender. However, the Act of **Settlement** in 1701 ensured Protestant succession to the throne, and Anne was succeeded by George I, great-grandson of James I.

Anselm, St (*c.* 1033–1109)

Italian philosopher-priest who became archbishop of Canterbury. He made the abbey of Bec, in Normandy, a centre of scholarship in Europe during his time as abbot from 1078. Appointed archbishop of Canterbury by **William II** of England in 1093, he was later forced into exile, but was recalled as archbishop of Canterbury by **Henry I**. Anselm holds an important place in the development of scholasticism.

Anselm was canonized in 1494, and his feast day is 21 April.

Anson, George, 1st Baron Anson (1697–1762)

English admiral who sailed round the world. In 1740 he commanded the South American squadron and attacked Spanish colonies and shipping. He returned home by circumnavigating the globe, loaded with £500,000 of Spanish treasure. Appointed to the Board of the Admiralty in 1745, he increased the efficiency of the British fleet, which contributed to its success in the **Seven Years' War** (1756–63) against France.

Anti-Corn Law League

An extra-parliamentary campaign group formed in September 1838 by Manchester industrialists to oppose the **Corn Laws**. Led by Liberals Richard **Cobden** and John **Bright**, the league argued for free trade and a halt to duties imposed on foreign corn imports.

The league initiated strategies for popular mobilization and agitation including mass meetings, lecture tours, pamphleteering, opinion polls, and parliamentary lobbying.

In June 1846 political pressure, the state of the economy, and the Irish potato famine prompted Prime Minister Peel to repeal the Corn Laws.

Anzio, Battle of

Beachhead invasion of Italy between 22 January and 23 May 1944 by Allied troops during World War II. Failure to use information obtained from deciphering German codes caused Allied troops to be stranded following German attacks. After five months, the breach of defences at Monte Cassino enabled the US 5th Army to dislodge the Germans from the Alban Hills and the Anzio force to begin its advance on Rome.

appeasement
Conciliatory policy by the British government, particularly by Neville Chamberlain, towards the Nazi and Fascist dictators in Europe in the 1930s in a bid to avoid war. It was strongly opposed by Winston Churchill, but the **Munich Agreement** of 1938 was generally hailed as a triumph of diplomacy. Appeasement ended when Germany occupied Bohemia-Moravia in March 1939, and in September of that year, when Germany attacked Poland, war was declared.

Arbroath, Declaration of
Declaration on 6 April 1320 by Scottish nobles of their loyalty to King Robert the Bruce and of Scotland's independence from England. It stated that Scotland had enjoyed 'an uninterrupted succession of 113 kings all of our own native and royal stock', and that the Scots would depose King Robert himself if he capitulated to the English, 'for it is not for glory, riches nor honours that we fight, but for freedom alone'.

In the 20th century, the Declaration of Arbroath has become a manifesto for Scottish nationalism.

Argyll, Archibald Campbell, 5th Earl of Argyll
(1530–1573)
Follower of the Scottish presbyterian **John Knox**. He supported Mary Queen of Scots from 1561 and commanded her forces after her escape from Lochleven Castle in 1568. Following her defeat at Langside, he revised his position, made peace with the regent, James Stuart, Earl of Murray, and became Lord High Chancellor of Scotland in 1572. He succeeded to the earldom in 1558.

Arnhem, Battle of
A battle between British and other Allied troops and the Germans at Arnhem, a Dutch town on the Rhine, during **World War II**.

On 17 September 1944 Allied parachutists were dropped in an attempt to capture bridges across the lower Rhine and clear the way for Allied troops to advance into Germany. The attempt failed, with some 7,600 casualties, and on 26 September **Montgomery** ordered a withdrawal.

Arthur, King

Legendary British king in the stories of Camelot and the knights of the round table. He is said to have been born in Tintagel, Cornwall, and buried in Glastonbury, Somerset. Camelot has been tentatively identified as a hill fort at South Cadbury in Somerset. Arthur was probably a 6th-century warlord and is credited with a great victory over the Saxons at Mount Badon, possibly in Dorset.

The King Arthur legends were developed in the 12th century by Geoffrey of Monmouth, Chrétien de Troyes, and the Norman writer Wace. Later writers who took up the theme include the anonymous author of Sir Gawayne and the Greene Knight (1346), Thomas Malory, Alfred Lord Tennyson, T H White, and Mark Twain.

Ashanti Wars

Four British expeditions of 1873–1901 to the interior of modern Ghana to seize control of trade in West Africa from the Ashanti people and end the slave trade there.

The first Ashanti War broke out in April 1873 when Garnet Wolseley was sent with 2,500 troops to defeat the Ashanti ruler, the Asantehene Kofi Karikari. This was settled on 14 March 1874 by the Treaty of Fomena whereby the Asantehene promised free trade and an end to human sacrifices. The agreement was broken, and in August 1896 the area was declared a British protectorate and the Asantehene was deported. The Ashanti territory was made part of the Gold Coast colony in September 1901.

Asquith, Herbert Henry, 1st Earl of Oxford and Asquith (1852–1928)

British Liberal politician, prime minister from 1908 to 1916. He introduced pensions for senior citizens and tried to give Ireland **Home Rule**.

Elected Liberal member of Parliament for East Fife in 1886, he became home secretary in **Gladstone's** 1892–95 government and in 1905 was made chancellor of the Exchequer. In 1908 he succeeded Campbell-Bannerman as prime minister.

Forcing through the radical budget of his chancellor David **Lloyd George** led Asquith into two elections in 1910. This resulted in the Parliament Act of 1911, which limited the right of the **Lords** to veto legislation.

Asquith's attempted Home Rule for Ireland Bill nearly led to civil war. Unity was re-established by the outbreak of World War I in 1914, and a coalition government was formed in May 1915. In December 1916 Asquith resigned as prime minister and was replaced by Lloyd George, who was more focused on war. The resignation caused a split in the **Liberal Party**, which went into steep decline after 1918, though Asquith remained its official leader until 1926.

Astor, Nancy Witcher Langhorne, Lady (1879–1964)

US-born British politician, the first female member of Parliament. She succeeded her husband as Conservative member for Plymouth in November 1919, after he went to the **Lords** as Viscount Astor. She remained an MP till 1945, championing women's rights, educational issues, and temperance.

> ❝ I married beneath me, all women do. ❞
>
> **Nancy Astor**, quoted in the *Dictionary of National Biography* 1961–1970

Atlantic, Battle of the

The continuous battle in the Atlantic Ocean between the Allies and Germany for control of the supply routes to the UK during **World War II**. The Allies destroyed nearly 800 U-boats, and at least 2,200 convoys of 75,000 merchant ships crossed the Atlantic protected by US naval forces. Prior to the US entry into the war in 1941, destroyers were supplied to the British under the Lend-Lease Act.

The Battle of the Atlantic began on 4 September 1939, the first night of the war, when the ocean liner *Athenia*, sailing from Glasgow to New York, was torpedoed by a German U-boat off the Irish coast.

Atlantic Charter

A declaration in 1941, by British prime minister **Churchill** and US president Roosevelt, of the principles that should govern the peace after **World War II**. The principles later formed the basis of the United Nations Organization's own charter. They included:

- the disarmament of aggressor states as a step towards general disarmament

- respect for the right of all peoples to choose their own governments
- no territorial changes to be made without the consent of the people affected
- the security of all nations by land or by sea
- international collaboration for the raising of economic standards.

Attlee, Clement, 1st Earl Attlee (1883–1967)
British Labour politician who as prime minister introduced major reforms after **World War II**. He was educated at Oxford and practised as a barrister from 1906 until 1909. Social work in London's East End led him to become a socialist, and in 1908 he joined the **Fabian Society**. After serving in **World War I** he became mayor of Stepney in east London (1919–20), and later Labour member of Parliament for Limehouse (1922–50) and West Walthamstow (1950–55).

In the first Labour government (1924) he was undersecretary for war and, in the second, chancellor of the Duchy of Lancaster and postmaster general (1929–31). In 1935 he became leader of the opposition. During World War II he was in the coalition government, serving as deputy prime minister from 1942. He became prime minister in July 1945 after a Labour landslide victory in the general election. From 1945 to 1951 he introduced a sweeping programme of nationalization and a whole new system of social services including the National Health Service (1948). Labour was returned to power with a much reduced majority in 1950 and was defeated in 1951. Attlee was made an earl in 1955 on his retirement as leader of the opposition.

> ❢ I think the British have the distinction above all other nations of being able to put new wine into old bottles without bursting them. ❢
>
> Prime Minister **Clement Attlee**, *Hansard*, 24 October 1950

Augustine of Canterbury, St (d. 605)
First archbishop of Canterbury. He was sent to England by Pope Gregory I to convert England to Christianity. He landed at Ebbsfleet in Kent in 597 and soon afterwards baptized Ethelbert, king of Kent, along with many of his subjects. He was appointed archbishop in 601, establishing his see at Canterbury. His feast day is 26 May.

Bacon, Francis, 1st Baron Verulam and Viscount St Albans (1561–1626)

English philosopher, politician, and writer, a founder of modern scientific research. Bacon was born in London, the nephew of Queen Elizabeth's adviser Lord **Burghley**. He studied law at Cambridge, and in 1596 became a Queen's Counsel. He helped secure the execution of the Earl of **Essex**, his patron, as a traitor in 1601, later arguing in *Apology* (1604) that his first loyalty was to his sovereign.

Knighted on the accession of **James I** in 1603, he became Baron Verulam in 1618 and Viscount St Albans in 1621. Having risen to Lord Chancellor, in 1618 he confessed to bribe-taking and spent four days in the **Tower of London**. From then on he devoted himself to science and writing, in both Latin and English.

Francis Bacon died after catching a cold while stuffing a chicken with snow in an early experiment in refrigeration.

His works include:

- *Essays* (1597, revised and enlarged in 1612 and 1625), famous for their pith and brevity
- *The Advancement of Learning* (1605), a pioneer work on scientific method
- *Novum Organum* (1620), in which he redefined the task of natural science seeing it as a means of empirical discovery and a method of increasing human power over nature
- *The New Atlantis* (1626), a description of a utopian state where scientific knowledge is systematically sought and exploited.

> ❛ If a man will begin with certainties, he shall end in doubts; but if he will be content to begin with doubts, he shall end in certainties.' ❜
>
> **Francis Bacon**, *Advancement of Learning*, Book I

Bacon, Roger (c.1214–1292)

English scholar and scientist who is popularly credited with having discovered gunpowder.

Bacon became a Franciscan monk and lectured in Paris and at **Oxford University**. In 1266, at the invitation of Pope Clement IV, he wrote three books covering all branches of knowledge. He also wrote about future discoveries, including aeroplanes, microscopes, telescopes, and steam engines, and promoted the use of latitude and longitude in mapmaking.

With his knowledge of astronomy Roger Bacon suggested changes to improve the Western calendar, which were finally carried out by Pope Gregory XIII in 1582.

Baden-Powell, Robert Stephenson Smyth, 1st Baron Baden-Powell (1857–1941)

British founder of the Scout Association. He famously commanded the garrison during the 217-day siege of **Mafeking** in the Second South African War (1899–1900). After 1907 he devoted his time to developing the Scout movement, which rapidly spread throughout the world. He began with a Scout camp for 20 boys on Brownsea Island, Poole Harbour, Dorset, in 1907. He published *Scouting for Boys* (1908) and about 30 other books. He was World Chief Scout from 1920. With his sister Agnes he also founded the Girl Guides, in 1910. Knighted in 1909, he was made Baron in 1929.

Balaclava, Battle of

A Russian attack on British positions near a Ukrainian town southeast of Sevastopol on 25 October 1854, during the Crimean War.

The battlefield consisted of two valleys divided by low hills. The British cavalry's Heavy Brigade was positioned in the south valley, while the Light Brigade was in the north valley. After a first Russian advance into the south valley was repulsed, the British general Lord **Raglan** ordered the Light Brigade to 'prevent the enemy carrying away the guns'. The instruction was unclear, and tragically misunderstood by Lord Lucan, the Light Brigade's commander. In the infamous **Charge of the Light Brigade**, he led his cavalry up the north valley between two rows of Russian artillery. Of the 673 British soldiers who took part,

Balaclava helmets were knitted hoods worn here by soldiers in the bitter weather.

there were 272 casualties. The brigade was saved from annihilation by French cavalry.

Baldwin, Stanley, 1st Earl Baldwin of Bewdley
(1867–1947)

British Conservative prime minister who secured equal voting rights for women and handled the **abdication crisis** of Edward VIII.

Baldwin was born in Bewdley, Worcestershire, the son of an iron and steel magnate. He was elected Unionist MP for his home town in 1908, and in 1916 was made parliamentary private secretary to Conservative leader Bonar Law. In 1919 he anonymously gave the Treasury £50,000, about 20% of his personal fortune, to cancel War Loans. He helped disrupt Lloyd **George's** coalition government in 1922, and, as chancellor in Bonar Law's government, achieved a settlement of war debts with the USA.

Prime minister in 1923–24 and again in 1924–29, Baldwin passed the Trades Disputes Act of 1927 after the **General Strike**, granted widows' and orphans' pensions, and introduced voting at 21 for women in 1928. He was premier for a third time from 1935 to 1937, and in 1936 dealt with the abdication crisis. He was later criticized for his failure to resist popular pressure to accommodate the dictators Hitler and Mussolini and for his failure to rearm more effectively.

> ❝ The only defence [against being bombed] is in offence, which means that you have to kill more women and children more quickly than the enemy if you want to save yourselves. ❞
>
> **Stanley Baldwin**, *Hansard*, 10 November 1932

Balfour Declaration

Statement of support for the setting up of a homeland for Jewish people. In a letter dated 2 November 1917, the British foreign secretary A J Balfour wrote to Lord Rothschild (chair of the British Zionist Federation): 'HM government view with favour the establishment in Palestine of a national home for the Jewish people'.

The Balfour Declaration helped provide the basis for the founding of the state of Israel in 1948.

ballot act

Legislation providing for secret ballots in elections. It was introduced by **Gladstone's** Liberal government in 1872 and opposed by landowners, who would no longer be able to monitor, and hence control, the voting of their tenants. They defeated the measure when it was first presented in the **Lords** in 1871 but William Forster eventually secured its passage in July 1872.

Bank of England

UK central bank founded by an act of Parliament in 1694 to finance **William III's** wars with France. The Bank was entrusted with issuing bank notes in 1844 and became the UK's central clearing bank. In 1946 it was nationalized by the Labour government.

Reforms announced in May 1997 gave the Bank operational independence to decide interest rates to meet inflation targets set by the chancellor of the Exchequer. The Bank's responsibility for managing the public debt was transferred to the Treasury.

Bannockburn, Battle of

Battle on 24 June 1314 at Bannockburn, near Stirling, in Scotland, in which the Scottish king **Robert the Bruce** defeated Edward II of England to secure Scotland's independence.

Edward led over 2,000 knights and 15,000 foot soldiers, including about 5,000 archers. Bruce had only 500 light cavalry and some 7,000 foot soldiers. He took up a defensive position behind a stream and dug pits to hamper the English cavalry. An unsuccessful night march to outflank the enemy left Edward's knights in boggy ground and the archers out of position in the rear. Bruce's pikemen blocked any further English advance and his cavalry routed the archers. The English suffered heavy casualties and 500 noblemen were taken for ransom.

Barebones Parliament

English assembly called by Oliver **Cromwell** to replace the '**Rump** Parliament' in July 1653. Although its members attempted to pass sensible legislation (civil marriage; registration of births, deaths, and marriages; custody of mentally ill), their attempts to abolish tithes, patronage, and the court of chancery, and to codify the

The assembly consisted of 140 members selected by the army and derived its name from one of its members, Praise-God Barbon.

law, led to the resignation of the moderates and to its dissolution in December 1653.

Barons' Wars

Two civil wars between kings of England and their barons in the 13th century:

- *1215–17* between King **John** and his barons, over his failure to honour the **Magna Carta**
- *1264–67* between Henry III, and the future **Edward I**, and their barons led by Simon de Montfort. At the Battle of Lewes on 14 May 1264 Henry III was defeated and captured. On 4 August 1265 Simon de Montfort lost the Battle of Evesham to Edward, Henry's son, and was killed.

Becket, St Thomas à
(1118–1170)

English archbishop of **Canterbury** who was murdered in Canterbury cathedral. Becket was chancellor to Henry II from 1155 till 1162, when he was appointed archbishop of Canterbury. Although a friend of Henry's, in 1164 Becket opposed the king's attempt to regulate the relations between church and state, and had to flee the country. He returned in 1170, but the reconciliation soon broke down. Encouraged by a hasty

Becket *Thomas à Becket is murdered in Canterbury Cathedral.*

> 6 No one shall set the sea between me and my Church. I did not come here to run away: anyone who wants me may find me. 9
>
> Attributed remark made by **St Thomas à Becket** to the knights who came to murder him at Canterbury Cathedral in December 1770

outburst from the king, four knights murdered Becket before the altar of Canterbury cathedral. He was declared a saint in 1172, and his shrine became the busiest pilgrimage site in England until the **Reformation** of the 16th century.

Bede, 'the Venerable' (c. 673–735)

English theologian and historian whose *Historia Ecclesiastica Gentis Anglorum* (*Ecclesiastical History of the English People*) of 731 is a primary source for early English history. It was translated into Old English by King **Alfred**.

Born at Monkwearmouth, in Durham, Bede entered the local monastery at the age of seven. He became a priest in Jarrow in about 703. Bede devoted his life to writing and teaching, and much of our knowledge of England in the Dark Ages before the 8th century is owed to his historical works and his painstaking research for accuracy. He was canonized in 1899.

Bedlam

Popular name for Bethlehem (or Bethlem) Royal Hospital, the first mental institution in Europe. The Priory of St Mary of Bethlehem was founded in Bishopsgate, London, in 1247. By the 14th century it was being used to house the mentally ill. The hospital site was later moved several times but kept the same name.

The present-day Bedlam is in West Wickham, Kent.

Beeching Report

The 1963 official report by Dr Richard Beeching (chair of the British Railways Board 1963–65), which resulted in the closure of hundreds of railway lines and several thousand stations. The plan was to close loss-making lines and improve the money-making routes. Networks in East Anglia, south Wales, and the West Country fared worst, whereas the densely populated southeast was less affected.

Berlin, Conference of

A conference in 1884–85 of the major European powers (France, Germany, the UK, Belgium, and Portugal) along with the USA to decide on the colonial partition of Africa. It was called by the German chancellor Otto von Bismarck. The parties also agreed on a neutral Congo Basin with free trade, and on the prohibition of the African **slave trade**.

Bevan, Aneurin (Nye) (1897–1960)

British Labour politician who started the **National Health Service** (NHS). Son of a Welsh miner, and himself a miner at 13, he was member of Parliament for Ebbw Vale from 1929 until his death. As minister of health in the post-World War II **Attlee** government, he inaugurated the NHS. He was minister of labour from January to April 1951, when he resigned (along with Harold Wilson) on the introduction of

Bevan *Aneurin Bevan speaks at a rally protesting against the Conservative government's action in the Suez Crisis.*

NHS charges and led a Bevanite faction against the government. In 1956 he became chief Labour spokesperson on foreign affairs, and in 1959 deputy leader of the **Labour Party**. He was an outstanding orator.

> ❢ He was like a fire in a room on a cold winter's day. ❢
>
> **Constance Cummings**, American actress, on Aneurin Bevan.
> Quoted in M Foot, *Aneurin Bevan*

Beveridge Report, the

The popular name for the 1942 report by the British economist William Beveridge that formed the basis for the social reform programme of the Labour government of 1945–50.

Properly called *Social Insurance and Allied Services* and also known as the *Report on Social Security*, it identified five 'giants': illness, ignorance, disease, squalor, and want. Beveridge proposed a scheme of social insurance from 'the cradle to the grave'. He recommended a national health service, social insurance and assistance, family allowances, and full-employment policies.

Bevin, Ernest (1881–1951)

British Labour politician who was chief creator of the Transport and General Workers' Union. He was the union's general secretary from 1921 to 1940.

> ❝ My [foreign] policy is to be able to take a ticket at Victoria Station and go anywhere I damn well please. ❞
>
> **Ernest Bevin**, *The Spectator*, April 1951

Appointed minister of labour and national service from 1940 in Winston Churchill's wartime coalition government, he organized the 'Bevin boys': men chosen by ballot to help the war effort by working in the coalmines. As foreign secretary in the Labour government of 1945–51, he played a leading part in the founding of the **North Atlantic Treaty Organization** (NATO).

Bill of Rights

An act of Parliament of 1689 that established Parliament as the foremost governing body. The Bill of Rights embodied the **Declaration of Rights**, which laid down the conditions under which William and Mary were offered the throne in the **Glorious Revolution**.

The Bill of Rights is the nearest approach to a written constitution that the United Kingdom possesses. Much of it was incorporated in the US constitution of 1788.

The act made it illegal, without Parliamentary consent, for the king to:

* suspend laws by royal authority
* levy money by royal prerogative
* maintain a standing army in peacetime.

The Bill also asserted:

* a right to petition the sovereign
* freedom of parliamentary elections
* freedom of speech in parliamentary debates and the necessity of frequent parliaments.

Bishops' Wars

Struggles between King **Charles I** of England and Scottish Protestants in 1638–40 over Charles's attempt to re-impose royal authority over the church in Scotland.

The dispute began when Archbishop **Laud**, with Charles's backing, tried to introduce the new Anglican prayer book into Scottish churches. Scottish

Protestants saw this as a challenge to the integrity of their church and agreed to resist. The Scots began mobilizing their forces for war and took Edinburgh and other key towns in March 1639. Charles was reluctant to call on Parliament to fund a war against the rebels, and the first Bishops' War was ended without a battle by the Treaty of Berwick in June 1639.

A second war started in August 1640 when the Scots invaded England, defeating Charles at Newburn and occupying Newcastle-upon-Tyne. Charles made peace with the Scots by the Treaty of Ripon in October 1640, but by then they controlled six English counties. He was obliged to pay them £3,600,000 and agree to reform of the English Church.

Black and Tans

The nickname of a special auxiliary force of the Royal Irish Constabulary employed by the British in 1920–21 to combat the **Sinn Féiners** (Irish nationalists) in Ireland. Among nationalists they were renowned for their brutality.

The name Black and Tans derives from the colours of their uniforms: khaki with black hats and belts.

Black Death

An epidemic of bubonic plague that ravaged Europe in the mid-14th century, killing between one-third and half of the population (about 75 million people). The disease was transmitted to humans by bacteria in fleas carried by migrating black rats. It came to England from France in August 1348 on a ship that docked at Weymouth. By the end of the winter of 1349 the plague had reduced England's population by a third.

The name Black Death was coined in England in the early 19th century.

Blackshirts

A term widely used to describe fascist paramilitary organizations, including Oswald Mosley's British Union of Fascists. Mosley's movement, founded in 1932, adopted the black shirt in imitation of Mussolini's fascist Squadristi and the Nazi SS (*Schutzstaffel*).

Blair, Tony (Anthony Charles Lynton) (1953–)

British politician, leader of the Labour Party from 1994, and prime minister from 1997.

A centrist and a Scot like his predecessor John Smith, he became Labour's youngest leader when he was elected to the post in July 1994. In 1995 he won approval for a new Labour Party charter, intended to distance the party from its traditional socialist base and promote 'social market' values. He and his party secured a landslide victory in the 1997 general election with a 179-seat majority.

Key initiatives of the Blair administration included Scottish and Welsh devolution, a peace agreement in Northern Ireland, and the creation of an elected mayor for London. However, in its economic strategy the Blair government differed little from its Conservative predecessor, imposing tight controls over public expenditure and, in the Private Finance Initiative, promoting 'public–private partnerships'.

Although he retained a high level of public approval during his first year as prime minister, Blair was criticized by some for governing in presidential style, for exercising too tight a control over his ministers and his party, and for making too much use of media 'spin doctors'.

> 6 The entire civilized world will not understand if we cannot put this together and make this work. 9
>
> **Tony Blair** on the peace negotiations in Northern Ireland, *Radio 5 Live*, 1 July 1999

Blenheim, Battle of

A decisive victory in the War of the Spanish Succession by British and Austrian troops led by General Marlborough over French and Bavarian armies near the Bavarian village of Blenheim on the River Danube. The battle, which took place on 13 August 1704, marked the turning point in the war.

The French had fortified the village, and the Allies attacked at about noon on 13 August. The Austrians struck at the Bavarians on the French left flank, before Marlborough drove a massive force – 90 cavalry squadrons, 23 infantry battalions, and supporting artillery – straight through the centre of the French line. The French were split from the Bavarians so that both could be dealt with separately. Marlborough then completed the move against Blenheim and captured most of the garrison, though most of the Bavarian forces were able to escape

Bligh, William (1754–1817)

English sailor and captain of HMS *Bounty*, whose crew mutinied against him. Bligh served with distinction in the **Napoleonic Wars** and accompanied Captain James **Cook** on his second voyage around the world (1772–74). In 1787 he commanded the *Bounty* on an expedition to the Pacific island of Tahiti to collect breadfruit-tree specimens. On the return voyage, the crew mutinied against harsh treatment. Bligh and those crew members loyal to him were cast adrift in a boat, and after many weeks reached Timor, near Java, having drifted 5,822 km/3,618 mi. Many of the mutineers settled in the Pitcairn Islands.

On his return to England in 1790 Bligh was exonerated from blame for his conduct. In 1805 he was sent to Australia as governor of New South Wales, where his discipline again provoked a mutiny (the Rum Rebellion, 1808). Recalled to Britain, he was made an admiral in 1811.

Blitz, the

From the German *Blitzkrieg* ('lightning war'), bombing raids on Britain by the German air force during **World War II** in 1940–41. An estimated 40,000 civilians were killed, 46,000 injured, and more than a million homes destroyed or damaged in the Blitz.

- The first air raid was in London on 7–8 September 1940, and raids continued for all but 10 nights until 12 November.
- The raids then targeted industrial cities such as Coventry (14 November), Birmingham, Portsmouth, and Liverpool.
- In spring 1941 the air defences began to take a larger toll on the attackers, because of improvements in radar for night fighters, and the raids fell away during the early summer.

Blood, Thomas (1618–1680)

Irish adventurer, known as Colonel Blood, who stole the crown jewels. In 1663 he tried to capture Dublin Castle, and in 1670 to assassinate the Duke of Ormonde. The next year, Blood and three accomplices stole the crown and orb from the **Tower of London**, but were soon captured. He was later pardoned by **Charles II**, and his estates, which had been confiscated, were restored to him.

Bloody Assizes

Courts held in the west of England under the Lord Chief Justice, Judge Jeffreys, known as 'the hanging judge', in 1685. The trials followed the

Duke of Monmouth's unsuccessful rebellion against **James II**. Monmouth was one of 320 rebels who were executed. Hundreds more were flogged, imprisoned, or transported.

Bloody Sunday
Shooting dead of 13 unarmed demonstrators in Londonderry, Northern Ireland, on 30 January 1972, by soldiers from the British Army's 1st Parachute Regiment. One wounded man later died from an illness attributed to the shooting. The demonstrators were taking part in a march to protest against the British government's introduction of internment without trial in Northern Ireland on 9 August 1971. The British government-appointed Widgery Tribunal found that the paratroopers were not guilty of shooting dead the 13 civilians in cold blood. In January 1998, however, British prime minister Tony Blair announced a new inquiry into the events of Bloody Sunday.

Boadicea
Alternative spelling of British queen **Boudicca**.

Boleyn, Anne (c. 1507–1536)
Queen of England from 1533 to 1536, the second wife of **Henry VIII**, and mother of **Elizabeth I**. Henry married Anne in 1533, after divorcing his first wife, **Catherine of Aragón**. Three years later, because she produced no male heir, Anne was accused of adultery and incest with her half-brother, a charge invented by **Thomas Cromwell**. She was declared guilty, sent to the Tower of London, and beheaded on 19 May 1536 at Tower Green.

> ❝ Never had a prince a more dutiful wife than you have in Anne Boleyn; with which name and place I could willingly have contented myself, if God and your Grace's pleasure had so been pleased. ❞
>
> **Anne Boleyn** in her last letter to Henry VIII, May 1536

Bolingbroke, Henry St John, 1st Viscount Bolingbroke (1678–1751)
British Tory politician and political philosopher who laid the foundations for 19th-century Toryism. Bolingbroke was foreign secretary between 1710 and

1714 and a **Jacobite** conspirator. When his plans to restore the 'Old Pretender' James Edward Stuart were ruined by Queen **Anne's** death in 1714, he fled abroad, returning in 1723.

> 6 Plain truth will influence half a score men at most ... while mystery will lead millions by the nose. 9
>
> **Henry St John Bolingbroke**, letter of 28 July 1721

Bondfield, Margaret Grace (1873–1953)
British trade unionist and Britain's first female cabinet minister. She helped to found the National Federation of Women Workers in 1906 and was active in the Cooperative Women's Guild. She became chair of the Trades Union Congress in 1923 and was twice a Labour member of Parliament between 1923 and 1931. She was appointed to the cabinet as minister for labour in 1929–31.

Bondfield was born in Somerset and began her political career in the National Union of Shop Assistants, serving as assistant secretary for ten years from 1898. She was the only female delegate to the Trades Union Congress of 1899.

Bonnie Prince Charlie
Scottish name for **Charles Edward Stuart**, pretender to the throne.

Bosworth, Battle of
Battle fought on 22 August 1485 (the last battle in the Wars of the **Roses**) in which **Richard III** was defeated and killed. The victor, Henry of Richmond, became **Henry VII**, the first **Tudor** king. The battlefield is near the village of Market Bosworth, 19 km/12 mi west of Leicester, England.

Richard was unhorsed in the battle and beaten to death as he lay there. This is a dramatic moment in Shakespeare's tragedy *Richard III*.

Boudicca, or Boadicea (d. AD 61)
Queen of the Iceni (native Britons) who rebelled against Romans. Her husband, King Prasutagus, had been a tributary to the Romans, but on his death the Romans seized the Iceni territory. They scourged Boudicca and raped her

❝I am not fighting for my kingdom and wealth now. I am fighting as an ordinary person for my lost freedom, my bruised body, and my outraged daughters. ❞

Boudicca to her army before the Icenian revolt AD 61, quoted by Tacitus

daughters. Boudicca raised the whole of southeastern England in revolt. Her armies sacked and burned Londinium (London), Verulamium (St Albans), and Camulodunum (Colchester), before she was beaten and her army nearly annihilated. In defeat, Boudicca poisoned herself.

Boudicca *Boudicca about to lead her warriors into combat with Roman forces.*

Bounty, mutiny on the
Naval mutiny in the Pacific in 1789 against British captain William **Bligh**.

Bow Street Runners
Informal police force organized in 1749 by Henry Fielding, chief magistrate at Bow Street in London. At first it was set up to assist the Bow Street Magistrates' court but from 1757 the force was funded by the government to cover the rest of London.

The Bow Street Runners formed the basis for the Metropolitan police force established by Robert Peel's government in 1829.

Boycott, Charles Cunningham (1832–1897)
English land agent in County Mayo, Ireland, who unwittingly gave the English language a new word. When he strongly opposed demands for agrarian reform by the Irish **Land League** in 1879–81, the peasants refused to work for him; hence the word boycott, meaning to isolate an individual, organization, or country, socially or commercially.

Boyne, Battle of the

The decisive battle of the War of English Succession, in which the exiled Catholic king **James II** was defeated by **William III**, a Protestant. The battle took place on 1 July 1690 by the River Boyne in eastern Ireland.

After obtaining aid from Louis XIV of France, James landed in Ireland where he had numerous supporters. His forces took up a position on the south side of the River Boyne. William sent his cavalry across the river in a frontal assault and routed James's army. Beaten, James fled to Dublin and then to France. The defeat put paid to any hopes of James's restoration to the English throne.

Bright, John (1811–1889)

British Liberal politician who campaigned for free trade, peace, and social reform. A Quaker mill-owner, he was among the founders of the **Anti-Corn Law League** in 1839, and was largely instrumental in securing the passage of the Reform Bill of 1867. He opposed the **Crimean War**, Palmerston's aggressive policy in China, and Disraeli's anti-Russian policy. During the American Civil War he was an outspoken supporter of the North.

❝ Force is not a remedy. ❞

John Bright, speech in Birmingham, 1880

Britain, ancient

The British Isles (excluding Ireland) from prehistoric times to the Roman occupation (1st century AD). Cave-dwelling hunter-gatherers in Britain at the end of the last Ice Age evolved into settled farming communities in the 3rd millennium BC. Stone-age society peaked in southern England early in the 2nd millennium BC, with the construction of the great stone circles of Avebury and Stonehenge. It was suc-ceeded by the Early Bronze Age Wessex culture, which established strong trading links with Europe. The Iron Age culture of the **Celts** dominated the last few centuries BC.

The Belgae (people from Gaul, north of the Seine and Marne rivers), who settled in southern Britain in the 2nd century BC, built the earliest British towns.

Britain, Battle of

A **World War II** aerial battle over Britain between German and British air forces from 10 July to 31 October 1940. The Germans had the advantage of using captured airfields in the Netherlands, Belgium, and France, which were in easy range of southeast England. On 1 August 1940 the Luftwaffe had about 4,500 aircraft of all kinds, compared with about 3,000 for the RAF. The Battle of Britain had been intended as a preliminary to the German invasion plan *Seelöwe* (Sea Lion), which Hitler abandoned on 10 October, choosing instead to invade the USSR.

PHASES IN THE BATTLE OF BRITAIN

- *10 July–7 August* preliminary phase
- *8–23 August* attack on coastal targets
- *24 August–6 September* attack on Fighter Command airfields
- *7–30 September* daytime attacks on London chiefly by heavy bombers
- *1–31 October* daytime attacks on London chiefly by fighters

---

British Museum

The UK's largest museum. Founded in 1753, it opened in 1759 in London at Montagu House in Bloomsbury. Rapid additions to the collection led to the construction of the present buildings, designed by Robert Smirke, between 1823 and 1847. Later extensions were the circular reading room, built in 1857, and the north wing, or Edward VII galleries, which date from 1914. In 1881 the Natural History Museum was transferred to South Kensington.

British National Party (BNP)

An extreme right-wing political party. It started as a breakaway movement from the **National Front**, but is now the leading far-right party in the UK. It has been blamed for incidents of violence against racial minorities.

Brunel, Isambard Kingdom (1806–1859)

English engineer and inventor, famous for his hugely ambitious projects unparalleled in engineering history.

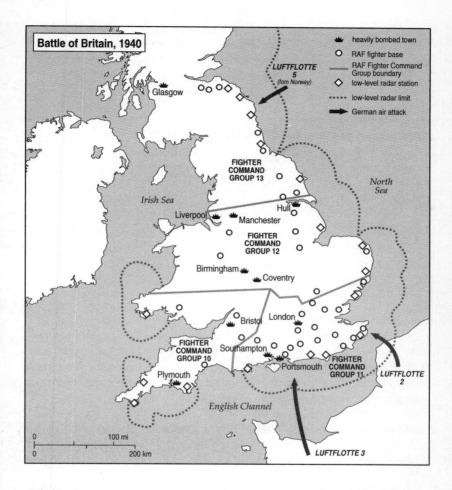

Battle of Britain, 1940

☠	heavily bombed town
○	RAF fighter base
▬	RAF Fighter Command Group boundary
◇	low-level radar station
····	low-level radar limit
➜	German air attack

LUFTFLOTTE 5 (fom Norway)

Glasgow

North Sea

FIGHTER COMMAND GROUP 13

Irish Sea

Liverpool
Hull
Manchester

FIGHTER COMMAND GROUP 12

Birmingham
Coventry

Bristol
London
Southampton

FIGHTER COMMAND GROUP 10

Portsmouth

FIGHTER COMMAND GROUP 11

LUFTFLOTTE 2

Plymouth

English Channel

LUFTFLOTTE 3

0	100 mi
0	200 km

At 19 he was appointed resident engineer on his father Marc Brunel's Thames Tunnel project. In 1833 he became engineer to the Great Western Railway, which adopted the 2.1-m/7-ft broad gauge on his advice. He built the Clifton Suspension Bridge over the River Avon at Bristol and the Saltash Bridge over the River Tamar near Plymouth. His shipbuilding designs include the *Great Western* (1837), the first steamship to cross the Atlantic regularly; the *Great Britain* (1843), the first large iron ship to have a screw propeller; and the *Great Eastern* (1858), which laid the first transatlantic telegraph cable.

Brunel was also responsible for building more than 2,600 km/1,600 mi of the permanent railway in the west of England, the Midlands, and South Wales. He constructed two railway lines in Italy, and acted as adviser on the construction of the Victoria line in Australia and on the East Bengal railway in India.

BRUNEL'S GREATEST ENGINEERING ACHIEVEMENTS

- Clifton Suspension Bridge, begun 1833, completed after his death
- *Great Western* (1837) – paddle-steamer that crossed the Atlantic in the unprecedented time of 15 days
- *Great Britain* (1843) – iron-hulled steamship, the first propeller-driven ship to cross the Atlantic
- *Great Eastern* (1858) – the first ship to be built with a double iron hull, and the largest ship in service until the end of the 19th century. It was driven by both paddles and a screw propeller.

Brussels, Treaty of
A 50-year treaty of economic, political, cultural, and military alliance made on 17 March 1948, between the UK, France, and the Benelux countries. In 1955 these were joined by West Germany and Italy. It was the forerunner of the **North Atlantic Treaty Organization** (NATO) and the European Community (now the **European Union**).

Buckingham, George Villiers, 1st Duke of Buckingham (1592–1628)
English courtier and influential adviser to **James I** and **Charles I**. Made duke in 1923 by James I, he negotiated Prince Charles's marriage to Henrietta Maria, sister of the French king. After Charles's accession, Buckingham attempted to form a Protestant coalition in Europe, which led to war with France. His policy on the French Protestants was attacked in Parliament. He failed to relieve the Protestants (Huguenots) besieged in La Rochelle in 1627, and when about to sail there for a second time, he was assassinated in Portsmouth.

Bunker Hill, Battle of
The first important battle between the British and colonists in the **American Revolution**. It was fought on 17 June 1775, near a small hill in Charlestown

(now part of Boston), Massachusetts. In fact, the battle took place on Breed's Hill, but is named after Bunker Hill as this was the more significant of the two. The British eventually succeeded in taking the top of the hill and driving off the Americans, but they suffered heavy losses.

> 6 Men, you are all marksmen – don't one of you fire until you see the whites of their eyes. 9
>
> **Israel Putnam**, US revolutionary soldier at the Battle of Bunker Hill in 1775

Burghley, William Cecil, 1st Baron Burghley (1520–1598)
English politician and chief adviser to **Elizabeth I**. He was secretary of state from 1558 and Lord High Treasurer from 1572. Burghley was largely responsible for the religious settlement of 1559, and took a leading role in the events preceding the execution of Mary Queen of Scots in 1587. He avoided a premature breach with Spain in the period leading up to the attack by the Spanish Armada in 1588, and did a great deal towards abolishing monopolies and opening up trade.

Burke, Edmund (1729–1797)
British Whig politician, political theorist and prolific writer, who famously supported the American colonists and the emancipation of Ireland, but denounced the French Revolution.

Born in Dublin, Ireland, Burke entered Parliament in 1765. He was quickly appointed private secretary to the prime minister, Lord Rockingham, and soon gained a reputation as one of the most eloquent and powerful speakers in the House. He was a leading figure in the impeachment of Warren Hastings, the governor general of India, for corruption in 1784. Altogether, his parliamentary career spanned more than 30 years.

Burke's basic political credo – that liberty is only possible within the strict framework of law and order – ensured that he has since been admired by British Conservatives as one of their main inspirational figures. His many writings include:

- *Thoughts on the Present Discontents* (1770), an attack on the government's attempts to coerce the American colonists

- *Reflections on the Revolution in France* (1790)

- *Letters on a Regicide Peace* (1795–97), in which he opposed peace with France.

---

6 To tax and to please, no more than to love and to be wise, is not given to men. 9

Edmund Burke, speech on American taxation in 1774

Burns, John Elliot (1858–1943)

British activist in the labour movement, and the first working-class member of the cabinet. Burns was born in London of Scottish parentage. He was sentenced to six weeks' imprisonment for his part in the Trafalgar Square demonstration on 'Bloody Sunday', 13 November 1887, and in 1889 he led the strike for the 'dockers' tanner' (wage of 6d per hour). An **Independent Labour** member of Parliament from 1892 to 1918, he held the cabinet post of president of the Local Government Board from 1906 to 1914.

Byng, John (1704–1757)

British admiral who was infamously tried and executed for his failure to accomplish his mission. When the French invaded the island of Menorca in 1756, Byng failed in the attempt to relieve Fort St Philip. He was court-martialled and shot. The French writer Voltaire ironically commented that it was done 'to encourage the others'.

---

6 I consider myself a victim destroyed to divert the indignation and resentment of an injured and deluded people. 9

John Byng on his court-martial and death sentence, quoted in *Dudley Pope At Twelve Mr Byng Was Shot*

Cabot, John (*c.*1450–1498)

Italian navigator and explorer, the first European to reach North America. Born Giovanni Caboto in Italy, he came to England in 1484 and settled in Bristol. He, with his three sons, was commissioned by **Henry VII** to find a new sea route to Asia. Cabot reached Cape Breton Island in Novia Scotia, Canada, in 1497, claiming it for England, though he thought he was in northeast Asia. He died at sea on another exploratory voyage, to Greenland.

Callaghan, (Leonard) James, Baron Callaghan of Cardiff (1912–)

British Labour prime minister from 1976 to 1979, a period of growing economic stress.

Callaghan was chancellor of the Exchequer between 1964 and 1967 and home secretary from 1967 to 1970 to Prime Minister Harold **Wilson**. As foreign secretary in 1974, he renegotiated the UK's membership of the European Community (now the **European Union**). He succeeded Wilson as prime minister in 1976, and the following year entered into an agreement with the Liberals (the 'Lib-Lab pact') to keep his government in office. Strikes in the so-called 'winter of discontent' of 1978–79 led to the government losing a vote of no confidence in the Commons, after the Liberals withdrew their support. Callaghan was forced to call an election in May 1979, at which his party was defeated by the Conservatives. In 1980 he resigned the Labour leadership, and in 1987 was made a life peer.

> ❝ Britain has lived too long on borrowed time, borrowed money, and even borrowed ideas. ❞
>
> **James Callaghan**, Sayings of the Week, the *Observer*, October 1976; as Prime Minister, he had applied to the International Monetary Fund for a $3.9 billion loan the week before

Campaign for Nuclear Disarmament (CND)

Independent British organization promoting the abolition of nuclear weapons. CND has consistently advocated unilateral British nuclear disarmament as a necessary step towards full-scale multilateral disarmament.

It was founded in 1958 by the philosopher Bertrand Russell and Canon John Collins, in the wake of an historic protest march to the government's Atomic Weapons Research Establishment, in Berkshire, in 1956.

CND membership peaked in the early 1980s, during a campaign against the stationing of US Pershing and cruise nuclear missiles on British soil.

Canning, George (1770–1827)

British Tory prime minister who in 1827 entered into a coalition with the Whigs. Canning entered Parliament in 1793 and quickly advanced under **Pitt the Younger**. He was made foreign secretary, but resigned after fighting a duel with the war minister, **Castlereagh**.

On Castlereagh's death in 1822, Canning again became foreign secretary and supported the national movements in Greece and South America. In 1827 he became prime minister. When **Wellington**, **Peel**, and other Tories refused to serve under him, he formed a coalition with the Whigs. He died in office.

Canterbury, archbishop of

Archbishop of the Church of England, the primate (archbishop) of all England, and first peer of the realm, ranking next to royalty. He crowns the sovereign, has a seat in the House of **Lords**, and is a member of the Privy Council. He is appointed by the prime minister. The first archbishop of Canterbury was **St Augustine** (601–04). The current holder of the office is George Carey, who succeeded Robert Runcie in 1991.

The archbishop of Canterbury's official residence is at Lambeth Palace, London, and his second residence is at the Old Palace, Canterbury.

Canute (c. 95–1035)

King of England from 1016, also known as Cnut the Great. Having invaded England in 1013 with his father, Sweyn, king of Denmark, he was acclaimed king on Sweyn's death in 1014 by his Viking army. Canute defeated **Edmund (II) Ironside** at Assandun, Essex, in 1016, and became king of all England on Edmund's death. He succeeded his brother Harold as king of Denmark in 1018, forced King Malcolm to pay homage by invading Scotland in about 1027, and conquered Norway in 1028.

The legend of Canute disenchanting his flattering courtiers by showing that the sea would not retreat at his command was first told by Henry of Huntingdon in 1130.

Caractacus (died *c.* AD 54)
British chieftain who led resistance against the Romans in southeast England in AD 43–51, before being defeated on the Welsh border. He was put on show in Claudius' triumphal procession, but was released as a tribute to his courage. He died in Rome.

Carson, Edward Henry, Baron Carson (1854–1935)
Anglo-Irish politician and lawyer who before World War I led the movement in Ulster to resist Irish **Home Rule**. The threat of armed rebellion against the Liberal government by his 'Ulster Volunteers' effectively wrecked the scheme by 1914. In 1915, he became attorney general in the coalition government and was a member of the war cabinet in 1917–18. He was created a life peer in 1921.

Carson was one of the leading legal and political figures of his day. He represented the Marquis of Queensbury in the 1895 case that ruined the career of Oscar Wilde.

Casement, Roger David (1864–1916)
British diplomat and Irish revolutionary who was executed for treason. Born in County Dublin, Casement joined the British consular service in 1892. He was knighted in 1911 for his exposé of the exploitation of plantation workers by Europeans in the Congo and Peru. On his retirement in 1913 he joined the Irish Volunteers and tried to raise support in Germany for Irish independence. He was captured in Ireland, sentenced to death,

British government agents circulated details of Casement's diaries, which revealed his homosexuality, in an attempt to discredit him.

and hanged as a traitor in August 1916. His remains were returned to Ireland in 1965.

Castlereagh, Robert Stewart, Viscount Castlereagh (1769–1822)

British Tory politician who helped the younger **Pitt** secure the union of England, Scotland, and Ireland in 1801. As chief secretary for Ireland, Castlereagh suppressed the rebellion of 1798, and as foreign secretary he coordinated European opposition to Napoleon and represented Britain at the Congress of Vienna of 1814–15.

He was twice secretary for war and the colonies but resigned in 1809 after a duel with the foreign secretary, **Canning**. His foreign policy favoured economic liberalism. At home he repressed the Reform movement, and popular opinion held him responsible for the **Peterloo massacre** of peaceful demonstrators in 1819. He committed suicide in 1822.

Catherine of Aragón (1485–1536)

The first queen of **Henry VIII** of England, from 1509 to 1533, and mother of **Mary I**. Born at Alcalá de Henares, Catherine was the youngest daughter of Ferdinand and Isabella of Spain. She married Henry's elder brother, Prince Arthur, in 1501 and after his death in 1502, married Henry on his accession to the throne in 1509. Of their six children, only Mary survived infancy. Catherine failed to produce a male heir and Henry divorced her without papal approval. The **Reformation** in England followed, and Catherine went into retirement until her death.

Catholic Emancipation

Acts of Parliament passed between 1780 and 1829 to ease the civil and political restrictions imposed on Roman Catholics from the time of **Henry VIII** and the **Reformation**. The election of the Irish Catholic Daniel **O'Connell** as member of Parliament for County Clare in 1828 led to full emancipation in 1829.

Cato Street Conspiracy

The unsuccessful plot hatched in Cato Street, London, to murder the Tory foreign secretary Robert **Castlereagh** and all his ministers on 20 February 1820. The leader, the radical Arthur Thistlewood (1770–1820), who intended to set up a provisional government, was hanged with four others.

Cavell, Edith (Louisa) (1865–1915)

English nurse and heroine of **World War I**. As matron of a Red Cross hospital in Brussels, Belgium, in World War I, she helped Allied soldiers escape to the Dutch frontier. She was court-martialled by the Germans and executed. The British government made much propaganda from her death, citing it as an example of German atrocities.

> ❝I realize that patriotism is not enough. I must have no hatred or bitterness towards any one. ❞
>
> **Edith Cavell**, last words on 12 October 1915, quoted in
> *The Times* on 23 October 1915

Caxton, William (c. 1422–1491)

The first English printer. He learned the art of printing in Cologne, Germany, in 1471 and set up a press in Belgium where he produced the first book printed in English, his own version of a French romance, *Recuyell of the Historyes of Troye*, in 1474. In 1476, he established himself in London, where he produced the first book printed in England, *Dictes or Sayengis of the Philosophres* (1477). The 100 or so books from Caxton's press in Westminster included:

- editions of **Chaucer**
- many texts from French and Latin that Caxton himself translated
- and others that he revised, such as Malory's *Morte d'Arthur*.

> ❝And certaynly our langage now used varyeth ferre from that which was used and spoken when I was borne. ❞
>
> **William Caxton**, 1490

Celts

Indo-European tribal people who settled in the British Isles and Ireland from about the 5th century BC. They originated in Alpine Europe about 1200 BC and spread throughout Europe and beyond. They had their own religion, led by **Druids**, and were known for their horsemanship and fierceness in battle. The

Celts were subjugated by the Roman invasion of Britain after AD 43, leaving only Ireland unscathed. The island of Iona is regarded as the cradle of the Celtic kingdom of Scotland.

The most important legacy of the Celtic presence is in language, both in place names, especially those of rivers, and in Scottish Gaelic, Irish Gaelic, Welsh, Manx, and Cornish.

Chamberlain, (Arthur) Neville (1869–1940)

British Conservative prime minister whose policy of **appeasement** towards Mussolini and Hitler failed to prevent the outbreak of World War II. As minister of health in 1923 and in 1924–29, Chamberlain concentrated on slum clearance. In 1931 he was appointed chancellor of the Exchequer in the national government, and in 1937 succeeded Stanley **Baldwin** as prime minister. Trying to stop the old Anglo-Irish feud, he agreed to return to Ireland those ports that had been occupied by the British navy.

In 1938 he went to Munich and reached a settlement with Hitler over Germany's territorial demands in Czechoslovakia. He was ecstatically received on his return, and claimed that the **Munich Agreement** brought 'peace in our time'. Within a year, however, the UK was at war with Germany. Chamberlain resigned in 1940 following the defeat of the British forces in Norway.

6 Peace with honour. I believe it is peace for our time. 9

Neville Chamberlain, speech from 10 Downing Street on 30 September 1938

Charge of the Light Brigade

Disastrous attack by the British Light Brigade cavalry against Russian artillery on 25 October 1854 during the Crimean War at the Battle of **Balaclava**.

Charles I (1600–1649)

In 1625 Charles succeeded his father **James I** of England (James VI of Scotland) as king of Great Britain and Ireland. He accepted Parliament's petition of right in 1628 curbing his powers of taxation, but then dissolved Parliament and ruled without it for 11 years. His advisers were **Strafford** and **Laud**, who persecuted the Puritans and provoked the Scots to revolt in the **Bishops' Wars**.

When the Short Parliament, summoned in 1640 to raise funds for Charles's war against the Scots, refused him these funds, Charles quickly dissolved it and imprisoned its leaders. The **Long Parliament** later that year rebelled. It declared extra-parliamentary taxation illegal, and voted that Parliament could not be dissolved without its own assent. Charles declared war on Parliament in 1642 – the beginning of the **Civil War** – but surrendered in 1646 and was beheaded in 1649.

Charles I *The trial of Charles I.*

> ❝ As a Christian, I must tell you that God will not suffer Rebels and Traytors to prosper nor his Cause to be overthrown. ❞
>
> **Charles I**, letter to Prince Rupert in 1645

Charles II (1630–1685)

King of Great Britain and Ireland from 1660, when Parliament accepted the restoration of the monarchy. He was the son of **Charles I**.

After Cromwell's victory in the **Civil War**, Charles withdrew to France. In 1660, with the collapse of Cromwell's republic, Charles issued the Declaration of Breda, promising a general amnesty. Parliament accepted, and Charles was proclaimed king on 8 May 1660.

In 1670 Charles signed the Secret Treaty of Dover, promising Louis XIV of France that he would declare himself a Catholic, re-establish Catholicism in England, and support the French king's projected war against the Dutch. In return Louis was to finance Charles and in the event of resistance to supply him with troops. War with the Netherlands followed in 1672, and at the same time Charles issued the Declaration of Indulgence, suspending all penal laws against Catholics.

In 1673 Parliament forced him to withdraw the Declaration and accept a Test Act excluding all Catholics from office, and in 1674 to end the Dutch war. Titus **Oates's** announcement of a 'popish plot' in 1678 caused a general panic, which Shaftesbury exploited to introduce his **Exclusion Bill**, excluding James, Duke of York, who was a Catholic, from the succession. Instead he hoped to substitute Charles's illegitimate son Monmouth. When Shaftesbury rejected a last compromise, Charles dissolved Parliament and ruled alone, financed by Louis XIV.

Charles Edward Stuart the Young Pretender or Bonnie Prince Charlie (1720–1788)
British prince and claimant to the thrones of Scotland and England. He was the grandson of **James II** and son of James, the Old Pretender.

In the **Jacobite** rebellion of 1745 Charles won the support of the Scottish Highlanders. His army invaded England but was beaten back by the Duke of Cumberland and routed at **Culloden** on 16 April 1746. Charles fled and for five months wandered through the Highlands with a price of £30,000 on his head before escaping to France. He visited England secretly in 1750 and settled in Italy in 1766.

> ❝ I am come home, sir, and I will entertain no notion at all of returning to that place whence I came, for I am persuaded my faithful Highlanders will stand by me. ❞
>
> **Charles Edward Stuart**, attributed remark on landing at Moindart in 1745

Chartism
A 19th-century radical movement, mainly of the working classes, which called for major changes to the British electoral system. It derived its name from the People's Charter, a six-point programme demanding:

- voting rights for all men
- electoral districts of equal size
- secret ballot
- annual parliaments
- abolition of the property qualification for voting eligibility
- payment for members of Parliament.

The Radical MP Thomas Attwood organized a National Convention in 1838 and the following year a petition was presented to the House of **Commons**. Parliament refused even to contemplate the petition and a subsequent petition of May 1842 met the same fate. About 60 Chartists were **transported** to Australia in 1842 after an abortive armed rising in response to these rejections.

Under the leadership of Fergus O'Connor, Chartism became a powerful expression of working class frustration, and a third petition was presented in 1848. The march and mass demonstration planned in support of the third chartist petition caused the government great alarm, and they threatened to use the military.

The long-term demise of Chartism was probably due to greater prosperity among the populace as a whole, lack of organization, and rivalry among the leadership of the movement.

Chaucer, Geoffrey (c. 1340–1400)

Medieval English poet, author of *The Canterbury Tales*. Chaucer presented English society as had never been done before, and he wrote in English rather than in French, the language of the court. Thus he developed English as a literary medium, and in doing so ensured that the Southeast Midland dialect used in London was the one ultimately to become standard English.

> Chaucer is buried in the Poets' Corner of Westminster Abbey.

Chaucer's early work shows formal French influence, as in the dream-poem *The Book of the Duchess* and his adaptation of the French allegorical poem on courtly love, *The Romaunt of the Rose*. More mature works reflect the influence of Italian realism, as in *Troilus and Criseyde*, adapted from the author Boccaccio.

The Canterbury Tales is a collection of stories told by a group of pilgrims on their way to Canterbury. It reveals Chaucer's

- genius for metre and characterization
- his knowledge of human nature
- and his stylistic variety, from urbane and ironic to simple and bawdy.

> ❢ She was a worthy womman al hir lyve, /
> Housbondes at chirche-dore she hadde fyve, /
> Withouten other companye in youthe. ❢
>
> **Geoffrey Chaucer**, *Canterbury Tales*, Prologue

child labour

Children employed to do the work of adults. In 19th-century Britain, thousands of children under ten, some as young as five, were employed by textile factories and mines, and forced to work in hazardous conditions, with little pay and sometimes for up to 16 hours a day. The first child-labour legislation was passed in England in 1802, but it was ineffective.

The **Factory Acts**, passed between 1819 and 1878, gradually enforced inspections, shortened hours, and raised the age at which children could work. In the UK in the mid-1990s, it was estimated that 1.5 million children were still working illegally.

Chiltern Hundreds, stewardship of Her Majesty's

The only means, apart from death or being voted out, for a British member of Parliament to vacate his or her seat.

British MPs may not resign. If they wish to leave office during a Parliament, they must apply for the stewardship of Her Majesty's Chiltern Hundreds of Stoke, Desborough, and Burnham or the stewardship of the Manor of Northstead. Although sinecures, these are technically offices of profit under the Crown, which disqualify the holder from sitting in Parliament. They are preserved for this purpose under the 1957 House of Commons Disqualification Act.

Chimney Sweepers Act

A law forbidding the use of children to sweep chimneys. It was passed in 1875 in Benjamin **Disraeli's** second ministry, partly in response to public outcry at the practice. Earlier attempts by Lord **Shaftesbury** (in acts of 1840 and 1864) had failed to curb the use of children to clean chimneys. Employers were now forbidden from taking on apprentices under the age of 16 and no one under the age of 21 was permitted to go up chimneys to clean them.

Churchill, Winston (Leonard Spencer) (1874–1965)

British Conservative prime minister and wartime leader (1940–45). In Parliament from 1900, at first as a Conservative, he became a Liberal MP in 1906.

A Conservative again from 1924, Churchill was made chancellor of the Exchequer under Baldwin and was prominent in the defeat of the **General Strike** of 1926. He was out of office from 1929 to 1939, as he disagreed with the Conservative policy over India and with **appeasement**.

From May 1940, during **World War II**, he headed an all-party administration as both prime minister and defence minister. He met the Soviet leader Stalin and US president Roosevelt in the Crimea at the Yalta Conference in February 1945 to draw up plans for the final defeat of Germany and its subsequent occupation. Already Churchill was worried by Soviet intentions in Eastern Europe, the 'iron curtain descending' as he later described it.

His government was defeated by a landslide in the 1945 elections and he became leader of the opposition. In October 1951 the Conservatives regained power, and Churchill again became prime minister until he resigned in April 1955. He remained an MP until 1964. In 1953 he was knighted and also received the Nobel Prize for Literature. His books include a six-volume history of World War II and a four-volume *History of the English-Speaking Peoples*.

---

6 From Stettin in the Baltic to Trieste in the Adriatic, an iron curtain has descended across the Continent. **9**

Winston Churchill, speech at Westminster College, Fulton, Missouri on 5 March 1946

Church of England

The established form of Christianity in England, a member of the Anglican Communion. It was dissociated from the Roman Catholic Church in 1534 under **Henry VIII**. The British monarch is still the supreme head of the Church of England today. Two archbishops head the provinces of Canterbury and York, which are divided into dioceses. The service book is the Book of Common Prayer.

In November 1992 the General Synod of the Church of England and the Anglican church in Australia voted in favour of the ordination of women, and the first women priests were ordained in England in 1994.

The main groups within the Church of England are the:

- Evangelical or Low Church, which maintains the church's Protestant character

- Anglo-Catholic or High Church, which stresses continuity with the pre-Reformation church and is marked by ritualistic practices and the use of confession

- liberal or modernist movement, concerned with the reconciliation of the church with modern thought
- Pentecostal Charismatic movement, emphasizing spontaneity and speaking in tongues.

Church of Scotland

The established form of Christianity in Scotland. Founded by John **Knox** and first recognized by the state in 1560, the church is based on the Protestant doctrines of the reformer Calvin. It went through several periods of episcopacy (government by bishops) in the 17th century, and those who adhered to episcopacy after 1690 formed the Episcopal Church of Scotland, an autonomous church allied to the Church of England.

In 1843 there was a split in the Church of Scotland (the Disruption), in which almost a third of its ministers and members left and formed the Free Church of Scotland. By an Act of Union of 3 October 1929, the Church of Scotland was united with the United Free Church of Scotland to form the United Church of Scotland.

Civil War, English

War between King **Charles I** and the Royalists (or Cavaliers) on one side and the Parliamentarians (or Roundheads) under Oliver **Cromwell** on the other. It was the culmination of a power struggle between the king and Parliament.

Hostilities began when Charles raised the royalist standard in Nottingham on 22 August 1642. After a series of battles, the turning point came in 1645 with the formation of the Parliamentarian **New Model Army**.

MAJOR CIVIL WAR BATTLES

- Edgehill, South Warwickshire, in October 1642. No conclusive outcome.
- Adwalton Moor in June 1643. Royalists took control of most of Yorkshire.
- Marston Moor in July 1644. Victory for the Parliamentarians.
- Naseby, near Leicester, in June 1645. New Model Army inflicts crushing defeat.
- Preston in August 1648. Cromwell leads the New Model Army to victory over the Scots.
- Worcester in 1651 Final defeat of the Royalist forces.

In 1646 Charles took refuge with the Scottish army based in the north of England, but was handed over as a prisoner to the Parliamentarians in January 1647. However, he escaped to the Isle of Wight, where he negotiated with a Scottish group for assistance to continue the war. Royalist rebellions and a further Scottish invasion of England in July 1648 followed, but they were suppressed. In 1649 Charles was tried and executed for treason. The following year his son **Charles II** who had recently been crowned in Scotland, led an unsuccessful invasion, and in 1651 the war ended in victory for the Roundheads.

Civil War battles, 1642–51

> 6 The utterly memorable Struggle between the
> Cavaliers (Wrong but Romantic) and the
> Roundheads (Right but Repulsive). 9
>
> **W C Sellar and R J Yeatman**, *1066 and All That*, Chapter 35

clan (from the Gaelic *clann* meaning 'children')
Social grouping based on kinship. Some traditional societies are organized by clans. Familiar examples are the Highland clans of Scotland. Theoretically each clan is descended from a single ancestor from whom the name is derived – for example, clan MacGregor ('son of Gregor').

Clans played a large role in the Jacobite revolts of 1715 and 1745, and their individual tartan Highland dress was banned from 1746 to 1782. Rivalry between clans was often bitter.

Clive, Robert, 1st Baron Clive (1725–1774)

British soldier and administrator who established British rule in India. Clive became a clerk in the East India Company's service in Madras in 1743, and then joined the army. During a dispute in 1751 over the succession to the Carnatic, an important trading region, Clive marched from Madras with 500 troops, seized Arcot, capital of the Carnatic, and defended it for seven weeks against 10,000 French and Italian troops. He then sallied out and relieved the British forces besieged in Trichinopoli. He returned to Britain a national hero, and was hailed as 'Clive of India'.

He returned to India in 1755 as governor of Fort St David. At Madras he learned that Suraj-ud-Daula, the new nawab of Bengal had driven the British from Calcutta and imprisoned his captives in the notorious Black Hole of Calcutta. Clive defeated the nawab's 34,000 strong army, with a force of only 1,900 troops. A subsequent victory at **Plassey** in June 1757 secured Bengal for the East India Company, and Clive was appointed governor of the province from 1757.

> 6 A savage old Nabob, with an immense fortune, a
> tawny complexion, a bad liver and a worse heart. 9
>
> Thomas Macaulay, English historian, essayist, poet, and politician,
> referring to Robert Clive, in *Historical Essays*

He came back to Britain on account of ill health in 1760, but was governor for a further year in 1765–66. On his return to Britain in 1766 his wealth led to allegations that he had abused his power. Although acquitted by a Parliamentary enquiry, he committed suicide.

CND
Abbreviation for **Campaign for Nuclear Disarmament**.

Coalbrookdale
An English village that is sometimes known as the 'cradle of the Industrial Revolution'. It is effectively a suburb of Telford, situated in the Severn Gorge. In 1709 Coalbrookdale became the world's most important iron-producing area following Abraham Darby's successful attempt to use coke – rather than coal or charcoal – to smelt iron in a blast-furnace. This allowed a massive increase in iron production.

Coalbrookdale Museum of Iron forms part of the Ironbridge Gorge World Heritage Site.

Cobbett, William (1763–1835)
English Radical politician and journalist, a supporter of the working class and Parliamentary reform.

After a period of army service in Canada, Cobbett lived in the USA as a teacher of English. In 1800 he returned to England, and with increasing knowledge of the sufferings of farm labourers became a Radical. From 1802 to 1835 he published his weekly *Political Register*, and in 1830 his crusading essays on the conditions of the rural poor were published as *Rural Rides*. He was imprisoned from 1809 to 1811 for criticizing the flogging of militiamen. After 1832 he represented Oldham in the Reformed Parliament.

Cobden, Richard (1804–1865)
British Liberal politician and economist, cofounder with John **Bright** of the **Anti-Corn Law League** in 1838.

A member of Parliament from 1841, Cobden believed in the abolition of privileges, a minimum of government interference, and the securing of international peace through free trade and by disarmament and arbitration. He opposed trade unionism and most of the factory legislation of his time, because he regarded them as opposed to liberty of contract. His opposition to the **Crimean War** made him unpopular. Cobden was largely responsible for the commercial treaty with France in 1860.

> 〝Are we to be the Don Quixotes of Europe, to go about fighting for every cause where we find that someone has been wronged?〞
>
> **Richard Cobden**, speech in the House of Commons, December 1854

Collins, Michael (1890–1922)

Irish revolutionary and founder of the Irish Free State. Born in County Cork, Collins became an active member of the Irish Republican Brotherhood, and in 1916 fought in the **Easter Rising**. In 1918 he was elected as a **Sinn Féin** member to the Dáil (the then illegal republican parliament), and became a minister in the Provisional government. He was also a founder and director of intelligence of the **Irish Republican Army**.

In 1921, Collins and Arthur Griffith (vice-president of the Irish republic declared in 1919) reluctantly signed a treaty with the British that recognized the partition of Ireland and granted dominion status to the new Irish Free State. This outcome, which fell short of independence for a 32-county republic, split the republican movement. Civil war ensued. Collins took command and crushed the opposition in Dublin and the large towns within a few weeks. When Griffith died on 12 August 1922, Collins became head of the state and the army, but he was ambushed near Cork on 22 August and killed.

Combination Acts

Laws passed in Britain in 1799 and 1800 making **trade unionism** illegal. They were introduced after the French Revolution out of fear that the unions would become centres of political agitation. The unions continued to exist, but claimed to be friendly societies or went underground. The acts were repealed in 1824.

Commons, House of

The lower, elected chamber in the UK **Parliament**. It originated in 1265 when Simon de **Montfort** included boroughs in his parliament, and in 1295 the **Model Parliament** established the Commons as a body whose members had full authority to act on behalf on those that they represent.

Commonwealth, the (British)

A voluntary association of 54 independent countries, many of which were once part of the British **Empire**. It was founded in 1931. Queen

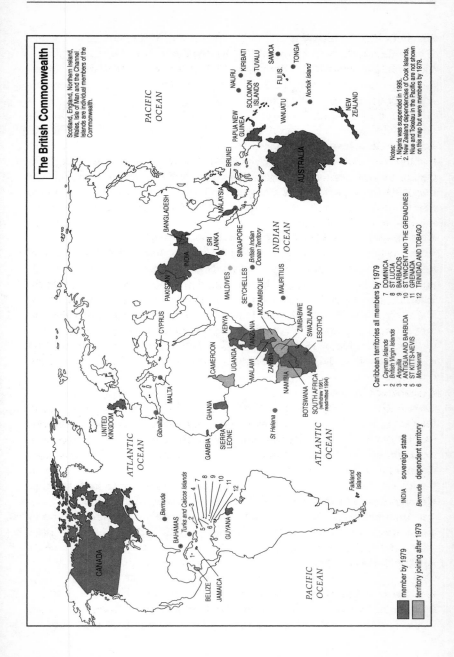

The British Commonwealth

Scotland, England, Northern Ireland, Wales, Isle of Man and the Channel Islands are individual members of the Commonwealth.

Caribbean territories all members by 1979

1. Cayman Islands
2. British Virgin Islands
3. Anguilla
4. ANTIGUA AND BARBUDA
5. ST KITTS-NEVIS
6. Montserrat
7. DOMINICA
8. ST LUCIA
9. BARBADOS
10. ST VINCENT AND THE GRENADINES
11. GRENADA
12. TRINIDAD AND TOBAGO

Notes:
1. Nigeria was suspended in 1995.
2. New Zealand dependencies of Cook Islands, Niue and Tokelau in the Pacific are not shown on this map but were members by 1979.

member by 1979

territory joining after 1979

INDIA   sovereign state

Bermuda   dependent territory

Elizabeth II is the formal head but not the ruler of 17 member states, while 5 have their own monarchs, and 31 are republics. The newest member is Mozambique, which was admitted in November 1995. Additionally, there are some 20 territories that are not completely sovereign but are dependencies of the UK or of other member states.

The Commonwealth has no charter or constitution, and ties, once important politically, militarily, and economically, are now mainly cultural and economic. However, it can make political statements by withdrawing membership. A recent example was Nigeria's suspension in November 1995 because of human-rights abuses. It was readmitted in May 1999. Fiji was readmitted in October 1997, ten years after its membership had been suspended because of discrimination against its ethnic Indian community.

Communist Party of Great Britain (CPGB)
British Marxist party founded in 1920, largely inspired by the Russian Revolution of 1917. The party enjoyed its greatest popularity in the 1930s and 1940s, particularly after Britain allied with the USSR during **World War II**. It had 18,000 members in 1939 and had two MPs elected in 1945. The party was split internally by the Soviet invasion of Hungary in 1956 and moved away from the USSR during the 1960s, particularly after the invasion of Czechoslovakia of 1968. Disbanded in 1991, the party was relaunched as 'Democratic Left', although some splinter factions still lay claim to the old name.

Connolly, James (1870–1916)
Irish socialist and revolutionary who was executed by the British. He helped found the Irish Socialist Republican Party in 1896, and in 1913 organized a strike of transport workers with the Irish Labour leader James Larkin. Connolly committed his small Irish Citizen Army to a joint operation with the Irish Republican Brotherhood, which resulted in the 1916 **Easter Rising**. He was commandant general of the Dublin Division in the Rising and was wounded in the fighting. News of his execution while sitting propped-up in a chair fuelled the indignation of Irish nationalists.

Conservative Party
One of the two major British parties. The name 'Conservative' replaced 'Tory' in general use from 1830. Traditionally the party of landed interests, it broadened its political base under **Disraeli's** leadership in the 19th century.

The present Conservative Party's free-market capitalism is supported by the world of finance and the management of industry. In the 1980s the party's economic policies increased the spending power of many, but also the gap between rich and poor. Nationalized industries were sold off, and the funding of local government was overhauled with the introduction of the poll tax, which led to riots on the streets. The Conservatives also favoured closer military and economic ties with the USA.

In 1990, Margaret **Thatcher**, Conservative prime minister since 1979, was forced out of office by her own party. The Conservatives continued in government under John Major and were re-elected in 1992. But the 1997 elections saw a landslide Labour victory, and Conservative support fell to 31%, its lowest level since 1832. John Major resigned as party leader, and was succeeded by William Hague.

> ❝ A Conservative government is an organized hypocrisy. ❞
>
> **Benjamin Disraeli**, British Conservative prime minister and novelist, in a speech on 17 March 1845

Cook, James (1728–1779)
British naval explorer who landed in Australia and claimed it for Britain. In 1759, he surveyed the St Lawrence River in North America. He set sail in 1768 on the *Endeavour* to Tahiti and went on to find and chart New Zealand and the Australian coast, returning to England in 1771. He made two more voyages, to the South Pacific and Antarctica (1772–75) and, in 1776, to the west coast of America by way of Hawaii, where he died in a fracas with the islanders.

> Unusually for those times, Cook's crews did not suffer from scurvy during the voyages, because he devised a diet that was high in vitamin C.

cooperative movement
A movement based on mutual assistance between groups of people in trade, manufacture, the supply of credit, housing, or other services. The principles of the cooperative movement were laid down in 1844 by the Rochdale Pioneers, under the influence of **Robert Owen**. In the UK the 1970s and 1980s saw a growth in the number of workers' cooperatives, set up in factories otherwise threatened by closure due to economic depression.

Copenhagen, Battle of

Famous sea victory by **Nelson**, who put his telescope to his blind eye and refused to see the signal to withdraw. The battle, between the British fleet under Sir Hyde Parker and the Danish fleet, took place on 2 April 1801 during the **Napoleonic Wars**.

> ❝ I have only one eye, I have a right to be blind sometimes … I really do not see the signal! ❞
>
> **Horatio Nelson**, at the Battle of Copenhagen, 1801

Corn Laws

Laws once used to control the export or import of cereals. Although mentioned as early as the 12th century, the Corn Laws only became significant in the late 18th century. After the **Napoleonic Wars**, with mounting pressure from a growing urban population, the laws aroused strong opposition because of their tendency to drive up prices. They were regarded by Radicals as benefiting wealthy landowners at the expense of the ordinary consumer. The **Anti-Corn Law League** was formed in 1838 to campaign against the laws. They were finally repealed by Robert **Peel** in 1846.

Cornwallis, Charles, 1st Marquis and 2nd Earl (1738–1805)

British general whose defeat at Yorktown in 1781 effectively ended the **American Revolution** and brought victory to the colonists. From 1786 to 1793 Cornwallis served as governor-general of India and again in 1805 till his death. In 1798 he was made viceroy of Ireland, where he put down the rebellion by Wolfe **Tone**. He succeeded to the earldom in 1762, and was made a marquis in 1792.

Corporation Act

A statute of 1661 that effectively excluded religious dissenters from public office. All magistrates in England and Wales were obliged to:

- take sacrament according to the Church of England
- swear an oath of allegiance
- renounce the Covenant by Scottish Protestants
- declare it treason to carry arms against the King.

These measures reflected the wishes of parliament rather than those of the king, **Charles II**. The Act was repealed in 1828.

Cranmer, Thomas (1489–1556)
English archbishop of Canterbury loyal to **Henry VIII**. A Protestant convert, Cranmer suggested in 1529 that the question of Henry VIII's marriage to **Catherine of Aragón** should be referred to the universities of Europe rather than to the pope. He was appointed archbishop of Canterbury in 1533 and declared the marriage null and void. Three years later he annulled Henry's marriage to Anne **Boleyn** in the same fashion. In 1540 he divorced Henry from Anne of Cleves and in the next year was instrumental in securing the condemnation of Catherine Howard, another of Henry's wives.

Cranmer was responsible for the issue of the Prayer Books of 1549 and 1552, and supported the succession of Lady Jane **Grey** in 1553. On the accession of the Catholic **Mary I**, he was tried and condemned for heresy. At first he recanted, but later resumed his position and was burned at the stake, first holding to the fire the hand which had signed his recantation.

> **6** This was the hand that wrote it, therefore it shall suffer punishment. **9**
>
> **Thomas Cranmer**, at the stake on 21 March 1556

Crécy, Battle of
The first major battle of the **Hundred Years' War**, in which Edward III of England defeated Philip VI of France. The two armies met on 26 August 1346 at the French village of Crécy-en-Ponthieu, 18 km/11 mi northeast of Abbeville.

Edward's forces were arranged in three divisions on foot, with Welsh archers and spearmen in the front ranks, who picked off the French knights as they rode forward. The battle resolved itself into a series of charges by the French knights, but the French were eventually beaten off.

Crimean War
A mid-19th century war between Russia and the allied powers of England, France, Turkey, and Sardinia. It was caused by British and French mistrust of Russia's ambitions in the Balkans. The battles of the River Alma, **Balaclava**, and Inkerman in 1854 led to a siege of the Black Sea port of Sevastopol,

---

PROGRESS OF THE CRIMEAN WAR

- *1853* Russia invaded the Balkans (from which they were compelled to withdraw by Austrian intervention) and sank the Turkish fleet at the Battle of Sinope on 30 November.
- *1854* Britain and France declared war on Russia, invaded the Crimea, and laid siege to Sevastopol (September 1854–September 1855); there followed the battles of Alma (20 September) Balaclava (25 October), and Inkerman (5 November).
- *1855* Sardinia declared war on Russia.
- *1856* The Treaty of Paris in February ended the war.

---

which, owing to military mismanagement, lasted for a year until September 1855. The war ended in early 1856. The scandal surrounding French and British losses through disease led to the organization of proper military nursing services by Florence Nightingale.

> ❝ The angel of death has been abroad throughout the land; you may almost hear the beating of his wings. ❞
>
> **John Bright**, speech in the House of Commons, February 1855, appealing for an end the Crimean War.

Cromwell, Oliver (1599–1658)

English general and politician who led the Parliamentary side to victory in the **Civil War** against the Royalists. Cromwell entered Parliament in 1629 and became active in the events leading up to war. He raised cavalry forces (called Ironsides) that helped defeat **Charles I's** troops at Marston Moor in 1644, and with **Fairfax** organized the **New Model Army**, which won decisively at **Naseby** in 1645.

Failing to reach a constitutional settlement with Charles I, Cromwell defeated the 1648 Scottish invasion at Preston. He declared Britain a republic ('the Commonwealth') in 1649, following the

---

Oliver Cromwell's head is buried in the grounds of Sidney Sussex College, Cambridge, but his body is interred on the site of the Tyburn gallows in London

execution of Charles. He also executed the leaders of the **Levellers**, who demanded radical reforms, and used terror to crush Irish clan resistance in 1649–50. He defeated the Scots, who recognized **Charles II**, at Dunbar in 1650 and Worcester in 1651.

In 1653, having forcibly expelled the corrupt 'Rump Parliament', Cromwell summoned a convention (called the **Barebones Parliament**), but it was soon dissolved for being too radical. Under a constitution drawn up by the army leaders, Cromwell became 'Lord Protector' (king in all but name). The Parliament of 1654–55 was dissolved as uncooperative, and after a period of military dictatorship, his last

Cromwell *A contemporary engraving showing Oliver Cromwell's achievements.*

Parliament offered him the crown, which he refused. As Protector, Cromwell established religious tolerance and raised Britain's prestige in Europe through an alliance with France against Spain.

❝I had rather have a plain russet-coated captain that knows what he fights for, and loves what he knows, than that which you call a gentleman and is nothing else.❞

Oliver Cromwell, letter to Sir William Spring, 1643

Cromwell, Thomas, Earl of Essex (*c.* 1485–1540)

English politician who drafted the legislation that made the Church of England independent of Rome. Originally in Lord Chancellor **Wolsey's** service, Cromwell became secretary to **Henry VIII** in 1534 and was created a baron in 1536.

Cromwell had Henry divorced from **Catherine of Aragón** by a series of acts that proclaimed Henry head of the church. From 1536 to 1540 Cromwell suppressed the monasteries and crushed all opposition to Protestantism. His mistake in arranging Henry's marriage to Anne of Cleves (to cement an alliance with the German Protestant princes against France and the Holy Roman Empire) led to his being accused of treason and beheaded.

> ❝ On light pretexts, by false accusations, they made me put to death the most faithful servant I ever had. ❞
>
> **Henry VIII**, six months after Cromwell's execution, quoted in Wriothesley's *Chronicle* of 1875 and Beckingsale's *Thomas Cromwell,* 1978

Culloden, Battle of

The defeat, in 1746, of **Charles Edward Stuart** by the Duke of Cumberland, which effectively ended the military challenge of the **Jacobite** rebellion. The battle was fought on a bleak stretch of moorland in Inverness-shire, Scotland.

The English front line began with a volley of musketry, after which the Jacobites, a mixture of French, Irish, and Scots, charged and broke through the first English line but were caught by the musket fire of the second line. They retired in confusion, pursued by the English cavalry who broke the Jacobite lines and shattered their force. About 1,000 of them were killed and a further 1,000 captured.

Cutty Sark

A famous British sailing ship, now in dry dock at Greenwich, London. Built in 1869, it was one of the tea clippers that in the 19th century sailed from Britain to China and competed to bring back its cargo the fastest. The biennial International Tall Ships Race is named after it.

Cymbeline or Cunobelin (lived 1st century AD)

King of the Catuvellauni tribe (AD 5–40), who fought against the Roman invasion of Britain. His capital was at Colchester, from which he ruled most of southeast England. He was the father of **Caractacus**.

D

danegeld

A tax imposed by Anglo-Saxon kings that was used to pay tribute to the Vikings. It was first exacted in 991 during the reign of **Ethelred the Unready**. After the **Norman Conquest** of 1066, the tax was revived and levied until 1162 to finance military operations.

Danelaw

The old name for that part of northern and eastern England settled by the **Vikings** in the 9th century. It occupied about half of England, from the River Tees to the River Thames. Within its bounds Danish law, customs, and language prevailed, rather than those of the West Saxons and Mercians. Its linguistic influence is still apparent in place names in this area.

Darling, Grace Horsley (1815–1842)

British 19th-century heroine. She was the daughter of a lighthouse keeper on the Farne Islands, off Northumberland. On 7 September 1838 the *Forfarshire* was wrecked. With her father, Grace Darling rowed through a storm to the wreck, saving nine lives. She was awarded a medal for her bravery.

Darnley, Henry Stewart or Stuart, Lord Darnley (1545–1567)

The second husband of **Mary Queen of Scots**, and father of **James I** of England (James VI of Scotland). Darnley married Mary, his first cousin, in 1565. On the advice of her secretary, David Rizzio, Mary refused him the crown matrimonial. In revenge, Darnley had Rizzio murdered in Mary's presence in 1566. A plot to kill Darnley was hatched by Bothwell, the third husband of Mary Queen of Scots, and he was assassinated in 1567. Mary's part in the plot remains a subject of controversy.

David I (1084–1153)

King of Scotland from 1124 who twice invaded England. The youngest son of **Malcolm III** Canmore and **St Margaret**, he was brought up in the English court of **Henry I**. He invaded England in support of Queen **Matilda**, but was defeated.

David II (1324–1371)

King of Scotland from 1329, son of **Robert the Bruce**. David was married at the age of four to Joanna, daughter of Edward II of England. After the defeat of the Scots by Edward III at Halidon Hill in 1333, the young David and Joanna were sent to France for safety. In 1346 David invaded England, was captured at the battle of Neville's Cross, and was imprisoned for 11 years.

D-Day

The day of the allied invasion of Normandy in **World War II**. Known as Operation Neptune, the assault took place on 6 June 1944 under the command of General **Montgomery**. It was the beginning of Operation Overlord, the invasion of Western Europe by Allied forces, under the supreme command of General Eisenhower. The Anglo-US invasion fleet landed on the Normandy beaches on the stretch of coast between the Orne River and St Marcouf. Artificial harbours known as 'mulberries' were constructed and towed across the Channel so that equipment and armaments could be unloaded. After overcoming fierce resistance the Allies broke through the German defences. Paris was liberated on 25 August, and Brussels on 2 September.

Declaration of Indulgence

A statement of government policy aimed at encouraging religious tolerance issued by decree of the monarch. There were four Declarations of Indulgence properly so called:

- decree of **Charles II**, in 1662, proclaiming his intention to introduce a bill suspending the penal laws against dissenters in the Church of England. The bill was defeated in the Lords;

- decree of Charles II, in 1672, guaranteeing freedom of worship and suspending all penal laws against Catholics and Protestant dissenters. His attempt was blocked by Parliament in 1673, obliging Charles to withdraw the Indulgence;

- decree of **James II**, in 1687, allowing full freedom of worship. It suspended the operation of the penal laws and remitted all penalties for ecclesiastical offences, thus endangering the Anglican monopoly of the church and state;

- decree of James II, in 1688, reinforcing his earlier Indulgence and ordering it to be read in all Anglican churches. It provoked fierce opposition within the Church of England and led to the arrest and trial of seven bishops.

Declaration of Rights
The statement issued by the Convention Parliament in February 1689, laying down the conditions under which the crown was to be offered to William III and Mary. Its clauses were later incorporated in the **Bill of Rights**.

Defender of the Faith
One of the titles of the English sovereign. It was conferred on **Henry VIII** in 1521 by Pope Leo X in recognition of the king's treatise against the Protestant Martin Luther. It appears on coins in the abbreviated form F.D. (Latin *Fidei Defensor*).

Depression, the
The world economic crisis precipitated by the Wall Street crash of 29 October 1929, when millions of US dollars were wiped off stock values by panic selling in a matter of hours. This forced the closure of many US banks and led to the recall of US overseas investments, with serious repercussions on the European economies. The UK and Germany, which were heavily in debt to the USA, were badly affected. The British economy remained depressed with high levels of unemployment until **World War II**, when armaments manufacture created more jobs.

Derby, Edward (George Geoffrey Smith) Stanley, 14th Earl of Derby (1799–1869)
British politician who in 1830 introduced the bill that abolished slavery in the British Empire. Originally a Whig, Derby joined the Tories in 1834, serving as secretary for war and the colonies in **Peel's** government. When Peel demanded the abolition of the **Corn Laws** in 1846, Derby resigned over the issue, splitting the Conservative Party. He was leader of the Conservatives from 1846 to 1868 and three times prime minister between 1852 and 1868, on each occasion as head of a minority government. During his third administration, the second **Reform Act** was passed. He inherited the title of Lord Stanley in 1834, became a peer in 1844, and succeeded to the earldom in 1851.

> ❝ The duty of an Opposition [is] very simple – to oppose everything, and propose nothing. ❞
>
> **Edward Stanley Derby**, speech in the House of Commons, 4 June 1841

Desmond Revolt

Two Catholic rebellions against Protestant rule in Ireland in 1569 and 1579. They were sparked by the proposed **plantations** of Munster and Connacht by Protestants. The Geraldine Clan rose in protest, led by Sir James Fitzmaurice, a cousin of the Earl of Desmond. The revolt was suppressed in 1573 and Fitzmaurice fled overseas.

He returned in 1579 to lead another Geraldine rising, but was soon killed. Gerald Fitzgerald, 15th Earl of Desmond, took up arms, with some military assistance from Philip II of Spain and Pope Gregory XIII, but the revolt was crushed and the Earl killed in 1583.

Despard Plot

A plot by the Irishman Edward M Despard in 1802 to seize the **Tower of London** and the **Bank of England** and assassinate King **George III**. The affair embarrassed the government not so much because of the seriousness of the plot itself, but because Admiral **Nelson** spoke in defence of the conspirators. Despard was executed on 21 February 1803. He and his fellow conspirators were the last people in England to be sentenced to be hanged, drawn, and quartered.

de Valera, Éamon (1882–1975)

Irish nationalist politician who was prime minister of the Irish Free State and later prime minister and president of the fully independent Republic of Ireland. De Valera was imprisoned for his part in the **Easter Rising**, and in 1917 was elected member of Parliament for East Clare, and president of

de Valera *Éamon De Valera, photographed on 1 January 1920.*

Sinn Féin. He authorized the negotiations of 1921, but refused to accept the ensuing treaty that divided Ireland into the Free State and the North.

In the civil war that followed, De Valera was arrested by the Free State government in 1923, and spent a year in prison. In

Throughout World War II, de Valera maintained a strict neutrality, rejecting an offer by Winston Churchill in 1940 to recognize the principle of a united Ireland in return for the Republic's entry into the war.

1926 he formed a new party, Fianna Fáil, which secured a majority in 1932. De Valera became prime minister and foreign minister of the Free State, and played the leading role in framing the present constitution of the Republic of Ireland by which the country became a sovereign independent state. He resigned after his defeat at the 1948 elections but was again prime minister in 1951–54 and 1957–59, and then president of the republic in 1959 and from 1966 to 1973.

disestablishment

The formal separation of a church from the State, so that the church is no longer recognized as the country's, or province's, official church. The Church of Ireland, created by **Henry VIII** in 1541, was a major source of grievance to Irish Catholics and was disestablished by Gladstone in 1869. The Welsh Anglican Church was disestablished in 1920 to become the Church in Wales. It thus gained its own archbishop and was detached from the province of Canterbury.

There have been several attempts to disestablish the Church of England. This would involve the abolition of both Royal Supremacy over the Church and the Prime Minister's right to advise the Crown on the appointment of bishops.

Disraeli, Benjamin (1804–1881)

British Conservative politician who established Conservative Central Office, the prototype of modern party organizations. Elected to Parliament in 1837, he was chancellor of the Exchequer in the three minority governments of Lord **Derby**. On Derby's retirement in 1868 Disraeli became prime minister but a few months later was defeated by **Gladstone** in a general election.

In 1874 Disraeli took office for the second time with a majority of 100.

His imperialist policies brought India directly under the crown, and he was personally responsible for purchasing control of the Suez Canal. In 1876 he accepted an earldom. The Bulgarian revolt of 1876 and the subsequent Russo-Turkish War of 1877–78 were concluded by the Congress of Berlin in 1878, where Disraeli was the principal British delegate and brought home 'peace with honour' and control of Cyprus. His government was defeated in 1880, and a year later he died.

As well as being a politician, Disraeli wrote popular novels which reflect an interest in social reform. They include *Coningsby* (1844) and *Sybil* (1845).

> ❝ Damn your principles! Stick to your party. ❞
>
> **Benjamin Disraeli**, Latham, *Famous Sayings*

Domesday or Doomsday Book

A record of the survey of England carried out in 1086 by officials of **William the Conqueror**. It was intended to assess land tax and other dues, ascertain the value of the crown lands, and enable the king to estimate the power of his barons. The name derives from the belief that its judgement was as final as that of Doomsday. The Domesday Book is preserved in two volumes at the Public Record Office in London.

Drake, Francis (c. 1540–1596)

English buccaneer, explorer, and naval hero. Having enriched himself as a pirate against Spanish interests in the Caribbean from 1567 to 1572, Drake was spon-

Drake *Contemporary mariners' instruments – an engraving to honour Drake's circumnavigation.*

sored by Elizabeth I for an expedition to the Pacific, sailing round the world in the *Golden Hind*, robbing Spanish ships as he went. He was knighted by **Elizabeth I**, was made mayor of Plymouth, and in 1584–85 represented the town of Bosinney in Parliament. In 1588 he helped to defeat the Spanish Armada as a vice admiral on the *Revenge*.

---

6 There is plenty of time to win this game [of bowls], and to thrash the Spaniards too. 9

Francis Drake, attributed remark

Druidism
The religion of the Celtic peoples of the pre-Christian British Isles and Gaul. The word is derived from the Greek *drus* ('oak'), a tree regarded by the Druids as sacred. The Druids taught the immortality of the soul and a reincarnation doctrine, and were expert in astronomy.

The Druids' stronghold was Anglesey, Wales, until they were driven out by the Roman governor **Agricola**. They existed in Scotland and Ireland until the coming of the Christian missionaries.

The Druids are thought to have offered human sacrifices. A possible example of this is Lindow Man, whose body was found in a bog in Cheshire in 1984.

Duncan I
King of Scotland who was defeated and killed by **Macbeth**. He succeeded his grandfather, Malcolm II, as king in 1034. He is the Duncan in Shakespeare's play *Macbeth* (1605).

Duncan II
King of Scotland, son of **Malcolm III** and grandson of **Duncan I**. He gained English and Norman help to drive out his uncle Donald III in 1094. He ruled for a few months before being killed by agents of Donald, who then regained power.

Dunkirk (French **Dunkerque**)
Northerly French seaport, the site of a massive evacuation in **World War II**. The seaborne withdrawal of British, French, and other Allied troops

in May–June 1940 was known as Operation Dynamo. After the ill-fated campaign on the Western Front in that year, it provided a much-needed boost to morale, particularly in Britain.

A motley 'fleet' of over 1,000 ships, from warships to private yachts, was assembled and sailed to Dunkirk. It was anticipated that perhaps 45,000 troops could be rescued before the Germans took the town. In the event, the Germans, thinking that the British troops penned inside Dunkirk could be safely left there, turned to complete their occupation of northern France. This leeway gave the British time to evacuate many more troops than had been believed possible, averting a potential disaster for the Allies. More than 338,000 soldiers were evacuated.

Dunstan, St (924–988)

English priest who set up a centre of learning at Glastonbury. He was abbot of Glastonbury from 945, and was made bishop of Worcester in 957 and of London in 959. He became archbishop of Canterbury in 960. St Dunstan's day is 19 May.

E

Easter Rising or Easter Rebellion

A republican insurrection that began in Dublin on Easter Monday, April 1916, and was an attempt to overthrow British rule in Ireland. It was led by Patrick Pearse of the Irish Republican Brotherhood (IRB) and James **Connolly** of **Sinn Féin**.

Arms from Germany intended for the IRB were intercepted, but the rising proceeded regardless with the seizure of the Post Office and other buildings in Dublin by 1,500 volunteers.

- The rebellion was crushed by the British Army within five days.

- Altogether 220 civilians, 64 rebels, and 134 members of the Crown Forces were killed.

- Pearse, Connolly, and about a dozen rebel leaders were subsequently executed in Kilmainham Jail.

- Others, including Éamon **de Valera**, were spared and given amnesty in June 1917.

> ❝ In the name of God, and of the dead generations from which she receives her old traditions of nationhood, Ireland through us summons her children to her flag and strikes for freedom. ❞
>
> **Patrick Henry Pearse**, proclamation at the
> General Post Office, Dublin in 1916

East India Company (British)

A commercial company chartered by Queen **Elizabeth I** and given a monopoly of trade between England and the Far East. By 1652 the company had some 23 factories in India. In the 18th century it became, in effect, the ruler of a large part of India, and a form of dual control by the company and a committee responsible to Parliament in London was introduced by Pitt's **India Act** of 1784. After the **Indian Mutiny** of 1857 the crown took complete control of the government of British India. The India Act 1858 abolished the company.

EC (European Community)
Former name, till 1993, of the **European Union** (EU).

Eden, (Robert) Anthony, 1st Earl of Avon (1897–1977)
British Conservative prime minister who resigned after the **Suez Crisis**. Eden was foreign secretary in the wartime coalition, formed in December 1940, and in the Conservative government elected in 1951. In April 1955 he succeeded **Churchill** as prime minister. When Egypt nationalized the Suez Canal in 1956 he authorized the use of force, and a joint Anglo-French force was sent to Egypt. It was withdrawn after pressure from the USA and the USSR, and Eden resigned in January 1957.

Edgehill, Battle of
First battle of the English **Civil War**. It took place in 1642, on a ridge in south Warwickshire, between Royalists under **Charles I** and Parliamentarians under the Earl of Essex. Both sides claimed victory.

Edmund (II) Ironside (c. 981–1016)
King of England who led the resistance to **Canute's** invasion. The son of **Ethelred II** 'the Unready', on Ethelred's death in 1016 Edmund was chosen as king by the citizens of London. Meanwhile, the Witan (the king's council) elected Canute. In the struggle for the throne, Canute defeated Edmund at Ashingdon, and they divided the kingdom between them. When Edmund died later the same year, Canute ruled the whole kingdom.

Education Acts
A series of measures in Britain from the late 19th century onwards aimed at providing everyone with an education.

- The 1870 Education Act was the beginning of state-financed education in England and Wales. Grants to charity schools were increased and local authorities were enabled to finance additional schools out of the rates.
- By 1891 elementary education was free and compulsory.
- H A L Fisher's 1918 Education Act aimed to raise the school leaving age to 14, with some provision for further training.

- Rab Butler's act of 1944 organized a Ministry of Education and intended that schooling be compulsory to the age of 16, though this took many years to achieve.
- The 1980s and 1990s saw a variety of Education Acts that restricted the ability of local authorities to determine the pattern of education by enforcing a National Curriculum and regular testing in all state schools.

Edward the Black Prince (1330–1376)

Prince of Wales who fought in the **Hundred Years' War**. The eldest son of Edward III of England, he fought at the Battle of **Crécy** in 1346 and captured the French king at Poitiers in 1356. He ruled Aquitaine from 1360 to 1371. In 1367 he invaded Castile and restored to the throne the deposed king, Pedro the Cruel. During the revolt that eventually ousted him, he caused the massacre of Limoges in 1370.

Edward I (1239–1307)

King of England who established English rule over Wales and secured recognition of his overlordship from the Scottish king. The son of Henry III (1207–72), he led the royal forces against Simon de **Montfort** (the Younger) in the **Barons' War** of 1264–67 and fought in the crusades. His reign saw Parliament move towards its modern form with the **Model Parliament** of 1295. He married Eleanor of Castile (1254–90) and then, in 1299, Margaret, daughter of Philip III of France. He was succeeded by his son Edward II (1284–1327).

Edward VII (1841–1910)

King of Great Britain and Ireland who was a renowned socialite. Edward was the eldest son of Queen **Victoria** and Prince Albert. His mother considered him too frivolous to take part in political life. In 1860 he made the first tour of Canada and the USA ever undertaken by a British prince. He married Princess Alexandra of Denmark in 1863, and they had six children. He succeeded to the throne in 1901.

Although Edward overrated his political influence, he contributed to the Entente Cordiale of 1904 with France and the Anglo-Russian agreement of 1907.

Edward VIII (1894–1972)

King of Great Britain and Northern Ireland who renounced the throne to marry an American divorcee, Mrs Wallis Simpson, causing the **abdication** crisis. The eldest son of **George V**, he received the title of Prince of Wales in 1910. He succeeded to the throne on 20 January 1936 and abdicated on 10 December 1936.

Edward was extremely popular as Prince of Wales, and he made fashion statements that changed the way men dressed in the Western world – soft collars, tweed sport jackets, cuffed trousers, low shoes, the Windsor knotted tie, and V-necked sweaters freed men from the starched look that characterized the turn of the century.

Edward the Confessor
(c. 1003–1066)

King of England who devoted himself to religion. He was the son of **Ethelred II** and lived in Normandy until shortly before his accession in 1042. During his reign, power was held by Earl Godwin and Godwin's son **Harold**. Edward rebuilt Westminster Abbey, which was consecrated in 1065, and he is buried there. He was canonized in 1161.

Edward's childlessness led ultimately to the Norman Conquest in 1066.

Elizabeth I (1533–1603)

Queen of England (1558–1603) who gave her name to a golden age of English history. She was the daughter of **Henry VIII** and **Anne Boleyn**.

During her Roman Catholic half-sister Mary's (**Mary I**) reign, Elizabeth's Protestant sympathies brought her under suspicion, and she lived in seclusion until on Mary's death she became queen. Through her Religious Settlement of 1559 Elizabeth enforced the Protestant religion by law.

Many attempts were made by Parliament to persuade her to marry or settle the succession. The rulers of European states made unsuccessful offers of marriage, and she used these bids to strengthen her power. She found courtship a useful political weapon, and she maintained friendships with,

> ❟ I know I have the body of a weak and feeble woman, but I have the heart and stomach of a king, and of a king of England too. ❟
>
> **Elizabeth I**, speech to the troops at Tilbury on the approach of the Armada in 1588

among others, the courtiers **Leicester**, Sir Walter **Raleigh**, and **Essex**. She was known as the Virgin Queen.

The arrival in England in 1568 of **Mary Queen of Scots** and her imprisonment by Elizabeth caused a political crisis, and a rebellion of the feudal nobility of the north followed in 1569. Friction between English and Spanish sailors hastened the breach with Roman Catholic Spain. An undeclared war with Spain continued until the landing of an English army in the Netherlands in 1585 and Mary's execution in 1587 brought it into the open. Philip of Spain's Armada (the fleet sent to invade England in 1588) met with total disaster. The Elizabethan age was expansionist in commerce and geographical exploration, and arts and literature flourished.

Elizabeth I *Queen Elizabeth I in Parliament.*

Elizabeth II (1926 –)

Queen of Great Britain and Northern Ireland. The elder daughter of **George VI**, she married her third cousin, the Duke of Edinburgh, in 1947. They have four children, Charles, Anne, Andrew, and Edward.

During **World War II**, she served in the Auxiliary Territorial Service. She succeeded to the throne on the death of her father in 1952 and was crowned on 2 June 1953.

With a fortune estimated at around £5 billion, Elizabeth is the richest woman in Britain, and probably in the world.

Empire, British

Former Empire made up of territories conquered or colonized by Britain. At its height in the 1920s, it occupied about a sixth of the landmass of the Earth.

The British Empire began in 1497 when the Italian seafarer John **Cabot** sailed across the Atlantic Ocean in the service of King Henry VII of England and reached Newfoundland. In 1583 the explorer Sir Humphrey Gilbert took possession of Newfoundland for **Elizabeth I**. In the centuries that followed, lands all around the world were annexed for reasons of commercial gain or national prestige. Empire builders included adventurers and explorers as well as military conquerors. By the 1920s the British Empire consisted of India, four self-governing countries known as dominions, and dozens of colonies and territories.

After **World War II** the empire began to break up as colony after colony became independent.

- India, the 'jewel in the imperial crown', was the first to acquire independence, dividing into two countries, India and Pakistan, in 1948.
- The rest of the colonies then followed, most of them becoming independent before 1980.
- With the return of Hong Kong to China in 1997, Britain was left with only 13 small dependencies.
- Today, these with 54 other independent countries form the **Commonwealth**.

enclosure

The takeover of common land as private property and the change of open-field systems to enclosed fields. It began in the 14th century and became widespread in the 15th and 16th centuries. For many, it caused poverty, homelessness, and rural depopulation, leading to riots in 1536, 1569, and 1607. A further wave of enclosures occurred between about 1760 and 1820.

ENCLOSURE ACTS

- *1603*: the first Enclosure Act.
- *1760–1820*: a new wave of enclosures by acts of Parliament reduced the yeoman class of small landowning farmers to agricultural labourers, or forced them to leave the land.
- *1876 onwards*: the enclosure of common land in Britain was limited by statutes.
- *1903*: the last major Enclosure Act.

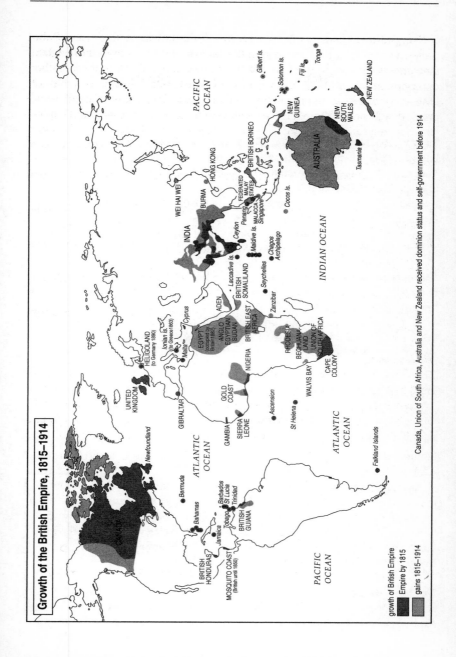

Growth of the British Empire, 1815–1914

growth of British Empire
Empire by 1815
gains 1815–1914

Canada, Union of South Africa, Australia and New Zealand received dominion status and self-government before 1914

Many farmers gained from enclosure. They were able to develop their property, cut costs, and increase yields and profits. From the 18th century, the general increase in food quality and productivity improved the health of the population, particularly those who lived in the towns and cities. However, numerous people lost their living, including the cottars who had previously lived on the edges of the commons, cultivating meagre plots.

Essex, Robert Devereux, 2nd Earl of Essex (1566–1601)

English soldier and politician and a one time favourite of Queen **Elizabeth I**. The son of Walter Devereux, 1st Earl of Essex, and stepson to Robert Dudley, Earl of **Leicester**, he succeeded to the earldom in 1576. Having distinguished himself in the Dutch fight against Spain, in 1599 he became Lieutenant of Ireland and led an army against Irish rebels under the Earl of Tyrone. But he fell from grace by making an unauthorized truce with Tyrone, was tried for treason, and was executed.

Ethelred (II) the Unready (968–1016)

Early king of England who fought the Danes. The son of King Edgar, he became king in 978, following the murder of his half-brother, Edward the Martyr. Ethelred tried to buy off the Danish raiders by paying **danegeld**. In 1002 he ordered the massacre of Danish settlers, provoking an invasion by Sweyn I of Denmark and his son, **Canute**. Ethelred's nickname is a corruption of the Old English 'unreed', meaning poorly advised.

European Union (EU)

European political and economic alliance, which the UK joined in 1973, following a referendum. Formerly called the European Community, its other members are Belgium, France, Germany, Italy, Luxembourg, the Netherlands, Denmark, the Republic of Ireland, Greece, Spain, Portugal, Austria, Finland, and Sweden.

A single market with free movement of goods and capital was established in January 1993. In September 1995 the EU's member nations stated their commitment to the attainment of monetary union by 1999, and in December of the same year they agreed to call the new currency: the euro. Eleven countries – all but the UK, Denmark, Sweden, and Greece – entered the single currency on 1 January 1999.

Exclusion Bills

A series of measures in the reigns of **Charles I** and **Charles II** intended to exclude Catholics from office.

- *June 1641* The first bill aimed to exclude bishops from sitting in parliament in order to weaken Charles I's support in the House of Lords. It was initially rejected by the Lords, but it was reintroduced after Charles attempted to arrest five MPs for treason. The bill became law in February 1642.

- *1678–81* A series of bills was proposed to bar Charles II's Catholic brother, James, Duke of York, from the throne. After the alleged 'Popish Plot' to murder Charles, a bill was introduced that would ensure the succession of his illegitimate son, the Duke of Monmouth. Charles dissolved parliament to prevent the bill's passage. A similar measure was introduced in 1680 but was rejected by the House of Lords. Charles summoned the next parliament to Oxford, but another exclusion bill was put forward in 1681 and Charles again dissolved parliament.

Fabian Society

UK socialist organization and forerunner of the **Labour Party**. It was started in London in 1884. The name derives from the Roman commander Fabius Maximus, known for his cautious tactics, and it refers to the evolutionary, reformist methods by which Fabians hope to attain socialism. Early members included George Bernard Shaw, and Beatrice and Sidney Webb (who founded the London School of Economics). The society helped to found the Labour Representation Committee in 1900, which became the Labour Party in 1906.

Factory Acts

Acts of Parliament that govern conditions of work, hours of labour, safety, and sanitary provision in factories and workshops in the UK. In the 19th century legislation was progressively introduced to regulate conditions of work. The first factory act was the Health and Morals of Apprentices Act of 1802. Much of the early legislation regulated conditions for women and children working in the textile industries. Men were only gradually brought within the protection of the law. Today, all employees, not only factory workers, are covered by the 1974 Health and Safety at Work Act, which is enforced by the Health and Safety Executive

Factory Acts in the UK: chronology

1802 Health and Morals of Apprentices Act, a first attempt to regulate conditions for workhouse children in the textile industry, is introduced.

1819 Factory Act prohibits children under nine working in cotton mills. Others are set an 11-hour maximum day.

1842 Mines Act prohibits employment of women and children under ten underground. Factory Act reduces hours for children and youths in textile factories.

1847 Factory Act imposes a maximum ten-hour day for women and young people in textile factories.

1853 Shift work for children is outlawed.

1901 Minimum working age increases to 12. Trade Boards are established to fix minimum wages, extended in 1918.

1909 First Old Age Pensions Act.
1911 National Insurance Act covers sickness and unemployment in vulnerable trades.
1931 'Means-tested' unemployment benefit is introduced.
1937 Factory Act limits workers under 16 to a 44-hour week and women to a 48-hour week.
1946 National Insurance Act provides comprehensive cover for industrial injuries.
1961 Factories Act extends safety regulations to all workplaces. Graduated pension scheme is introduced.
1965 Graduated redundancy payments are introduced.
1974 Health and Safety at Work legislation is extended to cover all workers.

Fairfax, Thomas, 3rd Baron Fairfax (1612–1671)

English general, commander in chief of the Parliamentary army in the **Civil War**. With Oliver **Cromwell** he formed the **New Model Army** and defeated **Charles I** at Naseby. He opposed the king's execution, resigned in protest against the invasion of Scotland in 1650, and participated in the restoration of **Charles II** after Cromwell's death. Knighted in 1640, he succeeded to the barony in 1648.

Falklands War

War between Argentina and Britain over disputed sovereignty of the Falkland Islands in the South Atlantic. It began when Argentina invaded and occupied the islands on 2 April 1982. On the following day, the United Nations Security Council passed a resolution calling for Argentina to withdraw. A British task force was immediately dispatched and, after a fierce conflict in which more than 1,000 Argentine and British lives were lost, the islands were returned to British rule on 14–15 June 1982.

Fawkes, Guy (1570–1606)

English conspirator in the **Gunpowder Plot** to blow up King **James I** and the members of both Houses of Parliament. Fawkes, a Roman Catholic convert, was arrested in the cellar underneath the House of Lords on 4 November 1605, tortured, and executed.

The Gunpowder Plot is still commemorated in Britain and elsewhere every 5 November with bonfires, fireworks, and the burning of the 'guy', an effigy.

Fenian movement

A 19th-century Irish republican secret society named after the Fianna, an Irish legendary warrior band. It was founded in the USA and Ireland in

1858. An uprising organized by Fenians in Ireland in 1867 and attacks on mainland Britain brought the Irish question to the attention of **Gladstone**, who introduced the **Home Rule** bill.

The name Fenian has been applied generally to supporters of Irish republicanism.

feudalism

The main form of social organization in medieval England. Based entirely on land, it involved a hierarchy of authority, rights, and power. A complex network of duties and obligations from royalty and the nobility at the top to the peasant **serfs** at the bottom was reinforced by the legal system and the Christian church.

With the growth of commerce and industry in the 13th century, feudalism began to break down, but it was not formally abolished in England till 1661.

Fire of London

A great fire that destroyed four-fifths of the City of London between 2 and 5 September 1666. It broke out in a bakery in Pudding Lane and spread as far west as the Temple. The fire destroyed 87 churches, including St Paul's Cathedral, and 13,200 houses, but fewer than 20 people lost their lives.

Fire of London *London burning in the Great Fire – as seen from Southwark.*

Flanders, Battle of

A series of military engagements in **World War I**, as the British advanced into Belgium and northern France from September to November 1918. They succeeded in driving the Germans out of the Benelux countries and back into Germany. The overall plan, conceived by the British commander **Haig**, was to develop attacks along the whole length of the British front as far as **Ypres**.

Fox, Charles James (1749–1806)

English Whig politician who ended the slave trade. The son of the 1st Baron Holland, he entered Parliament in 1769 as a supporter of the court, but went over to the opposition in 1774. He was secretary of state in 1782, and being a supporter of the French Revolution he led the opposition to **William Pitt the Younger's** war of intervention. As foreign secretary in 1806, he brought about the abolition of the **slave trade**. He opened peace negotiations with France, but died before their completion.

> ❝ Is peace a rash system? Is it dangerous for nations to live in amity ...? Must the bowels of Great Britain be torn out – her best blood be spilt – her treasure wasted – that you may make an experiment? ❞
>
> **Charles James Fox**, speech in the House of Commons in February 1800, arguing against war with France

Friends, Society of or Quakers

A Protestant sect whose members believe in nonviolence. Founded by George Fox in England in the 17th century, they were persecuted for their views, and many emigrated to form communities abroad; for example in Pennsylvania and New England. In the 19th century many Friends were prominent in social reform, for example, Elizabeth **Fry**. Quakers have exerted a profound influence on American life through their pacifism and belief in social equality, education, and prison reform.

- Their worship stresses meditation and the freedom of all to take an active part in the service (called a meeting, held in a meeting house).
- They have no priests or ministers.
- The name 'Quakers' may originate in Fox's injunction to 'quake at the word of the Lord'.

Frobisher, Martin (1535–1594)

English navigator and explorer who sought the Northwest Passage, a searoute round the top of America linking the Atlantic and Pacific Oceans. He made three expeditions, in 1576, 1577, and 1578, but did not achieve his goal. He fought against the Spanish Armada under **Drake** and was knighted in 1588 for helping to secure victory. He died fighting the Spanish in 1594.

Fry, Elizabeth (1780–1845)

English Quaker philanthropist who helped women prisoners and the poor. Born Elizabeth Gurney, in 1800 she married Joseph Fry, a London Quaker and relative of the Fry family of the Fry's chocolate business. From 1813 she began to visit and teach the women in **Newgate** prison who lived with their children in terrible conditions. She formed an association for the improvement of conditions for female prisoners in 1817, and for 25 years visited every ship carrying women convicts bound for Australia.

With her brother, Joseph Gurney, she worked on an 1819 report on prison reform. A pioneer for higher nursing standards and the education of working women, she campaigned for better housing and working conditions for the poor, and inspected mental asylums.

General Strike

In the UK, a nationwide strike called by the **Trades Union Congress** (TUC) on 3 May 1926 in support of striking miners. The cause of the strike was a royal commission report that recommended a cut in miners' wages. The mine-owners also expected miners to work longer hours. The miners' union, under the leadership of A J Cook, resisted with the slogan 'Not a penny off the pay, not a minute on the day'.

- A coal strike, started in early May 1926, swelled to include more than 2 million workers.

- The Conservative government under Stanley **Baldwin** used troops, volunteers, and special constables to maintain food supplies and essential services.

- After nine days the TUC ended the general strike, leaving the miners to fight on alone and in vain until November 1926.

- The Trades Disputes Act of 1927 made general strikes illegal.

George III (1738–1820)

King of Great Britain and Ireland whose rule was marked by the loss of the American colonies and the emancipation of **Catholics** in England. He succeeded his grandfather George II in 1760 and married Princess Charlotte Sophia of Mecklenburg-Strelitz in 1761. His intransigence led to the loss of America, for which he shared the blame with his chief minister Lord North. Possibly suffering from porphyria, he had repeated attacks of insanity, which became permanent from 1811.

> ❝ I desire what is good; therefore, everyone who does not agree with me is a traitor. ❞
>
> **George III**, Sir John Fortescue (ed) *The Correspondence of George III*

George IV (1762–1830)

King of Great Britain and Ireland who was notorious for his dissipation and extravagance. In 1820, he succeeded his father, **George III**, for whom he had been regent since 1811 during the king's period of insanity. In 1785 he had secretly married a Catholic widow, Maria Fitzherbert, but in 1795 also married Princess Caroline of Brunswick, in return for payment of his debts. He was a patron of the arts. His prestige was undermined by his dissolute behaviour and his treatment of Caroline (they separated in 1796).

George V (1865–1936)

King of Great Britain and Northern Ireland who changed the name of the royal household. He succeeded his father **Edward VII** in 1910. He became heir in 1892 on the death of his elder brother Albert, Duke of Clarence. In 1893 he married Princess Victoria Mary of Teck (Queen Mary), who had been engaged to his brother. During **World War I** he made several visits to the front. In 1917 he abandoned all German titles for himself and his family. The name of the royal house was changed from Saxe-Coburg-Gotha (popularly known as Brunswick or Hanover) to Windsor.

> ❝ I have many times asked myself whether there can be more potent advocates of peace upon the earth through the years to come than this massed multitude of silent witnesses to the desolation of war. ❞
>
> **George V**, referring to the mass war graves in Flanders in 1922, quoted in Gavin Stamp's *Silent Cities*

George VI (1895–1952)

King of Great Britain and Northern Ireland who succeeded his brother **Edward VIII** after the 1936 **abdication crisis**. The second son of **George V**, he was created Duke of York in 1920. He married Lady Elizabeth Bowes-Lyon (the 'Queen Mother') in 1923 they had two children: Elizabeth, who would become Queen, and Margaret. During **World War II**, he visited the battlefields of Normandy and Italy.

> ❝ We're not a family; we're a firm. ❞
>
> **George VI**, attributed remark

Gilbert of Sempringham, St (*c.* 1083–1189)

The founder of the Gilbertines, the only purely English religious order. As incumbent of Sempringham in Lincolnshire, he encouraged seven women of his parish to adopt a pattern of life similar to the rule of the Cistercians. In 1148 the order was approved by Rome, but later dissolved during the **Reformation**.

- By time of Gilbert's death, he had built 13 monasteries as well as orphanages and leper hospitals.
- He was canonized in 1202.
- His feast day is on 4 February.

Gladstone, William Ewart (1809–1898)

British Liberal prime minister who introduced elementary education (1870) and voting by secret ballot (1872) but failed to get his Home Rule for Ireland Bill passed. Gladstone entered Parliament as a Tory in 1833 and held ministerial office, but left the party in 1846 and after 1859 became a Liberal. He was twice chancellor of the Exchequer between 1852 and 1866, and prime minister for the first time from 1868 to 1874. He carried through reforms in education and in Ireland, and abolished the purchase of army commissions.

Gladstone strongly opposed Benjamin **Disraeli's** government's imperialist and pro-Turkish policy, and his Midlothian campaign of 1879 helped bring the government down. Gladstone's second government carried out the **Reform Act** of 1884 but lost prestige through its failure to relieve General **Gordon** in the Sudan.

Returning to office in 1886, Gladstone introduced his first Irish **Home Rule** Bill, which was defeated. In 1892 he formed his last government. His second Home Rule Bill was rejected by the Lords, and in 1894 he resigned. He led a final crusade against the massacre of Armenian Christians by the Turks in 1896.

Gladstone *The Right Honorable William Gladstone, Prime Minister*

> 6 All the world over, I will back the masses against the classes. 9
>
> **William Gladstone**, speech in Liverpool, 28 June 1886

Glencoe, Massacre of

Slaughter in Glencoe, Scotland, of 37 members of the MacDonald clan in 1692 by the Campbells, their hereditary enemies. **William III** had ordered all Highland chiefs to take an oath of allegiance before 1 January 1692, but the MacDonalds refused. Advised by the Master of Stair to wipe out the clan, the king quartered the Campbells on the MacDonalds. They lived amicably with their hosts for ten days, before turning on them.

> 6 Great stone of the glen, great is your right to be here. Yet if you but knew what would happen this night, you would be up and away. 9
>
> **Anonymous,** attributed to a soldier the night before the Massacre of Glencoe

Glendower, Owen (Welsh **Owain Glyndwr**) (*c.* 1350–1416)

Welsh nationalist leader. He led a rebellion against **Henry IV** of England, taking the title 'Prince of Wales' in 1400, and fought off English invasions in 1400–02. He gained control of most of the country and established an independent Welsh parliament. From 1405 onwards he suffered repeated defeats at the hands of Prince Hal, later **Henry V**. Glendower allied himself with Charles VI of France, who sent a force to Wales, but they too were beaten. Wales was reconquered by 1413 and Glendower went into hiding and disappeared from history.

Glorious Revolution

The removal of Catholic **James II** from the throne of England and his replacement by his Protestant daughter Mary and her husband **William of Orange** as joint sovereigns.

James had become increasingly unpopular on account of his unconstitutional behaviour and Catholicism. Arriving at Torbay on 5 November 1688, William rapidly gained support and James was allowed to flee to France after the army deserted him. Support for James in Scotland and Ireland was forcibly suppressed in 1689–90. In 1689 William and Mary accepted a new constitutional settlement, the **Bill of Rights**, which assured the ascendancy of parliamentary power over sovereign rule.

The Glorious Revolution: chronology

1669 James, Duke of York, heir to the English throne, is received into the Roman Catholic Church.

1678–81 Exclusion Crisis: following an alleged 'popish plot' to kill King Charles II and replace him with the Catholic James, three parliaments attempt to exclude James from the succession.

1685 6 February: Death of Charles II; accession of James II.

11 June–6 July: Monmouth's Rebellion: Charles II's illegitimate son invades southeast England and attempts to overthrow James II.

1688 10 June: Queen Mary gives birth to a son, James Edward, giving England the prospect of a second Catholic king.

30 June: Seven peers secretly invite the Protestant Prince William of Orange to invade England.

5 November: William of Orange lands at Torbay, southwest England, and advances towards London, gaining popular support.

10–11 December: James flees to France, but is stopped at Faversham, Kent, and taken back to London.

23 December: James makes a successful flight to France.

1689 13 February: William of Orange and his wife Mary (daughter of James II) are proclaimed King and Queen.

12 March: James II lands in Ireland in a bid to regain the throne.

1690 1 July: Battle of the Boyne: William defeats James; James returns to France.

Godiva or Godgifu, Lady (c. 1040–1080)

The wife of Leofric, Earl of Mercia, who, according to legend, rode naked through Coventry. Legend has it that her husband promised to reduce the heavy taxes on the people if she rode naked through the streets at noon. The grateful citizens remained indoors, but 'Peeping Tom' bored a hole in his shutters and was struck blind.

Gordon, Charles George (1833–1885)

British general who was besieged for ten months by the Mahdi's army in Khartoum, in the Sudan. From 1877 to 1880 Gordon was British governor of the Sudan. In 1884 he was sent to Khartoum to rescue English garrisons that were under attack by the Mahdi, Muhammad Ahmed. A relief expedition arrived on 28 January 1885 to find that Khartoum had been captured and Gordon killed two days before.

> ❝ I would sooner live like a Dervish with the Mahdi, than go out to dinner every night in London. ❞
>
> **Charles Gordon**, *Khartoum Journal*, 1883

Gordon Riots

Anti-Catholic riots in London between 2 and 9 June 1780. A mob of 50,000 Protestants led by Lord George Gordon marched on Parliament to present a petition against the Roman Catholic Relief Act of 1778.

- The mob attacked and destroyed houses and other property owned by Catholics.
- About 300 people were killed.
- After five days of rioting the army was called in to restore order.
- Gordon was charged with treason, but later acquitted.

Great Britain

The official name for England, Scotland, and Wales, and the neighbouring islands (except the Channel Islands and the Isle of Man). It dates from 1603, when the English and Scottish crowns were united under **James I** of England (James VI of Scotland). With Northern Ireland it forms the United Kingdom.

Greater London Council (GLC)

The elected local authority that governed London from 1965 to 1986. It was abolished by the Conservatives under Margaret **Thatcher**. Its powers devolved back to the borough councils or were transferred to unelected bodies.

Great Exhibition

The world fair held in Hyde Park, London, UK, 1851. It was described by its originator Prince Albert as 'the Great Exhibition of the Industries of All Nations', though over half the 100,000 exhibits were from Britain or the British Empire. More than 6 million people attended the exhibition. The exhibition hall, known as the Crystal Palace, was made of glass with a cast-iron frame.

Great Exhibition *The exterior of the Great Exhibition of 1851.*

Great Plague

A plague that swept London in 1665, the last major outbreak of bubonic plague in Britain. It reached its height in the autumn and subsided towards the end of the year. It claimed the lives of about 100,000 of London's 400,000 population.

Samuel **Pepys's** diary describes not only the horrors of the plague, but the upheaval it caused to life in the nation's capital.

Grenville, George (1712–1770)

English Whig politician, prime minister, and chancellor of the Exchequer, whose introduction of the **Stamp Act** of 1765 was one of the causes of the **American Revolution**. His government was also responsible for prosecuting the Radical John **Wilkes**.

Grenville, Richard (c. 1541–1591)

English naval commander and adventurer who died heroically aboard his ship *The Revenge* when it was attacked by Spanish warships.

- *1566–69:* Grenville fought in Hungary and Ireland.
- c. *1577:* he was knighted.
- *1585:* he commanded the expedition that founded Virginia, USA, for his cousin Walter **Raleigh**.
- *1586–88:* he organized the defence of England against the Spanish Armada.

Grey, Charles, 2nd Earl Grey (1764–1845)

British Whig prime minister who carried the Great **Reform** Bill (1832), which reshaped the parliamentary representative system, and the act that abolished slavery throughout the British Empire (1833). He entered Parliament in 1786, and in 1806 became First Lord of the Admiralty, and foreign secretary soon afterwards. Prime minister from 1830 to 1834, he was made an earl in 1807.

Grey, Lady Jane (1537–1554)

Queen of England for nine days (10–19 July 1553). The great-granddaughter of **Henry VII**, she married Lord Guildford Dudley, the son of the Duke of Northumberland, in 1553. When Edward VI died on 6 July 1553, Jane was persuaded by Northumberland, to accept the crown and was proclaimed queen four days later. Edward's sister **Mary I** had the support of the populace, and the Lord Mayor of London announced that she was queen on 19 July. Grey was executed on Tower Green.

Gulf War

A war between Iraq and a 28-nation coalition led by the USA and involving the UK, between 16 January and 28 February 1991. Iraq had invaded and annexed Kuwait on 2 August 1990 following a dispute over a shared oilfield, and the price of oil. Resolutions by the United Nations (UN) Security Council calling for immediate withdrawal of Iraqi troops went unheeded, as did peace initiatives by the UN and France.

- An air offensive lasting six weeks destroyed about one-third of Iraqi equipment and inflicted massive casualties.
- A 100-hour ground war followed, which effectively destroyed the remnants of the 500,000-strong Iraqi army in or near Kuwait.
- The UK deployed 42,000 troops during the war.

Gunpowder Plot

The Catholic conspiracy to blow up **James I** and his parliament on 5 November 1605. In 1604 the conspirators, led by Robert Catesby, took possession of a vault below the House of Lords where they stored barrels of gunpowder. Lord Monteagle, a Catholic peer, received an anonymous letter warning him not to attend Parliament on the following 5 November. A search was made, and Guy **Fawkes** was discovered in the vault and arrested. Several of the conspirators were killed as they fled, and Fawkes and seven others were captured and executed

Gunpowder Plot *Guy Fawkes and the conspirators of the Gunpowder Plot.*

Gwyn or Gwynn, Nell (Eleanor) (1650–1687)

English comedy actress who was the mistress of **Charles II**. She was an orange-seller at Drury Lane Theatre, London, before acting on the stage in 1665. The poet Dryden wrote parts for her. She became the king's mistress in 1669.

habeas corpus (Latin 'you may have the body')

Protection dating from the 1679 English Habeas Corpus Act against unlawful detention. It is defined as a writ directed to someone who has custody of a person, ordering him or her to bring the person before the court issuing the writ and to justify why the person is detained in custody. The main principles of habeas corpus were adopted in the US Constitution. The Scottish equivalent is the Wrongous Imprisonment Act of 1701.

Hadrian's Wall

A line of fortifications built by the Roman emperor Hadrian (reigned AD 117–38) across northern Britain from the Cumbrian coast on the west to the North Sea on the east. The wall itself ran from Bowness on the Solway Firth to Wallsend on the river Tyne, a distance of 110 km/ 68 mi. It was defended by 16 forts and smaller intermediate fortifications. It was breached by the **Picts** on several occasions and finally abandoned in about 383.

> Hadrian's Wall was declared a World Heritage Site in 1987.

Haig, Douglas, 1st Earl Haig (1861–1928)

Scottish military leader in **World War I**. Born in Edinburgh, Haig succeeded John French as army commander in chief in 1915. His **Somme** offensive in France in the summer of 1916 made considerable advances only at enormous cost to human life, and his **Passchendaele** offensive in Belgium from

> 6 Every position must be held to the last man: there must be no retirement. With our backs to the wall, and believing in the justice of our cause, each one must fight on to the end. 9
>
> **Douglas Haig**, order given on 12 April 1918

July to November 1917 achieved little with similar losses. He was created field marshal in 1917 and, after retiring, became first president of the British Legion in 1921.

Halifax, Edward Frederick Lindley Wood, 1st Earl of Halifax (1881–1959)

British Conservative foreign secretary associated with Chamberlain's **appeasement** policy. From 1926 to 1931 he was viceroy of India. He became Baron in 1925 and succeeded as Viscount in 1934. He received an earldom in 1944 for services to the Allied cause while ambassador to the USA between 1941 and 1946.

> ❝I often think how much easier the world would have been to manage if Herr Hitler and Signor Mussolini had been at Oxford.❞
>
> **Edward Halifax**, speech on 4 November 1937

Hamilton, Emma, Lady (c. 1761–1815)

English courtesan and, most famously, the mistress of Horatio **Nelson**. Born Amy Lyon, in 1782 she became the mistress of Charles Greville and in 1786 of his uncle Sir William Hamilton, the British envoy to the court of Naples, who married her in 1791. After Admiral Nelson's return from the Nile in 1798, during the Napoleonic Wars, she became his mistress. Their daughter, Horatia, was born in 1801.

Hanover, House of

German royal dynasty that ruled Great Britain and Ireland from 1714 to 1901. Under the Act of Settlement of 1701, the succession on the death of Queen **Anne** passed to the Protestant house of Hanover. On the death of Queen **Victoria**, the crown passed to **Edward VII** of the house of Saxe-Coburg (later called Windsor).

Hansard

The official report of the proceedings of the British Houses of Parliament. It is named after Luke Hansard, printer of the House of Commons *Journal* from 1774. The first official reports were published from 1803 by William **Cobbett** who, during his imprisonment, sold the business to his printer

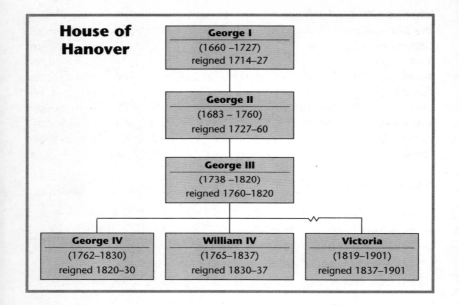

House of Hanover

George I
(1660 –1727)
reigned 1714–27

George II
(1683 – 1760)
reigned 1727–60

George III
(1738 –1820)
reigned 1760–1820

George IV
(1762–1830)
reigned 1820–30

William IV
(1765–1837)
reigned 1830–37

Victoria
(1819–1901)
reigned 1837–1901

Thomas Curson Hansard, Luke's son. The publication of the debates remained in the hands of the family until 1889.

The name *Hansard* was officially adopted in 1943 on the recommendation of a House of Commons Select Committee. *Hansard* is published by Her Majesty's Stationery Office and can now be consulted on the Internet.

Hardie, (James) Keir (1856–1915)

Pioneering Scottish socialist who was twice a Member of Parliament (1892–95 and 1900–15). He worked in the mines as a boy and in 1886 became secretary of the Scottish Miners' Federation. In 1888 Hardie founded the Scottish Parliamentary Labour Party. He entered Parliament as an Independent Socialist in 1892, and was the chief founder of the **Independent Labour Party** in 1893. He was chair of the newly formed **Labour Party** in 1906–08 and again in 1909–10.

A pacifist, Hardie strongly opposed the **South African War** and **World War I**, and his idealism in his work for socialism and the unemployed made him a popular hero.

Harold (II) Godwinson (c. 1020–1066)
The last Anglo-Saxon king of England. Harold succeeded his father Earl Godwin in 1053 as Earl of Wessex. In 1063 William of Normandy (**William the Conqueror**) tricked him into swearing to support his claim to the English throne. Harold succeeded **Edward the Confessor** as king in January 1066 and William prepared to invade. Meanwhile, Harold's treacherous brother Tostig joined the king of Norway in invading Northumbria. Harold routed and killed them at **Stamford Bridge** on 25 September. Three days later William landed at Pevensey, Sussex, and Harold was killed at the Battle of **Hastings** on 14 October.

Hastings, Battle of
A decisive battle between **William the Conqueror**, Duke of Normandy, and **Harold Godwinson**, King of England, on 14 October 1066. Harold was killed in the engagement and William was crowned king of England just over two months later on Christmas Day.

The battle site is 10 km/6 mi inland from Hastings, at Senlac, Sussex; it is marked by Battle Abbey.

- The Normans dominated the battle with archers supported by cavalry, breaking through the ranks of infantry.

- Both sides suffered heavy losses, especially the English whose army was decimated.

- Harold's death left England open to Norman rule.

Hastings, Warren (1732–1818)
Controversial British colonial administrator in India. A protégé of Lord **Clive**, who established British rule in India, Hastings carried out major reforms, and became governor general of Bengal in 1772 and governor general of India in 1774. He was impeached for corruption on his return to England in 1785, but acquitted ten years later.

Heath, Edward (Richard George) (1916–)
British Conservative prime minister who took the UK into the European Economic Community (EEC; now **European Union**). Born at Broadstairs, Kent, Heath was elected Conservative MP for Bexley in 1950. He became leader of the Conservative Party in 1965, won the June 1970 general election against all poll indications, and became prime minister of a

Conservative government. An enthusiastic 'European', Heath achieved his ambition of British entry to the EEC on 1 January 1973.

In the winter of 1973–74 his industrial and economic policies were directly challenged by miners' strikes, and in February he called a general election on the issue of 'Who governs Britain?'. This resulted in a Conservative defeat and the appointment of a Labour government.

Heath returned to the backbenches in 1975 and was a consistent critic of the **Thatcher** government of 1979–90, particularly on Europe. He remained critical of the European policy of Thatcher's successors, John Major and William Hague.

> **❝** We are the trade union for pensioners and children, the trade union for the disabled and the sick ... the trade union for the nation as a whole. **❞**
>
> **Edward Heath**, election speech in February 1974

Henderson, Arthur (1863–1935)
British Labour politician and trade unionist who helped change the Labour Party from a pressure group into a party of government. Born in Glasgow, Henderson worked for 20 years as an iron moulder in Newcastle. He was elected to Parliament in 1903 as Labour member for Rochdale, was the leader of the Labour Party in 1914–18 and home secretary in the first Labour

> Henderson worked for international disarmament and was awarded the Nobel Peace Prize in 1934.

government from 1924 to 1929. As foreign secretary in 1929–31 he accorded the Soviet government full recognition.

Henry I (1068–1135)
King of England from 1100, the youngest son of **William the Conqueror**. Henry succeeded his brother William II. He won the support of the Saxons by granting them a charter and marrying a Saxon princess, Matilda, daughter of **Malcolm III** of Scotland. An able

> Henry I is said to have died from eating too many lampreys. He could not resist eating large quantities, although they made him feel unwell.

administrator, he established a professional bureaucracy and a system of travelling judges.

Henry IV (1367–1413)

King of England from 1399, after **Richard II** was forced to abdicate. Originally Henry Bolingbroke, the son of John of Gaunt, he was banished in 1398 by Richard II. In 1399 he returned to head a revolt and be accepted as king by Parliament. However, he had difficulty in keeping the support of Parliament and the clergy, and had to deal with baronial unrest and Owen **Glendower's** rising in Wales.

Henry V (1387–1422)

King of England from 1413 to 1422, and victor at **Agincourt**. The son of **Henry IV**, he invaded Normandy in 1415 (during the **Hundred Years' War**), captured Harfleur and defeated a superior French force at Agincourt. He invaded again in 1417–19, capturing Rouen. His military victory forced the French into the Treaty of Troyes in 1420, which gave Henry control of the French government. He married Catherine of Valois in 1420 and was recognized as heir to the French throne by his father-in-law Charles VI, but died before him.

❝ Everyone knows I act in everything with kindness and mercy, for I am forcing Rouen into submission by starvation, not by fire, sword or bloodshed. **❞**

Henry V, to a delegation from Rouen during the siege of 1415

Henry VI (1421–1471)

King of England from 1422, the son of **Henry V.** He assumed royal power in 1442 and sided with the party opposed to the continuation of the **Hundred Years' War** with France. The unpopularity of the government after the loss of the English conquests in France encouraged Richard, Duke of York, and then his son Edward to claim the throne. Henry was deposed in 1461, taken prisoner in 1465, temporarily restored in 1470 but again imprisoned and then murdered.

Henry VI was eight months old when he succeeded to the English throne, and still a baby when his maternal grandfather, Charles VI, died, and he became titular king of France.

Henry VII (1457–1509)

King of England from 1485, after defeating and killing **Richard III** at the Battle of **Bosworth**. By marrying Elizabeth of **York** in 1486, Henry united the houses of **York** and **Lancaster**. Yorkist revolts continued until 1497, but Henry restored order after the Wars of the **Roses** using the **Star Chamber**.

Henry achieved independence from **Parliament** by amassing a private fortune through confiscations, crushing the independence of the nobility by a policy of forced loans and fines.

> ❛ The kings, my predecessors, weakening their treasure, have made themselves servants to their subjects. ❜
>
> **Henry VII** to Henry Wyatt, one of his councillors and father of the poet Sir Thomas Wyatt

Henry VIII (1491–1547)

King of England who married six times and split from the Church of Rome. He succeeded his father **Henry VII** in 1509 and married **Catherine of Aragón**.

Henry VIII *Henry VIII and his children, heirs to the throne.*

During the period 1513–29 Henry pursued an active foreign policy under the guidance of his Lord Chancellor, Cardinal **Wolsey**, who shared Henry's desire to make England stronger. Wolsey was replaced by Thomas **More** in 1529 for failing to persuade the pope to grant Henry a divorce. After 1532 Henry broke with papal authority, proclaimed himself head of the church in England, dissolved the monasteries, and divorced Catherine. He then married Anne **Boleyn**, whom he later had beheaded for adultery.

Although Henry laid the ground for the English **Reformation** by the separation from Rome, he had little sympathy with Protestant dogmas. He executed not only Roman Catholics, including Thomas **More**, for refusing to acknowledge his supremacy in the church, but also Protestants who maintained his changes had not gone far enough.

Henry's third wife, Jane Seymour, died of natural causes. He married Anne of Cleves in 1540 in pursuance of Thomas **Cromwell's** policy of allying with the German Protestants, but rapidly abandoned this policy, divorced Anne, and beheaded Cromwell. His fifth wife, Catherine Howard, was beheaded for adultery, and in 1542 Henry married Catherine Parr, who survived him.

HENRY VIII'S WIVES

- *1509–33:* Catherine of Aragón – divorced
- *1533–36:* Anne Boleyn – beheaded
- *1536–37:* Jane Seymour – died
- *1540:* Anne of Cleves – divorced
- *1540–42:* Catherine Howard – beheaded
- *1543–47:* Catherine Parr – outlived Henry

Hereward the Wake (11th century)

A legendary Saxon hero of the English resistance to the Normans. Outlawed by **Edward the Confessor** in 1062, Hereward returned home after 1066 to find his father dead, his brother murdered, and the Norman lord Peter de Bourne in possession. Hereward killed him in revenge and led 40 men to the last English strongpoint at the abbey on the Isle of Ely. When **William the Conqueror** took the island in 1071, Hereward retreated into the forest.

Highland Clearances
The forcible removal of tenants from large estates in Scotland from the mid-18th century, as landowners improved their estates by switching from arable to sheep farming. It led to hardship and widespread emigration to North America.

Hillsborough Agreement
Another name for the **Anglo-Irish Agreement**.

Home Guard
An unpaid force formed in Britain in May 1940 to repel the expected German invasion of **World War II**. Consisting of men aged 17–65 who had not been called up, it was part of the armed forces of the Crown and subject to military law.
* In 1944 the Home Guard was over 2 million strong.
* It was disbanded after the war, on 31 December 1945.
* It was revived in 1951.
* It ceased activity in 1957.

Home Rule, Irish
A movement to repeal the 1801 Act of **Union**, which joined Ireland to Britain, and to establish an Irish Parliament responsible for internal affairs. In 1870 Isaac Butt formed the Home Rule Association and the movement was led in Parliament from 1880 by Charles **Parnell**.

After **Gladstone's** Home Rule bills of 1886 and 1893 were both defeated, a third bill was introduced in 1912, which aroused fierce opposition in Ireland from the Protestant minority. From 1918 the call for an independent Irish republic replaced the demand for home rule. The Government of Ireland Act introduced separate Parliaments in the North and South in 1920, leading to the treaty of 1921 that established the Irish Free State.

Howe, Richard, 1st Earl Howe (1726–1799)
British admiral who in 1794 won the Glorious First of June victory over the French off the coast of Brittany in the French Revolutionary Wars. He com-

manded the Channel fleets in 1792–96 and fought against the colonists during the **American Revolution**.

Hudson's Bay Company

A chartered company founded in 1670 by the Englishman Prince Rupert to trade in furs with North American Indians. In 1783 the rival North West Company was formed, but in 1851 this was amalgamated with the Hudson's Bay Company.

The Hudson's Bay Company is still Canada's biggest fur company, but today also sells general merchandise through department stores and has oil and natural gas interests.

Hume, John (1937–)

The leader of the **Social Democratic and Labour Party** (SDLP) and one of the chief architects of the peace process in Northern Ireland. An MP since 1969, in 1993 he held talks with **Sinn Féin** leader, Gerry **Adams**, on the possibility of securing peace in Northern Ireland. This prompted a joint **Anglo-Irish** peace initiative, which in turn led to a general ceasefire in 1994. Despite the collapse of the ceasefire in 1996, Hume continued in his efforts to broker a settlement. This was achieved in 1998 with the Good Friday Agreement, and the SDLP polled strongly in the ensuing elections to the new Northern Ireland assembly. Hume shared the 1998 Nobel Peace Prize with the Ulster Unionist leader David Trimble for their efforts to further the peace process.

Humphrey, Duke of Gloucester (1391–1447)

An English prince, the youngest son of Henry IV, who founded the library at **Oxford University**. A renowned patron of learning, he was known as 'Good Duke Humphrey'. He clashed with his uncle, Cardinal Beaufort, over policy towards France, Humphrey favouring renewed war, and in the 1440s tried to have Beaufort removed from office. In 1447 Humphrey was accused of treason and died in prison five days later, possibly having been murdered.

Hundred Years' War

A series of conflicts between England and France from 1337 to 1453. Its origins lay with the English kings' possession of Gascony in southwest France and with trade rivalries over Flanders. Fears of French intervention in

Scotland, which England was trying to subdue, and Edward III's claim (through his mother Isabel, daughter of the French king Charles IV) to the throne of France sparked the war.

hunger march

A procession of the unemployed. It became a feature of social protest in Britain between World Wars I and II. The first hunger march took place in 1922 from Glasgow to London. Another followed in 1929. The National Unemployed Workers' Movement organized the largest demonstration, in 1932, with groups converging on London from all parts of the country, but the most emotive was probably the 1936 **Jarrow Crusade**.

Huskisson, William (1770–1830)

British Conservative politician and advocate of free trade. He served as secretary to the Treasury in 1807–09 and colonial agent for Ceylon (now Sri Lanka). He was active in the **Corn Law** debates and supported their relaxation in 1821.

William Huskisson was the first person to be killed by a train. He was struck at the opening of the Liverpool and Manchester Railway in 1830.

Independent Labour Party (ILP)

A British socialist party founded in Bradford in 1893 by the Scottish politician **Keir Hardie**. In 1900 it joined with trade unions and **Fabians** in founding the Labour Representation Committee, the nucleus of the **Labour Party**. Many members left the ILP to join the Communist Party in 1921, and in 1932 all connections with the Labour Party were severed. After World War II the ILP dwindled, eventually becoming extinct.

India Acts

Three major pieces of legislation that formed the basis of British rule in India until its independence in 1947.

Independent Labour Party *A plea to British workmen, from the Independent Labour Party.*

- The 1858 Act abolished the administrative functions of the British **East India Company**, replacing them with direct rule from London.

- The 1919 Act increased Indian participation at local and provincial levels but did not meet nationalist demands for complete internal self-government.

- The 1935 Act outlined a federal structure but was never implemented.

Indian Independence

The dissolving of British India by the India Independence Act of 1947. Under the act, the Indian subcontinent was divided into two new independent dominions, India (mostly Hindu) and East and West Pakistan (mostly Muslim). The creation of Pakistan was followed by violent clashes (the Punjab massacres), and a war between the two countries over Kashmir.

Indian Mutiny also Sepoy Rebellion or Mutiny

The revolt of Indian soldiers (Sepoys) in 1857–58 against the British in India. The uprising was confined to the north, from Bengal to the Punjab, and central India. It led to the end of rule by the British **East India Company** and its replacement by direct British Crown administration.

The majority of support for the mutiny came from the army and dethroned princes, but in some areas it developed into a peasant uprising and general revolt. It included the seizure of Delhi by the rebels, its siege and recapture by the British, and the defence of Lucknow by a British garrison.

Industrial Revolution

A rapid acceleration in technological and economic development that began in Britain in the second half of the 18th century. The traditional agricultural economy was overtaken by one dominated by manufacturing and heavy industry.

New materials – iron and steel – were used along with new energy sources, such as coal, and new machinery, particularly in the textile industry. Transport systems were revolutionized by steam trains, canals, and better roads. As cottage industries were

From 1830 to the early 20th century the Industrial Revolution that began in Britain spread throughout Europe and the USA and to Japan and the various colonial empires.

replaced by the factory system, new methods of labour organization were employed, bringing specialization, the division of labour, and the creation of the industrial working class.

New working conditions led to political changes as wealth and power were transferred from the landowner to the industrial capitalist. There were massive social changes brought about by migration from the countryside to the towns, a rising population, and the growth of urban areas.

Industrial Revolution: chronology

1701   The seed drill is invented by Jethro Tull.

1709   Abraham Darby introduces coke smelting to his ironworks at Coalbrookdale in Shropshire.

1712	The first workable steam-powered engine is developed by Thomas Newcomen.
1740	Crucible steelmaking is discovered by Benjamin Huntsman, a clockmaker of Doncaster.
1759	The first Canal Act is passed; by 1830 there are 6,500 km/4,000 mi of canals in Britain.
c. **1764**	The spinning jenny, which greatly accelerates cotton spinning, is invented by James Hargreaves in Blackburn.
1769	James Watt patents a more reliable and efficient version of the Newcomen engine.
1779	The spinning mule, which makes the production of fine yarns by machine possible, is developed in Bolton by Samuel Crompton.
1785	The power loom marks the start of the mechanised textile industry.
1825	The first regular railway services start between Stockton and Darlington in northeast England.
1829	With his steam locomotive *Rocket*, English engineer George Stephenson wins a contest to design locomotives for the new Manchester–Liverpool railway.
1851	Britain celebrates its industrial achievements in the Great Exhibition.

Invergordon Mutiny

An incident that occurred in the British Atlantic Fleet at Cromarty Firth, Scotland, on 15 September 1931. Ratings refused to prepare the ships for going to sea after the government cut their pay. The pay cuts were subsequently reviewed.

IRA

Abbreviation for **Irish Republican Army**.

Irish partition

The division of Ireland in 1921 into the Irish Free State and Northern Ireland. After World War I **Sinn Féin** became the dominant force in Irish politics. Irish representatives returned in the general election of December 1918 met in an independent parliament (Dáil Éireann) in Dublin, and affirmed the independence of the country. From 1919 to 1921 there was guerrilla warfare against the British army, especially by the **Irish Republican Army** (IRA).

A truce was declared in 1921, and in the same year a parliament for the six northeastern counties of Ireland was established. The Anglo-Irish Treaty was signed on 6 December 1921, establishing the dominion status of the other 26 counties, and the Irish Free State came into being.

Irish potato famine

A five-year famine in Ireland that resulted from the failure of the potato crop. During the 17th and 18th centuries the potato was the staple diet of the Irish peasantry. In 1846 the potato crop failed, and this was followed by a famine that was to last until 1851. Nearly a million people died from diseases caused by malnutrition, and more emigrated to the USA. The British government was slow to provide relief, fuelling Irish hostility.

Irish Republican Army (IRA)

A militant Irish nationalist organization, the paramilitary wing of **Sinn Féin**, whose aim is to create a united Irish socialist republic including Ulster.

The IRA was founded in 1919 by Michael **Collins** as the successor to the Irish Volunteers, a militant nationalist body dating from 1913. During the War of Irish Independence of 1919–21 it employed guerrilla tactics against British forces in Ireland. It was declared illegal in 1936, but came to the fore again in 1939 with a bombing campaign in Britain.

The IRA's activities intensified from 1968, as the civil-rights disorders ('the Troubles') in Northern Ireland increased. It carried out bombings and shootings in Northern Ireland as well as bombings in mainland Britain and on British military bases in continental Europe.

> In 1984 the IRA blew up the Brighton hotel where Prime Minister Thatcher and members of her cabinet were staying during the Conservative Party conference, but she escaped unharmed.

In August 1994 the IRA announced a cessation of its military activities, in response to the Anglo-Irish peace initiative. In July 1997 it declared a permanent ceasefire.

HISTORY OF THE IRA

- *1919* The IRA was begun by Michael Collins.
- *1969* The IRA split into two wings, one 'official' and the other 'provisional'. In time, the Provisionals became the dominant force who spoke for the IRA.
- *1974* The Irish Republican Socialist Party, with its paramilitary wing, the Irish National Liberation Army (INLA), split from the IRA. In April *1995* the INLA announced that it was renouncing the use of violence.
- *1997–8* 'Continuity IRA' and 'Real IRA', republican splinter group opposed to the IRA's ceasefire, carried out a number of bomb attacks.

Jack the Ripper

The popular name for the unidentified mutilator and murderer of at least five female prostitutes in the Whitechapel area of London in 1888.

The murders provoked public outrage and the police were heavily criticized. This later led to a reassessment of police procedures. Jack the Ripper's identity has never been discovered, although several suspects have been proposed, including members of the royal household.

Jacobite

A supporter of the royal house of Stuart after the deposition of **James II** in 1688. Jacobites include the Scottish Highlanders who rose unsuccessfully in 1689, and those who rose in Scotland and northern England in 1715 under the leadership of James Edward Stuart and followed his son Charles Edward Stuart in an invasion of England from 1745 to 1746. After the defeat at **Culloden**, the Jacobites disappeared as a political force.

James I (1566–1625)

King of England from 1603 and Scotland (as James VI) from 1567. The son of **Mary Queen of Scots** and her second husband, Lord **Darnley**, he succeeded to the Scottish throne on the enforced abdication of his mother and assumed power in 1583. He established a strong centralized authority, and in 1589 married Anne of Denmark.

As successor to **Elizabeth I** in England, he alienated the Puritans by his High Church views and Parliament by his assertion of divine right. He was also unpopular because of his favourites, such as **Buckingham**, and his schemes for an alliance with Spain. He was succeeded by his son **Charles I**.

> ❮ A custom loathsome to the eye, hateful to the nose, harmful to the brain, dangerous to the lungs. ❯
>
> **James I** on tobacco smoking in *A Counterblast to Tobacco,* 1604

James II (1633–1701)

King of England and Scotland (as James VII) who lost the throne to **William of Orange**. The second son of **Charles I**, he succeeded his brother, **Charles II**, in 1685. He had become a Catholic in 1671, which led first to attempts to exclude him from the succession, then to the rebellion by the Duke of Monmouth, and finally to the Whig and Tory leaders' invitation to William of Orange to take the throne in 1688. James fled to France, then led an uprising in Ireland in 1689, but after defeat at the Battle of the **Boyne** (1690) remained in exile in France.

> ❝ I have often heretofore ventured my life in defence of this nation: and I shall go as far as any man in preserving it in all its just rights and liberties. ❞
>
> **James II** to the Privy Council on becoming king in 1685

Jamestown

The first permanent British settlement in North America. It was established by Captain John Smith in 1607 and was the capital of Virginia from 1624 to 1699. The first Anglican church in North America was built in Jamestown and the first slaves on the continent also arrived there.

In Jamestown Festival Park there is a replica of the original Fort James, and models of the ships *Discovery, Godspeed*, and *Constant* that carried the 105 pioneers.

Jarrow Crusade

A protest march in 1936 from Jarrow to London against the many job losses caused by the closure of Palmer's shipyard in Jarrow. It was led by the Labour MP Ellen Wilkinson and proved a landmark event of the 1930s **Depression**.

In 1986, on the 50th anniversary of the event, a similar march was held to protest at the high levels of unemployment in the 1980s.

Jellicoe, John Rushworth, 1st Earl Jellicoe (1859–1935)

British admiral who commanded the Grand Fleet in 1914–16 during **World**

War I. The only action he saw was at the inconclusive battle of **Jutland**. As First Sea Lord in 1916–17 he failed to press for the introduction of the convoy system to combat attacks by German U-boats. He was made Earl in 1925.

Jenkins's Ear, War of

A war in 1739 between Britain and Spain that started because of Britain's unlawful trade in Spanish America. The name derives from the claim of Robert Jenkins, a merchant captain, that his ear had been cut off by Spanish coastguards near Jamaica. The incident was seized on by opponents of Robert **Walpole** who wanted to shame his government's antiwar policy and force war with Spain.

Jews in Britain

England was the last major European country to be reached by the Jews, and it was the first to expel them. Many Jews came to England with **William the Conqueror** in 1066 and settled in large towns. Some became wealthy as merchants and moneylenders, and this led to their unpopularity. They were expelled from England by Edward II in 1290 and did not return until 1656.

By the late 1990s, there were about 300,000 Jews in Britain. Many have made important contributions to business and the arts.

John I ('Lackland') (1167–1216)

King of England from 1199 and acting king from 1189 during the absence of his brother **Richard I** ('the Lion-Heart') on the Third Crusade. John plotted against Richard and was complicit in the death in 1203 of his own nephew Arthur, Duke of Brittany, a rival for the English throne.

John lost Normandy and almost all the other English possessions in France to Philip II of France by 1205, and provoked Pope Innocent III to excommunicate England from 1208 to 1213 over John's attempt to limit the papacy's right of interference in the appointment of English bishops, which traditionally was the preserve of the king. His repressive policies and excessive taxation brought him

John was nicknamed '**Lackland**', probably because, as the youngest of Henry II's five sons, it was difficult to find a portion of his father's French possessions for him to inherit.

into conflict with his barons, and he was forced to seal the **Magna Carta** in 1215. His repudiation of this charter led to the first **Barons' War**, during which he died.

John Bull

An imaginary figure who is a personification of England. He is represented in cartoons and caricatures as a prosperous farmer of the 18th century. The name was popularized by Dr John Arbuthnot's political satire *History of John Bull* (1712), advocating the Tory policy of peace with France.

Jutland, Battle of

World War I naval battle between British and German forces on 31 May 1916, off the west coast of Jutland. Its outcome was indecisive, but the German fleet remained in port for the rest of the war.

- a.m.

  German fleet entered the North Sea to entice British battle cruisers to the Norwegian coast and destroy them.

- p.m.

  The British took the bait and a long-range gunnery duel then took place in which the British lost battle cruisers and sustained damage to their flagship.

  The British turned away to draw the Germans north and bring them against Admiral Jellicoe's larger force.

  The fleets met, and a general melee ensued during which another British battle-cruiser was sunk. However, the Germans realised they were out-gunned and fled.

  Jellicoe, fearful of torpedos in the failing light of evening, decided not to follow.

❝ I had always to remember that I could have lost the war in an afternoon. ❞

John Rushworth, 1st Earl Jellicoe, attributed remark, referring to the Battle of Jutland

---

K

Keble, John (1792–1866)

Anglican priest and religious poet in memory of whom Keble College, Oxford, was founded in 1870. Keble was professor of poetry at Oxford from 1831 to 1841. His sermon on the decline of religious faith in Britain, preached in 1833, heralded the start of the Oxford Movement, a Catholic revival in the Church of England. He wrote four of the *Tracts for the Times* (theological treatises in support of the movement), and his book of poems, *The Christian Year* (1827), was very popular in the 19th century.

Kells, Book of

An 8th-century illuminated manuscript of the Gospels produced at the monastery of Kells in County Meath, Ireland. It is now in Trinity College library, Dublin.

Kidd, 'Captain' William (c. 1645–1701)

Scottish pirate whose execution marked the end of 200 years of the British government's condoning of piracy. Kidd spent his youth privateering for the British against the French off the North American coast, and in 1695 was given a royal commission to suppress piracy in the Indian Ocean. Instead, he joined a group of pirates in Madagascar. In 1699, on his way to Boston, Massachusetts, he was arrested, taken to England, and hanged.

Kidd *Captain Kidd hanging in chains.*

‹ This is a very false and faithless generation. ›

'Captain' (William) Kidd, last words before being hanged in 1702. He
had only surrendered on the sure promise of a free pardon

King's/Queen's Champion

A ceremonial office that is held by virtue of possessing the lordship of
Scrivelsby, Lincolnshire. A document of 1332–33 described the champion
as 'an armed knight on horseback to prove by his body, if necessary, against
whomsoever, the King who is crowned that day is the true and right heir of
the kingdom'. Sir John Dymoke established his right to champion the
monarch on coronation day in 1377 and it is still held by his descendant.
This office was last performed on the coronation of King George IV in 1821,
at a banquet in Westminster Hall.

Kitchener, Horatio Herbert, 1st Earl Kitchener of Khartoum (1850–1916)

Irish general whose face appeared on **World War I** army recruitment
posters. He defeated the Sudanese at the Battle of Omdurman in 1898 and
reoccupied Khartoum. In South
Africa, he was commander in
chief from 1900 to 1902 during
the **South African War**. He conducted the war there by a
scorched-earth policy and created the earliest concentration
camps for civilians. Appointed
war minister on the outbreak of
World War I, he modernized the
British forces and was successful in his campaign calling for voluntary
recruitment.

Kitchener countered Boer guerrilla
warfare by putting the non-combatants
who supported them in concentration
camps. About 26,000 women and
children who had been interned died
of sickness.

knighthood, orders of

The fraternity that carries with it the rank of knight. Admission is granted as a
mark of royal favour or as a reward for public services. During the Middle
Ages the fraternities fell into two classes: religious, which included the
Templars and the Knights of St John, who had taken religious vows; and sec-
ular, knights who were engaged in the service of a prince or great noble.
Knights wore the badge of their patron or the emblem of their patron saint.

The Order of the Garter, founded in 1348, is the oldest order now in existence. Among the many other British orders are:

- the Order of the Bath, founded in 1725
- the Order of the British Empire (OBE), founded in 1917
- the Order of Merit (OM), founded in 1902.

Knox, John (*c.* 1505–1572)
Scottish Protestant reformer, founder of the Church of Scotland. Originally a Roman Catholic priest, Knox is thought to have been converted by the reformer George Wishart. In England he assisted in compiling the Prayer Book, as a royal chaplain to **Henry VIII** from 1551. On Mary's accession in 1553 he fled the country and in 1557 was, in his absence, condemned to be

John Knox's books include *First Blast of the Trumpet Against the Monstrous Regiment of Women* (1558).

burned. While in exile he met the great Protestant leader John Calvin in Geneva. In 1559 he returned to Scotland to promote Presbyterianism. He was tried for treason but acquitted in 1563.

Labour Party
British political party based on socialist principles, originally formed to represent workers. It was founded in 1900 at a conference representing the trade unions, the **Independent Labour Party**, and the **Fabian Society** and in 1906 gained 29 seats in Parliament. By 1922 it was recognized as the official opposition, and in 1924 formed a minority government for a few months under the party's first secretary Ramsay **MacDonald**.

In 1936–39 there was dissension within the party, and Aneurin **Bevan** and others were expelled for advocating an alliance of all left-wing parties against the government of Neville **Chamberlain**. Labour supported Winston **Churchill's** wartime coalition, but in 1945 withdrew and took office for the first time as a majority government led by Clement **Attlee**. Under Labour, the welfare state was developed by **nationalization** of essential services and industries, a system of **national insurance** was established, and in 1948t the **National Health Service** was founded.

Defeated in 1951, Labour was again in power in 1964–70 and 1974–79 but then remained out of office for 18 years. It returned to government in May 1997 after a landslide election victory under the leadership of Tony **Blair**, who promoted the party as 'New Labour'.

❛ The honest truth is that if this Government were to propose a massacre of the first-born, it would still have no difficulty in getting it through the Commons. ❜

Diane Abbott, Labour MP, on the perils of landslide victories and 'Stepford Backbenchers' (backbenchers with unquestioning allegiance); *Independent on Sunday*, 12 July 1998

Lancaster House Agreement
Accord reached at a conference held in September 1979 at Lancaster House, London, to enable a smooth transition to the independent state of Zimbabwe in 1980. Britain and representative groups of Rhodesia, includ-

ing the white **Rhodesian** government under Ian Smith and black nationalist groups, participated.

Lancaster, House of

English royal house, a branch of the **Plantagenets**. It began in 1267 when Edmund, the younger son of Henry III, was granted the earldom of Lancaster. This became a duchy for Henry of Grosmont, who died in 1361, and it passed to John of Gaunt in 1362 by his marriage to Blanche, Henry's daughter. John's son, **Henry IV**, established the royal dynasty of Lancaster in 1399. He was followed by two more Lancastrian kings, **Henry V** and **Henry VI**, before Lancastrian succession was disputed by the House of **York** in the Wars of the **Roses**.

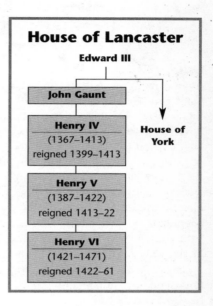

House of Lancaster

Edward III

John Gaunt

Henry IV
(1367–1413)
reigned 1399–1413

House of York

Henry V
(1387–1422)
reigned 1413–22

Henry VI
(1421–1471)
reigned 1422–61

Land League

Irish peasant-rights organization, formed in 1879 by Michael Davitt and Charles **Parnell** to fight against tenant evictions. By skilful use of the boycott against anyone who took a farm from which another had been evicted, it forced **Gladstone's** government to introduce a law in 1881 restricting rents and granting tenants security of tenure.

Latimer, Hugh (c. 1485–1555)

English bishop who was burned for heresy. After his conversion to Protestantism in 1524 he was imprisoned several times but was protected

❝ Be of good comfort, Master Ridley, and play the man; we shall this day light such a candle, by God's grace, in England as I trust shall never be put out. ❞

Hugh Latimer, attributed remark, to Nicholas Ridley as they were about to be burned at the stake by Cardinal Thomas **Wolsey** and Henry VIII. Latimer was appointed bishop of Worcester in 1535, but resigned in 1539. Under Edward VI his sermons denouncing social injustice won him great influence, but he was arrested in 1553, once Mary was on the throne, and two years later he was burned at the stake in Oxford.

Laud, William (1573–1645)

Archbishop of Canterbury from 1633, who was executed for treason. Laud's High Church policy, his support for **Charles I's** unparliamentary rule, his censorship of the press, and his persecution of the **Puritans** all aroused bitter opposition. His strict enforcement of the statutes against enclosures and of laws regulating wages and prices further alienated the propertied classes. Laud's attempt to impose the use of the Prayer Book on the Scots precipitated the English **Civil War**. Impeached by Parliament in 1640, he was imprisoned in the Tower of London, condemned to death, and beheaded.

Laud *William Laud, Archbishop of Canterbury, prior to his death in 1645.*

> ❝ I laboured nothing more than that the external public worship of God, too much slighted in most parts of this kingdom, might be preserved. ❞
>
> **William Laud** at his trial in 1644

Lawrence, Thomas Edward (1888–1935)

British soldier and scholar who became famous as 'Lawrence of Arabia'. Appointed to the military intelligence department in Cairo, Egypt, during **World War I**, he took part in negotiations for an Arab revolt against the Ottoman Turks, and in 1916 attached himself to the emir Faisal. He became a guerrilla leader of genius, combining raids on Turkish communications with the organization of a joint Arab revolt, described in his book *Seven Pillars of Wisdom* (1926).

At the end of the war he was disappointed by the Paris Peace Conference's failure to establish Arab independence. He joined the Royal Air Force in 1922 under an assumed name to escape attention and in 1935 he died in a motorcycle accident.

> ❝ It's the most amateurish, Buffalo-Billy sort of performance, and the only people who do it well are the Bedouin. ❞
>
> **T E Lawrence**, letter in 1917, describing an attack on a Turkish train

Leicester, Robert Dudley, Earl of Leicester (*c.* 1532–1588)

English courtier who was a favourite of **Elizabeth I**. His father, the Duke of Northumberland, was executed for supporting Lady Jane **Grey's** claim to the throne, and he himself was briefly imprisoned in the **Tower of London**. In 1564 Elizabeth made him Earl of Leicester. He led the disastrous military expedition of 1585–87 sent to help the Netherlands against Spain, but despite this failure, he retained the favour of the queen. Elizabeth gave him command of the army prepared to resist the threat of Spanish invasion in 1588.

Elizabeth might have married Leicester had he not been already married to Amy Robsart. When Amy died in 1560 after a fall downstairs, Leicester was suspected of murdering her. In 1578 he secretly married the widow of the Earl of Essex.

Levellers

Members of a democratic movement, led by John Lilburne, in the English **Civil War**. Their programme included the establishment of a republic, government by a parliament with one elected house, religious tolerance, and sweeping social reforms.

The Levellers found wide support among Cromwell's **New**

'True Levellers' (or Diggers) were a 17th-century radical sect that attempted to seize and share out common land. They were denounced by the Levellers because of their more radical methods, but the support they attracted alarmed the government. They were dispersed in 1650.

Model Army and the yeoman farmers, artisans, and small traders, and proved a powerful political force from 1647 to 1649. Cromwell's refusal to implement their programme led to mutinies by Levellers in the army. These were ruthlessly put down in 1649, ending the movement.

Liberal Party

British political party, the successor to the Whig Party. In the 19th century it represented the interests of commerce and industry. Its outstanding leaders were **Palmerston**, **Gladstone**, and **Lloyd George**.

During the Liberals' first period of power, from 1830 to 1841, they promoted parliamentary and municipal government reform and the abolition of slavery, but their laissez-faire theories led to the harsh **Poor Law** of 1834. Liberal pressure forced Peel to repeal the **Corn Laws** of 1846, thereby splitting the Tory party.

From 1914 the Liberal Party declined, and the rise of the **Labour Party** pushed it into the middle ground. After World War II it was reduced to a handful of MPs. A revival began under the leadership of Jo Grimond and continued under Jeremy Thorpe.

Between 1977 and 1978 the Liberal leader David Steel entered into an agreement to support Labour in any vote of confidence in return for consultation on measures undertaken.

> David Steel was the first party leader in British politics to be elected by party members who were not MPs.

After the 1987 general election, Steel suggested a merger of the Liberal Party and the Social Democratic Party (SDP). The new Liberal Democrat Party was formed on 3 March 1988, with Paddy Ashdown elected leader. In 1999, Ashdown was replaced by Charles Kennedy.

licensing laws

Legislation governing the sale of alcoholic drinks. From the late 19th century, temperance and nonconformist movements lobbied for tighter restrictions on the consumption of alcohol. In Wales, Sunday closing was enforced from 1881, and in 1913 Scotland was permitted to hold local referenda on licensing issues.

Restrictions on pub hours in England were initially introduced as a temporary measure during **World War I**, not as a morality act but to improve efficiency on the home front. However, the regulations were retained after the war.

Liverpool, Robert Banks Jenkinson, 2nd Earl Liverpool
(1770–1828)
British Tory prime minister who, while successful abroad, caused serious unrest at home. He entered Parliament in 1790, became foreign secretary, was twice home secretary, then war minister, and prime minister from 1812 to 1827. His government conducted the **Napoleonic Wars** to a successful conclusion, but its ruthless suppression of freedom of speech and of the press aroused such opposition that between 1815 and 1820 revolution frequently seemed imminent.

Livingstone, David
(1813–1873)
Scottish missionary and explorer. In 1841 he went to Africa, reaching Lake Ngami in 1849. He followed the Zambezi to its mouth, saw the Victoria Falls, and travelled to East and Central Africa. From 1866 he tried to find the source of the River Nile, and reached Ujiji in Tanganyika in November 1871. The British explorer Henry Stanley joined him there. Livingstone died in Old Chitambo (now in Zambia) and was buried in Westminster Abbey, London.

Livingstone *Dr David Livingstone.*

Livingstone not only mapped a great deal of the African continent but also helped to end the Arab slave trade.

Llewelyn I (1173–1240)
Prince of Wales from 1194 who drove out the English. He extended his rule to all Wales not in Norman hands, driving the English from northern Wales in 1212, and taking Shrewsbury in 1215. During the early part of Henry III's reign Llewelyn was several times attacked by English armies. He was married to Joanna, the illegitimate daughter of King John.

Lloyd George, David, 1st Earl Lloyd-George of Dwyfor
(1863–1945)

British Liberal prime minister during and after **World War I**. Born in Manchester of Welsh parentage, he entered parliament in 1890. During the **Boer War**, he was prominent as a Boer sympathiser. A pioneer of social reform and the welfare state, as chancellor of the Exchequer he introduced old-age pensions in 1908 and health and unemployment insurance in 1911. His 1909 budget (with graduated direct taxes and taxes on land values) provoked the Lords to reject it, and resulted in the **Parliament Act** of 1911 limiting their powers.

Lloyd George held ministerial posts during World War I until 1916 when there was an open breach between him and Prime Minister **Asquith**, and he became prime minister of a coalition government. In the postwar 1918 elections he achieved a huge majority over Labour and Asquith's followers.

High unemployment, intervention in the Russian Civil War, and use of the military police force the **Black and Tans** in Ireland eventually eroded his support as prime minister. The creation of the Irish Free State in 1921 and his pro-Greek policy against the Turks caused the collapse of his second coalition government in 1922. He was made an earl in 1945.

> ❝ Four spectres haunt the poor – old age, accident, sickness and unemployment. We are going to exorcise them. We are going to drive hunger from the hearth. We mean to banish the workhouse from the horizon of every workman in the land. ❞
>
> **David Lloyd George**, speech, 1910

local government

The part of government that deals mainly with matters concerning the inhabitants of a particular area or town. It is usually financed at least in part by local taxes.

The Municipal Reform Act in 1835 established elected councils, although their powers remained small. In country areas local government was in the hands of the justices of the peace until the Local Government Act in 1888 set up county councils.

Under the Local Government Act of 1972 the counties were subdivided into districts each with a district council, replacing the former county borough, and urban and rural district councils. Since 1997, reorganization proposals have emphasized single-tier unitary bodies, each providing a full range of local services. In April 1998 47 unitary authorities were created in England, replacing former borough or city councils that were part of two-tier structures. In 1997 the government announced plans to introduce directly elected mayors for the major cities, beginning with London in the year 2000.

LOCAL GOVERNMENT ACTS

- *1835* Municipal Reform Act established the rule of elected councils.
- *1888* Local Government Act set up county councils and county boroughs.
- *1894* Local Government Act set up urban and rural district councils, and parish councils in the rural districts.
- *1972* Local Government Act established the upper range of local government for England on a two-tier basis: 46 counties, with London and six other English cities created metropolitan areas.
- *1974* Local Government Act set up a Commission for Local Administration, creating an ombudsman for complaints about local government.

Locarno, Pact of

A pact, initiated by the British foreign secretary Austen Chamberlain and signed in London on 1 December 1925, that settled the question of French security. The signatories to the diplomatic documents, which had been initialled in Locarno, Switzerland, on 16 October 1925, were Britain, France, Belgium, Italy, and Germany. The pact guaranteed Germany's frontiers with France and Belgium, and following the signing Germany was admitted to the League of Nations.

Lollard

A follower of the English religious reformer John **Wycliffe** in the 14th century. The name comes from the Dutch *lollaert* ('mumbler'), applied to earlier European groups accused of combining pious pretensions with heretical belief. They were active from about 1377. After the passing of the statute *De* *heretico comburendo* ('The Necessity of Burning Heretics') in 1401 many Lollards were burned, and in 1414 they raised an unsuccessful revolt in London, known as Oldcastle's Rebellion.

- The Lollards condemned the doctrine of the transubstantiation of the bread and wine of the Eucharist.
- They advocated the diversion of ecclesiastical property to charitable uses.
- They denounced war and capital punishment.

Londonderry, Siege of

A siege of some 20,000 Protestants by the Jacobite forces of **James II** in Londonderry, Ulster, in 1689. They held out for 105 days, from 17 April to 30 July, before relief came and the Jacobites were driven off.

London Working Men's Association (LWMA)

A 19th-century campaigning organization for political reform in Britain. It was founded in June 1836 by William Lovett and others, who drew up the first version of the People's Charter (see **Chartism**). It was founded in the belief that popular education, achieved through discussion and access to a cheap and honest press, was a means of obtaining political reform. By 1837 the LWMA had 100 members.

Long Parliament

English Parliament that continued through the **Civil War**. The Royalists withdrew before the outbreak of war in 1642 and the Presbyterian moderates who wanted to negotiate with **Charles I** were excluded in 1648. The remaining **'Rump'** ruled England until expelled by Oliver Cromwell in 1653. Reassembled in 1659–60, the Long Parliament initiated the negotiations for the **restoration** of the monarchy.

Lords, House of

The unelected upper chamber of the UK **Parliament**. Its 665 or so members comprise temporal peers (hereditary and life peers) and spiritual peers (the two archbishops and 24 bishops). The Lords Temporal are Conservative, Labour, Liberal Democrat, or 'cross-benchers' (independents). They also include the 'law lords' who exercise the judicial role of the House of Lords as the final court of appeal in both civil and criminal cases. The Lords are presided over by the Lord Chancellor, who is also a law lord.

The House of Lords was originally the more important of the two Houses of Parliament. In the latter half of the 19th century and the early part of the 20th there were increasing clashes between Lords and **Commons**, culminating

In April 1998 there were 304 Conservative hereditary peers in the House of Lords compared with only 17 Labour.

in the rejection by the upper House of **Lloyd George's** People's Budget in 1909. This resulted in the passing of the **Parliament Act** of 1911, which restricted the powers of the Lords in that they may delay a bill passed by the Commons but not reject it.

In 1997 the Labour government announced its intention to end the right of hereditary peers to sit and vote in the chamber, with the long-term aim of creating a democratically elected second chamber. In 1999, the number of hereditary peers was reduced from some 750 to fewer than 100.

> ❝ People behave curiously when offered the extremely attractive option of being murdered today or threatened with murder tomorrow. ❞
>
> **Viscount Cranborne**, Conservative leader in the House of Lords, on the introduction of a Bill to abolish the voting rights of the hereditary peerage in a reformed second chamber; *Daily Telegraph*, 13 October 1998

Luddite

A member of a group involved in machine-wrecking riots in northern England between 1811 and 1816. The organizer of the Luddites was referred to as General Ludd, but may not have existed. Many Luddites were hanged or transported to penal colonies, such as Australia.

The movement, which began in Nottinghamshire and spread to Lancashire, Cheshire, Derbyshire, Leicestershire, and Yorkshire, was primarily a revolt against the unemployment caused by the introduction of machines in the **Industrial Revolution**.

Lusitania

British ocean liner sailing from New York to Liverpool that was sunk by a German submarine off the Irish coast on 7 May 1915. Some 1,200 people lost their lives, including 128 Americans. This act of aggression helped to bring the USA into **World War I** in 1917.

Macbeth (c. 1005–1057)

King of Scotland, the subject of Shakespeare's tragedy *Macbeth*. The son of Findlaech, ruler of Moray and Ross, he was commander of the forces of **Duncan I**, whom he killed in battle in

Shakespeare's *Macbeth* was based on the 16th-century historian Holinshed's *Chronicles*.

1040 to take the Scottish crown. His reign was prosperous until Duncan's son **Malcolm III** led an invasion and killed him at Lumphanan in Aberdeenshire.

Macdonald, Flora (1722–1790)

Scottish heroine who rescued Prince **Charles Edward Stuart**, the Young Pretender, after his defeat at Culloden in 1746. Disguising him as her maid, she escorted him from her home, on South Uist in the Hebrides, to France. She was arrested and imprisoned in the Tower of London, but released in 1747.

MacDonald, (James) Ramsay (1866–1937)

The first Labour prime minister. Born in Scotland, the son of a labourer, he became first secretary of the new Labour Party in 1900. He was elected to Parliament in 1906 and led Labour until 1914, when his opposition to **World War I** lost him the leadership. He was leader again in 1922, and in January 1924 he formed a government dependent on the support of the Liberal Party. When support was withdrawn in October of the same year, MacDonald was forced to resign. He returned to office in 1929, again as leader

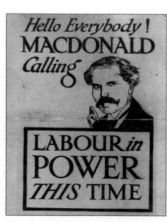

MacDonald *Ramsay MacDonald on a Labour Party poster of November 1924, for the General Election.*

of a minority government, which collapsed in 1931 during an economic crisis. MacDonald left the Labour Party to form the **National Government** with backing from both the Liberals and Conservatives. He resigned the premiership in 1935.

Macmillan, (Maurice) Harold, 1st Earl of Stockton (1894–1986)

British Conservative prime minister whose realization of the 'wind of change' in Africa advanced the independence of former colonies. Macmillan entered Parliament in 1924, and during the interwar years was one of the severest critics of his party leaderships' policy of **appeasement**. After World War II, as minister of housing from 1951 to 1954 he achieved the construction of 300,000 new houses a year. He became chancellor of the Exchequer in December 1955 and is popularly remembered for the introduction of Premium Savings Bonds. He became prime minister on the

Macmillan was known as Supermac, a nickname coined by the cartoonist Vicky.

resignation of Anthony **Eden** after the Suez Crisis, and led the Conservative Party to victory in the 1959 elections on the slogan 'You've never had it so good' (borrowed from a US election campaign).

In 1963 Macmillan attempted to negotiate British entry into the European Economic Community (EEC), but was blocked by the French president Charles de Gaulle. Much of his career as prime minister was spent defending the UK's retention of a nuclear weapon, and he was responsible for the purchase of US Polaris missiles in 1962.

> 6 The wind of change is blowing through this continent. 9
>
> **Harold Macmillan**, speech in Cape Town on 3 February 1960

Mafeking, Siege of

A long siege of the British-held town (now Mafikeng) by the Boers during the **South African War**. It lasted from 12 October 1899 to 17 May 1900.

The British garrison of about 750 soldiers under Colonel Robert **Baden-Powell**, 1,700 townspeople, and about 7,000 Africans, were besieged by a

10,000-strong Boer force. The siege was not pressed very hard, and the only serious attack attempted by the Boers failed. Inside the town, Baden-Powell organized the population to keep

The Mafeking celebrations led to the coining of a new verb – 'to maffick', meaning 'to celebrate intemperately'.

life going more or less as normal to maintain morale: there were tea-parties, concerts, and polo matches. Eventually, after seven months, a British column arrived to disperse the Boers and relieve the town. The announcement of the relief of Mafeking led to wild scenes of celebration across Britain.

Magna Carta (Latin 'great charter')

The charter granted by King **John** in 1215, traditionally seen as guaranteeing human rights against the excessive use of royal power. As a reply to the king's demands for excessive feudal dues and attacks on the privileges of the church, Archbishop Langton proposed to the barons the drawing-up of a binding document in 1213. John

Four original copies of Magna Carta exist today, one each in Salisbury and Lincoln cathedrals and two in the British Library.

was forced to accept this at Runnymede (in Surrey) on 15 June 1215.

Malcolm III, called Canmore (c. 1031–1093)

King of Scotland who killed **Macbeth**. The son of **Duncan I**, he fled to England in 1040 when the throne was usurped by Macbeth. He recovered southern Scotland, slew Macbeth in battle in 1057, and was crowned the following year. He was killed at Alnwick while invading Northumberland, England.

Mappa Mundi

A 13th-century symbolic map of the world. It is circular and shows Asia at the top, with Europe and Africa below and Jerusalem at the centre (reflecting Christian religious rather than geographical belief). It was drawn by David de Bello, a canon at Hereford Cathedral, England, who left the map to the cathedral, where it was used as an altarpiece.

Marconi Scandal

A scandal in 1912 in which British chancellor **Lloyd George** and two other government ministers were found by a French newspaper to have dealt in shares of the US Marconi company shortly before it was announced that the

Post Office had accepted the British Marconi company's bid to construct an imperial wireless chain. A parliamentary select committee concluded that the decision to adopt Marconi's tender was not the result of ministerial corruption. The scandal did irreparable harm to Lloyd George's reputation.

Margaret, St (c. 1045–1093)

Queen of Scotland, the granddaughter of King Edmund Ironside of England. She went to Scotland after the Norman Conquest, and soon afterwards married **Malcolm III**. The marriage of her daughter Matilda to **Henry I** united the Norman and English royal houses.

Through her influence, the Lowlands, until then purely Celtic, became largely anglicized. She was canonized in 1251 in recognition of her support for the church.

Marlborough, John Churchill, 1st Duke of Marlborough (1650–1722)

English soldier and military strategist, the hero of the Battle of **Blenheim**. He was created a duke in 1702 by Queen **Anne**, and given the Blenheim mansion in Oxfordshire in recognition of his services, which included defeating the French at Blenheim, outside Vienna, in 1704. The return of the Tories to power and his wife's quarrel with the queen led to his dismissal as army commander in chief in 1711, and his flight to Holland to avoid charges of corruption. He returned in 1714.

> ❝ I have not time to say more, but beg you will give my duty to the Queen, and let her know her army has a glorious victory. ❞
>
> **John Churchill, 1st Duke of Marlborough**, letter to his wife after the Battle of Blenheim in 1704

BATTLES OF THE MARNE

- **First Battle** 6–9 September 1914. The German advance was halted by French and British troops under the overall command of the French general Joseph Joffre.
- **Second Battle** 15 July–4 August 1918. The German advance was defeated by British, French, and US troops under the French general Henri Pétain, and German morale crumbled.

Marne, Battles of the
Two **World War I** battles along the River Marne, in northern France, in which the British and Allies repulsed German offensives.

Married Women's Property Acts
Laws passed in Britain in 1870 and 1882, granting women basic rights in the division of property between husband and wife. Until 1870 common law decreed that a wife's property, including money and shares, passed to her husband. The new laws allowed women to retain their earnings and to retain the property they owned at the time of their marriage.

Marshall rebellion
A rebellion led by Richard Marshall, Earl of Pembroke, against Henry III in 1233–34. It was sparked by the king's employment of French advisers, the *poitevins*, and was widely supported in Wales. However, in Ireland the royalists predominated, and Marshall was captured and killed by Irish royalists. English bishops procured a settlement under which Henry dismissed the *poitevins* and replaced them with Marshall's brother, Gilbert.

Marston Moor, Battle of
A battle in the English **Civil War** in which the Royalists were well beaten by the Parliamentarians and Scots. It took place on 2 July 1644 on Marston Moor, 11 km/7 mi west of York. The Royalist forces were commanded by Prince Rupert and William Cavendish; their opponents by Oliver **Cromwell** and Lord Leven. Lord **Fairfax**, on the right of the Parliamentarians, was routed, but Cromwell's cavalry charges proved decisive.

Mary I called Bloody Mary (1516–1558)
Catholic queen of England who sanctioned the persecution and killing of Protestants. She was the eldest daughter of **Henry VIII** by **Catherine of Aragón**. When Edward VI died in 1553, Mary secured the crown without difficulty in spite of the conspiracy to substitute Lady Jane **Grey**. In 1554 Mary married Philip II of Spain, and as a devout Roman Catholic obtained the restoration of papal supremacy. She was succeeded by her half-sister **Elizabeth I**.

Mary II (1662–1694)
Queen of England, Scotland, and Ireland who ruled jointly with **William III**. She was the Protestant elder daughter of the Catholic James II, and in 1677

Mary II *King William III and his wife, Queen Mary II.*

was married to her cousin William of Orange. After the 1688 revolution she accepted the crown with William.

During William's absences from England she took charge of the government, and showed courage and resource when invasion seemed possible in 1690 and 1692.

Mary Queen of Scots (1542–1587)

Queen of Scotland (1542–67) who was executed for plotting against **Elizabeth I**. Also known as Mary Stuart, she was the daughter of James V of Scotland. Mary's connection with the English royal line from Henry VII made her a threat to Elizabeth I's hold on the English throne, especially as she was a champion of the Catholic cause.

> ❝ O Lord my God, I have trusted in thee; / O Jesu my dearest one, now set me free. / In prison's oppression, in sorrow's obsession, / I weary for thee. ❞
>
> **Mary Queen of Scots**, written in her *Book of Devotion* before her execution, quoted in Swinburne (trans) *Mary Stewart V*

In 1567, Mary's second husband, Lord **Darnley**, was assassinated in a conspiracy by the Earl of Bothwell, who shortly afterwards married Mary. A rebellion followed, and Mary abdicated and was imprisoned. She escaped in 1568, raised an army, and after its defeat at Langside fled to England, only to be imprisoned again. A plot against Elizabeth I devised by Anthony Babington led to Mary's trial and execution at Fotheringay Castle in 1587.

Mary Rose

English warship, built for **Henry VIII** of England, which sank off Southsea, Hampshire, on 19 July 1545, with the loss of most of the 700 on board. The wreck was located in 1971, and raised for preservation in dry dock in Portsmouth harbour (where it had originally been built) in 1982. The cause of the disaster is not certain, but the lower gun ports were open after firing, and that, combined with overcrowding, may have caused the sinking.

Preserved in the accumulated silt of the wreck were over 19,000 objects, including leather and silk items, a unique record of Tudor warfare and daily life.

Matilda, the Empress Maud (1102–1167)

Claimant to the throne of England. Matilda was recognized during the reign of her father, **Henry I**, as his heir. On Henry's death, in 1135, the barons elected her cousin Stephen to be king. Matilda invaded England in 1139, and was crowned by her supporters in 1141. Civil war ensued until Stephen was finally recognized as king in 1153, with Henry II (Matilda's son) as his successor.

Maundy money

Money presented by the British sovereign to poor, elderly people each year on Maundy Thursday, the Thursday before Easter in the Christian calendar. The ceremony of the sovereign washing pilgrims' feet on that day in commemoration of Jesus washing the apostles' feet was observed from the 4th to the 18th century until the time of **William III**.

The number of people who receive Maundy money each year is always the same as the age of the sovereign.

Melbourne, (Henry) William Lamb, 2nd Viscount Melbourne (1779–1848)

British Whig prime minister who was an adviser to the young Queen **Victoria**. A Viscount in 1829, Melbourne was Home Secretary in 1830–34, prime minister in 1834 and again from 1835 to 1841.

For 20 years Melbourne was married to Lady Caroline Ponsonby: the novelist Lady Caroline Lamb and sometime mistress of Lord Byron.

Mercia

An Anglo-Saxon kingdom that emerged in the 6th century. By the late 8th century it dominated all of England south of the River Humber, but from about 825 came under the power of Wessex. Mercia eventually came to denote an area bounded by the Welsh border, the Humber, East Anglia, and the Thames.

Merthyr Uprising

Revolt, triggered by poverty and falling wages, of miners and ironworkers in Merthyr Tydfil, Wales, in 1831. They took possession of the town for three days until the military arrived to put down the rising, killing 16 of them. One of the ringleaders, Richard Lewis, popularly known as Dic Penderyn, was condemned to death.

Minden, Battle of

A victory by a combined British and Hanoverian army over the French during the **Seven Years' War**. The battle took place on 1 August 1759 at Minden, 70 km/44 mi west of Hannover, Germany. Due to mismanagement of the Allied cavalry, the French were able to withdraw in good order, but at a loss of over 7,000 casualties and 43 guns. Allied losses were some 2,700; over half of these were in the six English battalions.

To this day, the descendants of the English battalions who fought at the Battle of Minden wear a rose in their caps on the anniversary of the battle.

Mines Act

Legislation from 1842 regulating working conditions and safety standards for coalminers in Britain. After the nationalization of the coal industry 1946, the National Coal Board was responsible for ensuring adequate safety standards and proper working conditions for miners. In the coal strikes of the 1970s and 1980s, the withdrawal of a certification of safety was often as crucial as the withdrawal of labour.

IMPROVEMENTS IN MINE SAFETY STANDARDS

- *1842* The first act prohibited the employment of females and of boys below the age of 10.
- *1850* Inspection of mines was introduced.
- *1851* Royal School of Mines was established to train inspectors.
- *1860* The lower age-limit for boys working in the mines was raised to 12.
- *1872* Various safety measures, including a requirement that a manager of mines be correctly trained and certified, were introduced.
- *1908* The working day was limited to eight hours.
- *1930* The working day was reduced further to seven and a half hours.

Model Parliament

The first English parliament to include representatives from outside the clergy and aristocracy. It was set up in 1295 by **Edward I** because he needed the support of the whole country against his enemies, Wales, France, and Scotland. His aim was to raise money for military purposes, and the parliament did not pass any legislation. As well as bishops, earls, and barons it included the lower clergy and representatives of the shires, cities, and boroughs (two knights from every shire, two representatives from each city, and two burghers from each borough).

Montfort, Simon de, the Younger (*c.* 1208–1265)

English soldier who led the opposition to Henry III during the second **Barons' War**. Born in Normandy, he arrived in England in 1230, and was granted the earldom of Leicester. Initially one of Henry's favourites, he married the king's sister Eleanor in 1238. He later disagreed with the king's administrative policies, and in 1264 he

> Simon de Montfort the Younger was the son of Simon de Montfort who led a crusade against the Albigensian heretics in southern France.

defeated and captured Henry at the battle of Lewes, in Sussex. In 1265, as head of government, he summoned the first parliament in which the towns were represented. He was killed at the Battle of Evesham in the same year.

> **❝ Command your souls to God, for our bodies are the foe's. ❞**
>
> **Simon de Montfort**, last words to his supporters at the battle of Evesham, 1265

Montgomery, Bernard Law, 1st Viscount Montgomery of Alamein (1887–1976)

English soldier who commanded the 8th Army in North Africa in the second Battle of El **Alamein** in 1942 during **World War II**. At the start of the war Montgomery led part of the British Expeditionary Force in France and took part in the evacuation from **Dunkirk** in 1940.

His victory over the Germans at El Alamein enabled a rapid Allied advance into Tunisia.

Promoted to field marshal in 1944, Montgomery was commander of the British troops in northern Europe and received the German surrender in 1945. He was created 1st Viscount Montgomery of Alamein in 1946.

More, (St) Thomas (1478–1535)

English politician and scholar who was executed for refusing to accept the king as head of the church. From 1509 he was favoured by **Henry VIII** and employed on foreign embassies. He was a member of the privy council from 1518 and was knighted in 1521.

On the fall of Cardinal **Wolsey** he became Lord Chancellor, but resigned in 1532 because he could not agree with the king on his ecclesiastical policy and marriage with Anne **Boleyn**. In 1534 he refused to take the oath of supremacy to Henry VIII as head of the church, and after a year's imprisonment in the **Tower of London** he was executed. More was canonized in 1935.

> More was also a patron of artists, including Holbein, and a prolific author. The title of his political book *Utopia* (1516) has come to mean any supposedly perfect society.

> 6 I pray you, master Lieutenant, see me safe up, and my coming down let me shift for my self. 9
>
> **Thomas More**, ascending the scaffold, quoted in Roper's *Life of Sir Thomas More*

Morgan, Henry (*c.* 1635–1688)

Welsh buccaneer in the Caribbean. He made war against Spain, capturing and sacking Panama in 1671. In 1675 he was knighted and appointed lieutenant governor of Jamaica.

Morton, James Douglas, 4th Earl of (1516–1581)

Scottish noble who was regent for and executed by James VI (**James I** of England). From 1563 to 1566 Morton was Lord Chancellor under **Mary Queen of Scots**, but was instrumental in the murder of her favourite, Rizzio, in 1566. He may also have been involved in the murder of her husband, Lord **Darnley**. He joined the rebellion against Mary in 1567 and defeated royalist forces at the battles of Carberry Hill and Langside. From 1572 to 1578 he was a successful regent for the young James VI, but he was later executed, allegedly for his part in the murder of Darnley, the king's father.

Mountbatten, Louis Francis Albert Victor Nicholas, 1st Earl Mountbatten of Burma (1900–1979)

English admiral and administrator who was the last viceroy and governor general of India. He was a great-grandson of Queen Victoria. In 1942, during **World War II**, Mountbatten became chief of combined operations. He was appointed commander in chief in southeast Asia in 1943, and in September 1945 he accepted the surrender of 750,000 Japanese troops. In India, in 1947–48, he oversaw that country's transition to independence. He was chief of UK Defence Staff from 1959 to 1965. He was killed by an **IRA** bomb aboard his yacht off the Republic of Ireland.

> 6 I can't think of a more wonderful thanksgiving for the life I have had than that everyone should be jolly at my funeral. 9
>
> **Louis Mountbatten**, quoted in R Hough's *Mountbatten*

Munich Agreement

Pact signed on 29 September 1938 in Munich by Neville **Chamberlain** for the UK and Adolf Hitler for Germany compelling Czechoslovakia to surrender its Sudeten-German districts (the sudeten) to Germany. The agreement was also signed by Edouard Daladier (France) and Benito Mussolini (Italy). Chamberlain claimed it would guarantee 'peace in our time', but it did not prevent Hitler from seizing the rest of Czechoslovakia in March 1939 and the outbreak of **World War II** later that year.

> After the war the Sudeten was returned to Czechoslovakia, and over 2 million German-speaking people were expelled from the country.

❦ We have seen today a gallant, civilized and democratic people betrayed and handed over to a ruthless despotism. ❧

Clement Attlee, British Labour politician, speech in the House of Commons during the Munich debate in October 1938

Municipal Corporations Act

An English act of Parliament of 1835 that laid the foundations of modern local government. The act made local government responsible to a wider electorate of ratepayers through elected councils. Boroughs incorporated in this way were empowered to take on responsibility for policing, public health, and education, and were subject to regulation and auditing to reduce corruption. Similar acts were passed for Scotland in 1833 and Ireland in 1840.

Napoleonic Wars

A series of European wars (1803–15) between, on the one side, Britain and its allies (the German states, Spain, Portugal, Russia), and, on the other, France. After the French Revolutionary Wars, Napoleon I was aiming to conquer Europe, and at one time nearly all of Europe was under French domination. Napoleon was finally defeated at the Battle of **Waterloo** in 1815.

- During the Napoleonic Wars, the annual cost of the British army was between 60% and 90% of total government income.

- About half of Napoleon's army was made up of foreign mercenaries, mainly Swiss and German.

Naseby, Battle of

A decisive battle of the English **Civil War** in which the Royalists, led by Prince Rupert, were defeated by the Parliamentarians ('Roundheads') under Oliver **Cromwell** and General Fairfax. It was fought on 14 June 1645 near the village of Naseby, 32 km/20 mi south of Leicester.

- Prince Rupert's cavalry broke the Parliamentary right wing and then recklessly pursued them towards the village of Naseby.

- On the other wing, Cromwell's cavalry routed the force opposing them and then turned inward to take the Royalist infantry in the flank.

- Prince Rupert, returning from his chase, found the battle over.

- About 1,000 Royalists were killed and 5,000 taken prisoner, together with all their artillery.

National Front (NF)

An extreme right-wing British political party. The NF was formed in 1967 from a merger of the League of Empire Loyalists and the British National Party. It attracted attention during the 1970s through the violence associated with its demonstrations in areas with large black and Asian populations. In national elections in the 1970s, the NF, standing on a platform of repatriation of coloured immigrants and national autonomy, won 3% of the vote but has since attracted minimal support. In 1982 its leading figure, John Tyndall, left to form a new **British National Party**.

National Government

A government of Labour, Liberal, and Conservative MPs that formed in 1931, after a rapidly declining economic situation led to a split in the Labour government.

The Labour leader, Ramsay **MacDonald**, was prime minister of the National Government but the majority of his own party refused to support him. He resigned as prime minister in 1935 and was succeeded by the Conservative Stanley **Baldwin**.

In 1940 the National Government was replaced by a wartime coalition government led by Winston Churchill.

National Health Service (NHS)

Government provision of medical care on a national scale. The National Health Service Act of 1946 was largely the work of Aneurin **Bevan**, Labour minister of health. It instituted a health service from July 1948 that sought to provide free medical, dental, and optical treatment as rights. Since then, both Labour and Conservative governments have introduced charges for some services.

Between 1989 and 1994 the number of NHS staff nurses and midwives on hospital wards fell by 13%, or about 50,000, while the number of managers increased by 400%, or more than 18,300.

The NHS still provides free hospital care, but limited charges are made for doctors' prescriptions, eye tests and spectacles, and dental treatment, except for children and people on very low incomes.

National Insurance Act

An act of Parliament that, for the first time, provided insurance for workers against ill health and unemployment. It was introduced by the Liberal chancellor **Lloyd George** in 1911. The schemes were contributory, with employer, employee, and the state making regular contributions. The act was in two parts:

- Part I introduced compulsory health insurance for all manual workers aged between 16 and 70 and nonmanual workers with incomes below £250 a year who did not claim exemption.

- Part II provided insurance against unemployment for 2 million workers but excluded domestic servants, agricultural workers, and nonmanual workers exempt from Part I.

nationalization

A policy of bringing a country's essential services and industries under public ownership, which in the UK was pursued especially by **Attlee's** Labour government of 1945–51. Legislation was passed nationalizing the **Bank of England**, coal, and most hospitals in 1946; transport and electricity in 1947; gas in 1948; and iron and steel in 1949.

In 1953 the Conservative government provided for the return of road haulage to private enterprise and for decentralization of the railways. It also denationalized iron and steel in 1953, but these were renationalized by the next Labour government in 1967. In 1977 **Callaghan's** Labour government nationalized the aircraft and shipbuilding industries. With the advent of a Conservative government 1979, the process was reversed in the form of **privatization**.

Under Tony **Blair**, Labour pledged to restore vital utilities to public ownership or public control but did not commit itself to full nationalization based on the post-1945 model. Once in power, it retreated from its former stance and announced a number of privatization measures, including:

- the Royal Mint
- the Commonwealth Development Corporation
- Air Traffic Control.

national service

Conscription into the British armed forces in peacetime, introduced shortly before **World War II** and again in 1947. It ended in 1962.

NATO

Abbreviation for **North Atlantic Treaty Organization**.

Navigation Acts

Acts of Parliament passed from 1381 to protect English shipping from foreign competition and to ensure monopoly trading between Britain and its colonies. The last one was repealed in 1849, with coastal trade exempt until 1853. The Navigation Acts helped to establish England as a major sea power, but were one of the causes of the **American Revolution**.

THE NAVIGATION ACTS

■ *1650* 'Commonwealth Ordinance' forbade foreign ships to trade in English colonies.

■ *1651* This act forbade the importation of goods except in English vessels or in vessels of the country of origin of the goods. This led to the Anglo-Dutch War of 1652–54.

■ *1660* All colonial produce was required to be exported in English vessels.

■ *1663* Colonies were prohibited from receiving goods in non-English vessels.

Nelson, Horatio, 1st Viscount Nelson (1758–1805)

England's most famous naval hero. He joined the navy in 1770. During the Revolutionary Wars against France he lost the sight in his right eye in 1794 and lost his right arm in 1797.

He became a rear admiral and a national hero after the victory off Cape St Vincent, Portugal. In 1798 he tracked the French fleet to Aboukir Bay where he almost entirely destroyed it. Promoted to vice admiral in 1801, he won a decisive victory over Denmark at the Battle of **Copenhagen**, and negotiated peace with Denmark. On his return to England Nelson was created a viscount.

In 1803 he received the Mediterranean command and for nearly two years blockaded Toulon. He defeated the Franco-Spanish fleet at **Trafalgar**, near Gibraltar, in 1805 but was killed in the battle. He is buried in St Paul's Cathedral, London.

❝ You must hate a Frenchman as you hate the devil. ❞

Horatio Nelson to a midshipman under his command on
HMS *Agamemnon* in the western Mediterranean in 1793.
Quoted in Robert Southey's *Life of Nelson*, Chapter 3

Newgate

A grim prison that stood on the site of the **Old Bailey** central criminal court in London. Originally a gatehouse (hence the name), it was established in the 12th century, rebuilt after the Great Fire of 1666, and again in 1780. Between 1783 and 1868 public executions were held outside Newgate prison. It was demolished in 1903. One of the cells is preserved in the Museum of London.

New Model Army

An army created in 1645 by Oliver **Cromwell** to support the cause of Parliament during the English **Civil War**. It was characterized by organization and discipline. Thomas **Fairfax** was its first commander.

Nightingale, Florence (1820–1910)

English nurse, the founder of nursing as a profession. She was born in Florence, Italy, and trained in Germany and France. In 1854 she took a team of nurses to Scutari (now Üsküdar, Turkey) and reduced the **Crimean War** hospital death rate from 42% to 2%. Her self-sacrificing services to the wounded made her name famous throughout Europe. In 1856 she founded the Nightingale School and Home for Nurses in London. In 1907 she was awarded the Order of Merit.

Florence Nightingale was the author of the classic *Notes on Nursing* (1860), the first textbook for nurses.

Nightingale *A young Florence Nightingale.*

❝ It may seem a strange principle to enunciate as the very first requirement in a Hospital that it should do the sick no harm. ❞

Florence Nightingale, *Notes on Hospitals*

nonconformist

Originally, a member of the **Puritan** section of the Church of England clergy who, in the Elizabethan age, refused to conform to certain practices, such as wearing the surplice and kneeling to receive Holy Communion. After 1662 the term was confined to those who left the church rather than conform to the Act of Uniformity, which required the use of the *Prayer Book* in all churches. It is now applied mainly to members of the Free churches.

Norfolk, Thomas Howard, 3rd Duke of (1473–1554)

The brother-in-law of **Henry VII** and a leading Catholic politician under **Henry VIII**. He led various campaigns against the French in the 1520s and returned to England to oppose **Wolsey**. Appointed Lord High Admiral in 1531, he served at the Battle of Flodden. He was arrested in 1546 when his son, Henry Howard, Earl of Surrey, claimed during Henry VIII's last illness that Norfolk should be protector for the young Edward VI. His son was beheaded, but the duke was saved by Henry's own death, and he was released by **Mary I**.

> Norfolk's nieces Anne Boleyn and Catherine Howard married Henry VIII, and Norfolk proved his loyalty to the king by his willingness to preside over their trials and executions for adultery.

Norfolk, Thomas Howard, 4th Duke of (1536–1572)

A Catholic peer who hoped to marry **Mary Queen of Scots** and have her declared heir to **Elizabeth I**. He was implicated in the **Northern Rebellion** of 1569 but released. He was arrested after the failure of the Ridolfi Plot, a conspiracy to replace Elizabeth I with Mary, and executed.

Norman Conquest

The invasion and settlement of England by the Normans, following the victory of **William the Conqueror** at the Battle of **Hastings** in 1066.

By about 1072 the Norman hold on the kingdom was firmly established and the affairs of church and state were completely in Norman hands. The English lost their landed possessions and were excluded from

> The Norman Conquest turned England away from Scandinavia and towards France, and brought England more closely into the European stream of political thought.

administrative posts. William introduced feudal land tenure: the granting of a definite piece of land in return for definite services. In 1085 he instigated the compilation of the **Domesday Book**, a recorded survey of land and property in the English shires.

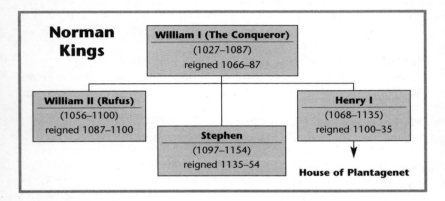

North Atlantic Treaty Organization (NATO)

A Western military alliance of which the UK is a member. It was set up in April 1949 to provide for the collective defence of the major Western European and North American states against the perceived threat from the USSR. The collapse of communism in eastern Europe from 1989 prompted a radical review of NATO's policy and defence strategy. In June 1999 NATO mounted the biggest military operation in Europe after World War II, when its forces took over the Serbian province of Kosovo to keep the peace in the region.

After the Eastern European Warsaw Pact was disbanded in 1991, an adjunct to NATO, the North Atlantic Cooperation Council, was established, including former Soviet republics, with the aim of building greater security in Europe.

In March 1999, former Warsaw Pact members Poland, Hungary, and the Czech Republic officially joined NATO.

Northcliffe, Alfred Charles William Harmsworth, 1st Viscount Northcliffe (1865–1922)

British newspaper proprietor who originated the picture paper. Born in Dublin, Northcliffe left school at the age of 16. He founded the *Daily Mail* in 1896, and in 1903 revolution-ized popular journalism with the *Daily Mirror*, the first picture paper. He was made a baron in 1905 and in 1908 he obtained control of *The Times*.

Northcliffe supported the removal of **Asquith** as prime min-ister in 1916 and **Lloyd George**

Northcliffe, who liked to be known as 'The Napoleon of Fleet Street', had a brother Harold Sidney Harmsworth, who was associated with him in many of his newspapers. Harold later became 1st Viscount Rothermere.

appointed him head of the British War Mission in the USA in 1917. Created viscount, he was made director of propaganda in enemy countries in 1918.

Northern Rebellion or Rebellion of the Earls
A rising led by the earls of Northumberland and Westmorland in support of **Mary Queen of Scots** in 1569–70. They called for Mary to be declared **Elizabeth I's** successor and for the restoration of Catholicism. The bishop of Durham was seized and the Catholic mass was restored, but when the promised Spanish support did not arrive the rising was put down. The earls fled to Scotland but 400 other rebels were executed.

Notting Hill riots
Racial battles involving up to 2,000 youths in the Notting Hill area of London in August and September 1958. The riots were the culmination of the attacks by whites against blacks that were

The Notting Hill riots influenced the development of the Commonwealth Immigrants Act of 1962, which restricted immigration of non-whites.

common in the area in the late 1950s. Along with a similar riot in Nottingham in 1958, the Notting Hill riots brought racial issues to the fore and were cited as arguments for controlling further immigration.

Nuffield, William Richard Morris, 1st Viscount Nuffield (1877–1963)
English manufacturer and philanthropist, the founder of the motor industry in Oxford. Starting with a small cycle-repairing business, in 1910 he designed a car that could be produced cheaply, and built up Morris Motors Ltd at Cowley, Oxford.

He endowed Nuffield College, Oxford, in 1937 and the Nuffield Foundation for medical, social, and scientific research in 1943. He was cre-ated Baron in 1934, and Viscount in 1938.

O

Oates, Titus (1648–1705)

English priest and conspirator. He entered the Jesuit colleges at Valladolid, Spain, and St Omer, France, as a spy in 1677–78, and on his return to England announced he had discovered a 'Popish Plot' to murder **Charles II**, burn London, and put the Catholic **James II** on the throne. Although this story was almost entirely false, many innocent Roman Catholics were executed between 1678 and 1680 on Oates's evidence.

Occam or Ockham, William of (c. 1300–1349)

English philosopher, logician, and theologian. Born at Ockham, Surrey, he became a Franciscan monk and was known as 'the Invincible Doctor'. He was imprisoned in Avignon, France, on charges of heresy in 1328 but escaped to Munich, Germany, where he died.

The principle of reducing assumptions to the absolute minimum is known as Occam's razor.

> ❝ *Entia non sunt multiplicanda praeter necessitatem* (No more things should be presumed to exist than are absolutely necessary). ❞
>
> **William of Occam**, statement that came to be known as Occam's razor

O'Connell, Daniel (1775–1847)

Irish lawyer and politician, known as 'the Liberator'. In 1823 he formed the Catholic Association, to campaign for **Catholic emancipation** and the repeal of the 1801 Act of **Union** between Britain and Ireland.

He achieved the first objective in 1829, when the ban on Catholics holding public office was lifted after his election as member of Parliament for County Clare. In his attempt to oppose the Union, he organised mass meetings all over Ireland, and formed an alliance with the Whigs in Britain, but was jailed for sedition.

On his release from prison, the **Irish potato famine** of 1845–46 pushed the repeal of the Union into the background.

Offa (died *c.* 796)

King of the Anglo-Saxon kingdom of Mercia (west-central England) from 757 to 797. Offa conquered Essex, Kent, Sussex, and Surrey, defeated the Welsh and the West Saxons, and established Mercian supremacy over all ofEngland south of the River Humber. He also built the earthwork known as Offa's Dyke along the Welsh border to defend his frontier in the west.

Official Secrets Act

A British law that prohibits the disclosure of confidential material from government sources by employees. The 1989 act replaced Section 2 of an act of 1911, which had long been accused of being too wide-ranging. Prosecution under criminal law is now reserved for material that the government claims is seriously harmful to national security.

However, it remains an absolute offence for a member or former member of the security and intelligence services (or those working closely with them) to disclose information about their work. There is no public-interest defence, and disclosure of information already in the public domain is still a crime.

> Journalists who repeat disclosures that are in breach of the Official Secrets Act are themselves in breach of the Act and liable to prosecution.

Old Bailey

The popular name for the Central Criminal Court in London. Situated in Old Bailey Street in the City of London, off Ludgate Hill, it was established on the site of **Newgate** prison in 1834.

'Old Contemptibles'

The name proudly adopted by British veteran soldiers of **World War I** who survived the retreat from Mons in 1914 and other early battles.

> The name Old Contemptibles arose from the German Kaiser Wilhelm's outburst that his forces in Belgium had been held up by 'Sir John French's contemptible little army'.

Old Bailey *The Statue of Justice on top of the Central Criminal Court, or Old Bailey.*

O'Neill, Hugh, 2nd Earl of Tyrone
(*c.*1550–1616)

Irish chieftain and rebel who plotted against **Elizabeth I** and **James I**. O'Neill was brought up in England at the house of Sir Henry Sidney. In 1602, he supported a Spanish invasion force that had landed in Ireland to instigate a revolt against Elizabeth, but was defeated at the battle of Kinsale. He made his peace with James I, but was soon suspected of planning sedition once more. He fled from Ireland in 1607 and died in Rome.

open-field system

A farming system in lowland areas of England during the Middle Ages. A village would normally have three large fields throughout which each farmer's land was distributed in scattered strips, while another area was set aside for common grazing. Two fields would be cultivated each year, usually with corn, and the third left fallow to recover its fertility. The strips, intended to share good and bad land fairly, made efficient farming difficult, and common grazing made it easy for disease to spread quickly among livestock.

By the early 19th century, **enclosure** meant that most farmland had been consolidated into individual holdings. A form of the open-field system survives at Laxton in Nottinghamshire.

Opium Wars

Two wars waged by Britain against China to enforce the opening of Chinese ports to trade in opium. Opium from British India paid for Britain's imports from China, such as porcelain, silk, and, above all, tea.

- *First Opium War 1839–42* resulted in the cession of Hong Kong to Britain and the opening of five treaty ports. Later, other European states were also given concessions.
- *Second Opium War 1856–60* followed with Britain and France in alliance against China, when there was further Chinese resistance to the opium trade. China was forced to give the European states greater trading privileges, at the expense of its people.

Orange Order
A sectarian lodge in Northern Ireland named after **William of Orange** and pledged to maintain Protestant ascendancy in the province. It was established in 1795 as a revival of the Orange Institution of 1688, formed in support of William's victory at the Battle of the **Boyne**, an event commemorated on 12 July every year by Protestant parades.

ordeal, trial by
In medieval Britain and elsewhere, a method of testing the guilt of an accused person based on the belief in heaven's protection of the innocent. Such ordeals included:

- walking barefoot over heated iron
- dipping the hand into boiling water
- swallowing consecrated bread (causing the guilty to choke).

In one trial ordeal, the accused would be bound and thrown into cold water; if he or she sank, it would prove innocence, but remaining afloat showed guilt.

Ordovices
A Celtic tribe in central and northwest Wales that resisted Roman occupation between AD 43 and 78. They supported **Caractacus**. Their frequent revolts eventually subsided in AD 78, but they remained under a form of military occupation and were never really romanized.

Orléans, Siege of
A siege of the well-fortified and strategically important city of Orléans, in central France, by English forces during the **Hundred Years' War**. It lasted from 12 October 1428 until 8 May 1429. Joan of Arc arrived on 29 April and inspired French forces to defeat the English and liberate the city. Control of Orléans would have given England access to France south of the Loire.

Oswald, St (c. 605–642)

King of Northumbria who helped further the cause of Christianity. Oswald became king in 634, after killing the Welsh king Cadwallon. During exile on the Scottish island of Iona he became a Christian convert, spreading the word in northern England with the help of St Aidan. Oswald was defeated and killed by King Penda of Mercia. He is commemorated on 9 August.

Owen, Robert (1771–1858)

British socialist, father of the **cooperative movement**. Born in Wales, Owen became manager in 1800 of a mill at New Lanark in Scotland, where, by improving working and housing conditions and providing schools, he created a model community. He stopped child employment and established sickness and old-age insurance for his workers. As stated in his book *A New View of Society* (1813), he believed that personal character was wholly determined by environment.

❝ Providence now evidently designs to effect the destruction of ignorance and misery, and firmly establish the reign of reason, intelligence and happiness. ❞

Robert Owen, *A New View of Society,* 1813

From 1817 Owen proposed 'villages of cooperation', self-supporting communities run on socialist lines, which, he believed, would ultimately replace private ownership. He later attempted to run such a community in the USA (called New Harmony). In 1833 he organized the Grand National Consolidated Trades Union, intending that the unions should take over industry and run it on a cooperative basis.

Oxford University

The oldest British university and one of the oldest in Europe. It was established during the 12th century. The earliest existing college was founded in 1249. After suffering from land confiscation during the **Reformation**, the university was reorganized by **Elizabeth I** in 1571.

The university's main library was founded in 1409 by **Humphrey**, Duke of Gloucester. It was restored and enlarged from 1598 to 1602 by Thomas Bodley and is called the Bodleian after him. The New Bodleian, with a capacity of 5 million books, was opened in 1946.

Paine, Thomas (1737–1809)

English left-wing political writer who believed in republicanism, deism, the abolition of slavery, and the emancipation of women. Paine went to America in 1774, where his pamphlet *Common Sense* (1776) ignited passions in the **American Revolution**. In 1787 he returned to Britain and wrote *The Rights of Man* (1791) in support of the French Revolution. In 1792 Paine was indicted for treason and escaped to France to represent Calais in the National Convention. While there, Paine wrote *The Age of Reason* (1793). Paine returned to the USA in 1802 and died in New York.

> ❢ The sublime and the ridiculous are often so nearly related, that it is difficult to class them separately. ❢
>
> **Thomas Paine,** *The Age of Reason,* 1793

Palestine, mandate

A commission in 1922 from the League of Nations to Britain to administer Palestine. Before the defeat of the Turks in **World War I**, Palestine had been under Ottoman control. Under the terms of the **Balfour Declaration** of 1917 Britain was committed to help create a national homeland for Jewish people. Britain administered Palestine during a period of increasing unrest between Jewish and Arab settlers. The British remained in Palestine until 1948, when Palestine was partitioned to create a new Jewish state, Israel.

Palmerston, Henry John Temple, 3rd Viscount Palmerston (1784–1865)

English politician. He entered Parliament as a **Tory** in 1807 and was secretary-at-war from 1809 to 1828. He broke with the Tories in 1830 and sat in the **Whig** cabinets of the 1830s and 1840s as foreign secretary. His policy was marked by distrust of France and Russia, and backing for Belgian and Turkish independence.

As prime minister from 1855 to1858, he rectified Aberdeen's mismanagement of the **Crimean War**, suppressed the **Indian Mutiny**, and carried through the Second **Opium War**.

During his second term in office from (1859–65), he was responsible for the warship *Alabama* going to the Confederate side in the American Civil War. He was popular with the people, but his high-handed attitude annoyed Queen **Victoria** and other ministers.

> ❛ Die, dear doctor! That's the last thing I shall do. ❜
>
> **Viscount Palmerston's** last words

Pankhurst family

The family most closely identified with the **suffragette** movement. Emmeline Pankhurst (1858–1928) was its leader. Her daughters Christabel (1880–1958) and Sylvia (1882–1960) were also suffragettes. In 1903 Emmeline formed the Women's Social and Political Union. She used militant methods and was imprisoned several times. During **World War I**, Emmeline and Christabel helped to mobilize women to help with the war effort; Sylvia was a pacifist. After the war, Emmeline lectured in the United States and Canada and Christabel devoted herself to a religious movement.

Following the Italian invasion of Ethiopia in 1935, Sylvia devoted her life to Ethiopian independence. Her works include *The Suffrage Movement* (1931) and a biography of her mother, published in 1935.

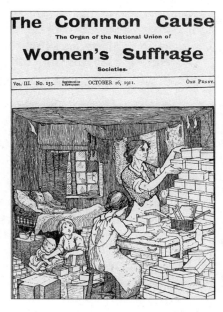

Pankhurst family *Front page of a pamphlet supporting the Pankhursts' efforts for equal opportunities for women.*

> ❝ Deeds, not Words. ❞
>
> Slogan of the Women's Social and Political Union

Park, Mungo (1771–1806)

Scottish explorer of the River Niger. Funded by the African Association, Park travelled to Africa in 1795 to follow the course of the Niger River and spent 18 months there. He did not achieve his goal of reaching Timbuktu, but proved that it was feasible to travel through the interior of Africa. He wrote an account of his experiences, *Travels in the Interior Districts of Africa* (1797). He disappeared and probably drowned during a second African expedition.

parliament

The legislative body of a country, whose name comes from the French for 'speaking'. The UK Parliament is usually dated from 1265, but its powers were not established until the late 17th century. It comprises the House of **Commons** and the House of **Lords**. Parliament meets in the Palace of

---

EVOLUTION OF THE UK PARLIAMENT

- *1066–1265* Norman kings held Great Councils of noblemen, sometimes including knights (who represented shires).
- *1265* **Simon de** Montfort's Parliament included burgesses (who represented boroughs) as well as knights.
- *1300s* Burgesses and knights met separately from the barons, forming the House of Commons; Parliament acquired the right to legislate.
- *1640, 1688* Revolutions abolished all royal claim to tax or legislate without parliamentary consent. Whig and Tory parties emerged.
- *1707* English and Scottish parliaments united.
- *1801* English and Irish parliaments united, until 1922.
- *1911* **Parliament Act**; introduction of pay for MPs.
- *1969* All men and women over 18 receive the vote.
- *1999* Devolution of Scottish Parliament and formation of the Welsh Assembly.
  Irish Assembly formed.
  First stage of reform of the House of Lords completed, with the election of 75 peers to form an interim House.
- *2000* Irish Assembly dissolved following failure to reach agreement on IRA decommissioning of weapons.

Westminster, London. A public bill that has been passed is an **act of Parliament**.

Parliament Act

An **act of Parliament** passed in October 1911 that took away power from the House of **Lords** and gave more authority to the House of **Commons**. It was introduced after the Lords rejected **Lloyd George's** radical People's Budget of 1909 and made it possible to present a bill for royal assent without the approval of the Lords. The Act also reduced the maximum life of a parliament from seven years to five, but any parliament may extend its own life, as happened during both world wars.

Parnell, Charles Stewart (1846–1891)

Irish nationalist politician. Born in Avondale, County Wicklow, Parnell was elected member of Parliament for Meath in 1875. He supported a policy of obstruction and violence to attain **Home Rule**, and became the president of the Nationalist Party in 1877. In 1879 he approved the **Land League**; he was imprisoned for his beliefs in 1881. In 1887 he was falsely accused in *The Times* of involvement in the murder of Lord Frederick Cavendish, chief secretary to the Lord Lieutenant of Ireland. Three years later his affair with a married woman, Katherine O'Shea, caused another scandal. For fear of losing the support of **Gladstone**, Parnell's party deposed him. He died suddenly of rheumatic fever at the age of 45.

> ❝ No man has a right to fix the boundary of the march of a nation; no man has a right to say to his country – thus far shalt thou go and no further. ❞
>
> **Charles Stewart Parnell**, giving a speech in Cork in 1885

Passchendaele, Battle of

World War I battle fought near Ypres, southern Belgium. A British offensive, begun on 31 July 1917, met fierce resistance from the German forces. Severe rains reduced the trenches to mud, and the battle went on for more than three months. British casualties numbered nearly 400,000. The name is often erroneously applied to the whole of the Battle of **Ypres**, but Passchendaele was in fact just part of that battle.

Patrick, St (*c.* 389–*c.* 461)

Patron saint of Ireland, said to have taken Christianity there. Aged 16, British-born Patrick was carried off by pirates to six years' slavery in Antrim, Ireland, before escaping either to Britain or Gaul to train as a missionary. He landed again in Ireland in 432 or 456, and his work was a vital factor in the spread of Christian influence there.

- Legend has it that St Patrick drove all the snakes from Ireland.
- St Patrick's Day is on March 17.
- It is said that St Patrick used the three-leaved shamrock to explain the Holy Trinity.
- Of Patrick's writings only his *Confessio* and an *Epistola* survive.

patronage

Power to give a favoured appointment to an office or position in politics, business, or the church; or sponsorship of the arts. Patronage was for centuries bestowed mainly by individuals (often royal or noble) or by the church. Political patronage has largely been replaced by a democratic system of meritocracy (in which selection is by open competition) but patronage survives in the political honours system (awards granted to party supporters) and in the appointment of university professors and leaders of national corporations.

Peasants' Revolt

The rising of the English peasantry in June 1381. It was sparked off by the imposition of a new **poll tax**, three times the rates of that imposed in 1377. Wat **Tyler** and John Ball, rebels from southeast England, led the march on London and demanded reforms. The authorities put down the revolt by deceit and force.

Peel, Robert (1788–1850)

British Conservative politician who, as home secretary during the 1820s, founded the modern police force. He also introduced Roman **Catholic**

> ❛I may be a Tory, I may be illiberal, but ... Tory as I am, I have the further satisfaction of knowing that there is not a single law connected with my name which has not had as its object some mitigation of the severity of our criminal system. ❜
>
> **Robert Peel**, speaking in the House of Commons in 1827

emancipation in 1829. Peel was prime minister from 1834 to 1835 and from 1841 to 1846, when his repeal of the **Corn Laws** caused him and his followers to break with the **Conservative Party**. He formed a third party standing between the Liberals and Conservatives; the majority of the Peelites, including **Gladstone**, subsequently joined the Liberals.

peerage

Holders, in descending order, of the titles of duke or duchess, marquess or marchioness, earl or countess, viscount or viscountess, and baron or baroness. Peers are allowed to take a seat in the House of **Lords**.

In the late 19th century the peerage was augmented by the Lords of Appeal in Ordinary (nonhereditary life peers) and, from 1958, by a number of specially created life peers of either sex (usually long-standing members of the House of **Commons**). Since 1963 peers have been able to disclaim their titles, usually to enable them to take a seat in the Commons.

> ❝ One of those hassles in life is that no one understands the difference between a viscount and a lord. ❞
>
> 3rd Viscount Thurso, writing in *The Independent*, 1 February 1997

Peninsular War

War of 1808–14 caused by Napoleon's invasion of Portugal and Spain. British forces under Sir Arthur Wellesley (the Duke of **Wellington**) combined with Spanish and Portuguese resistance and succeeded in defeating the French at Vimeiro in 1808, Talavera in 1809, Salamanca in 1812, and Vittoria in 1813. The war was ended by Napoleon's forced abdication in 1814.

Penn, William (1644–1718)

English Quaker leader, who founded Pennsylvania. Born in

Penn *William Penn.*

London, he joined the Society of **Friends** in 1667, and was imprisoned several times for his beliefs. He wrote *No Cross, No Crown* (1669) while in prison. In 1681 he obtained a grant of land in America (in settlement of a debt owed by King **Charles II** to his father) on which he established Pennsylvania as a refuge for persecuted Quakers. He wrote a liberal constitution for the colony and governed it until his return to England in 1684.

> ❝ Men are generally more careful of the breed of their horses and dogs than of their children. ❞
>
> **William Penn,** *Reflexions and Maxims,* pt 1, no 85

penny post

The first national pre-paid postal service, introduced in Britain in 1840. Until then, postage was paid by the recipient according to the distance travelled. Rowland Hill of Shrewsbury suggested the new service, which would be paid for by the sender of the letter or package according to its weight. The first adhesive stamp, the Penny Black, was introduced in May 1840. It bore the sovereign's portrait in the manner of coins.

Pepys, Samuel (1633–1670)

English naval administrator and diarist. His *Diary* (1660–69) is a unique record of the daily life of the period, the historical events of the **Restoration**, the manners and scandals of the court, administration of the British Navy, and Pepys's own interests, weaknesses, and intimate feelings.

The original manuscript of the *Diary* is in six volumes, containing more than 3,000 pages. It includes accounts of the **Great Plague** of London (1665) and the **Fire of London** (1666). The *Diary* was written in cipher (a form of shorthand) and was not deciphered until 1825.

> ❝ Strange to see how a good dinner and feasting reconciles everybody. ❞
>
> **Samuel Pepys,** *Diary,* 9 November 1665

Percy, Henry 'Hotspur' (1364–1403)

English soldier, son of the 1st Earl of Northumberland, who led the rebellion against **Henry IV**. In repelling a border raid, he defeated the Scots at

Homildon Hill, Durham, in 1402 but was captured. King Henry IV refused to pay the ransom. In 1403 Percy was killed at the Battle of Shrewsbury while on his way to join Owain **Glendower** in Wales in revolt against Henry IV . Legend has it that he was killed by Prince Hal (later **Henry V**).

Peterloo massacre

Events in St Peter's Fields, Manchester, England, on 16 August 1819, when a peaceful open-air meeting for parliamentary reform was charged by cavalry soldiers. The 60,000-strong crowd, which included many women and children, was unarmed and entirely peaceful. Local magistrates, concerned that the Radical politician Henry Hunt was to speak, sent in the yeomanry to arrest him. In the crush and panic that followed, 11 people were killed and 500 wounded. The 'massacre' caused an outcry, but the government stood by the magistrates. The name was given in analogy with the Battle of **Waterloo**.

Philby, Kim (Harold Adrian Russell) (1912–1988)

British intelligence officer from 1940 and Soviet double agent from 1933. Philby was head of anticommunist espionage from 1944 to 1946, then liaison officer in Washington from 1949 to 1951, until he was confirmed to be a double agent and asked to resign. Named in 1963 as having warned fellow double agents Guy Burgess and Donald Maclean that their activities were known, he fled to the USSR and became a Soviet citizen and a general in the KGB. A fourth member of the ring was Anthony Blunt. Philby's autobiography, *My Secret Life,* was published in 1968.

❝ To betray, you must first belong. I never belonged. ❞

Kim Philby writing in *The Sunday Times*, 17 December 1967

Pict

Roman term for a member of the peoples of northern Scotland, possibly meaning 'painted' (tattooed). Of pre-Celtic origin, and speaking a Celtic language that died out in about the 10th century, the Picts are thought to have inhabited much of England before the arrival of the **Celts**. They were united with the Celtic Scots under the rule of Kenneth MacAlpin in 844. Their greatest monument is a series of carved stones, whose symbols remain undeciphered.

Pilgrimage of Grace

Rebellion against **Henry VIII** from 1536 to 1537, which originated in Yorkshire and Lincolnshire. The uprising was directed against the king's policies, including the dissolution of the monasteries and the effects of the **enclosure** of common land. At the height of the rebellion, the rebels controlled York and included the archbishop there among their number. A truce was arranged in December 1536 and the rebels dispersed, but their demands were not met, and a further revolt broke out in 1537. Its suppression led to the execution of over 200 of the rebels, including the leader, Robert Aske.

Pilgrim Fathers

The emigrants who sailed from England on the *Mayflower* in 1620 to found the first colony in New England, North America. Of the 102 passengers, about a third were **Puritan** refugees. They landed at Cape Cod in December and decided to stay, moving on to find New Plymouth harbour and founding the Massachusetts colony. About half of the Pilgrims died over the winter, before they received help from American Indians. The survivors celebrated the first Thanksgiving in the autumn of 1621.

Pitt, William, 'the Elder', 1st Earl of Chatham (1708–1778)

British Whig prime minister, also known as 'the Great Commoner'. Pitt entered Parliament in 1735 and led the Patriot faction opposed to the Whig prime minister Robert **Walpole**. Pitt attacked Walpole's successor, Carteret, over the War of the Austrian Succession. Pitt was appointed prime minister in 1756 on the outbreak of the **Seven Years' War**. In 1759, the 'year of victories', the French were expelled from India and Canada. In 1761 Pitt wished to declare war on Spain, but **George III** disagreed and Pitt resigned. He was again recalled to form an all-party government in 1766 and made 1st Earl of Chatham the same year. He collapsed during his last speech in the House of **Lords**, opposing the withdrawal of British troops from the United States.

> ❝ If I were an American, as I am an Englishman, while a foreign troop was landed in my country I would never lay down my arms – never, never, never!'
>
> **William Pitt 'the Elder'**, speaking in the House of Commons in 1777

Pitt, William, 'the Younger' (1759–1806)

British **Tory** prime minister. Second son of William **Pitt 'the Elder'**, he entered Parliament aged 22 and became Britain's youngest prime minister in 1783. He reformed the country's finances and negotiated reciprocal tariff reduction with France, but underestimated the revolution there and, from 1793, became embroiled in wars with France.

After the 1798 Irish revolt, Pitt tried to solve the Irish question by the Act of **Union** of 1801, but **George III** rejected the **Catholic emancipation** Pitt had promised as a condition, and Pitt resigned in 1801. Returning to office in 1804, he organized an alliance with Spain, Austria, Russia, and Sweden against Napoleon. Pitt died shortly after hearing of Napoleon's victory at Austerlitz. He was buried in Westminster Abbey.

> ❝ Necessity is the plea for every infringement of human freedom. It is the argument of tyrants; it is the creed of slaves. ❞
>
> **William Pitt 'the Younger'**, speaking in the House of Commons in 1783

Plaid Cymru

Welsh nationalist political party established in 1925, dedicated to an independent Wales. Its name is Welsh for 'Party of Wales', and the party was set up to safeguard the country's culture, language, and economic life. It has contested parliamentary elections in Wales since 1929, but did not gain representation in Westminster until 1966, when it won Carmarthen. This seat was lost in 1970, but in the two general elections of February and October 1974 Plaid Cymru won two and three seats respectively. Four Plaid Cymru MPs were returned in the 1997 general election.

The Labour Party's 1997 devolution proposals for Wales were criticized by Plaid Cymru as being too cautious. Nevertheless, the party supported the 'Yes' vote in the subsequent referendum.

Plantagenet

English royal house which reigned from 1154 to 1399. The name comes from the nickname of Geoffrey, Count of Anjou (1113–1151), father of Henry II, who often wore in his hat a sprig of broom, *planta genista*. In the 1450s, Richard, Duke of York, took 'Plantagenet' as a surname to emphasize his superior claim to the throne over that of **Henry VI**.

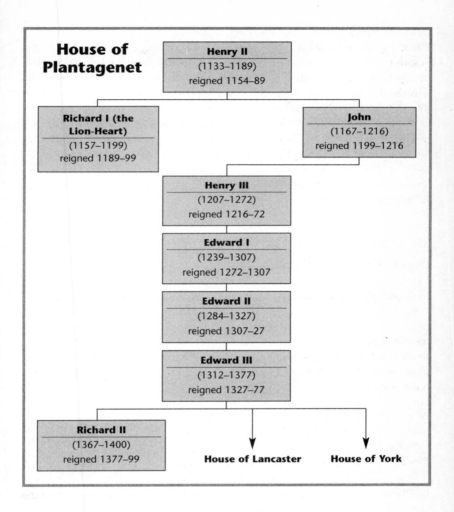

Plantation of Ireland

The colonization and conquest of Ireland by English and Scottish settlers from 1556 to 1660. The settlers were encouraged to settle in **Ulster**, which led to several rebellions by the Irish and the Anglo-Irish aristocracy, particularly in 1563, 1580, 1598, and 1641. Oliver **Cromwell** eventually defeated Ireland, killing about two-thirds of the Irish population. He rewarded his soldiers with vast estates there.

Plassey, Battle of

British victory under Robert **Clive** over the Nawab of Bengal, Suraj Dowla, on 23 June 1757. This brought Bengal under the control of the **East India Company** and hence under British rule. The battle took place at the former village of Plassey, about 150 km/95 mi north of Calcutta. Although outnumbered, Clive won the battle with minimal losses through Suraj's impetuous squandering of his

The nawab's army included 35,000 foot soldiers, 18,000 cavalry, and 50 guns. Clive's forces numbered just 3,000, of which he lost 72.

advantage in an all-out bombardment that exhausted his ammunition. Clive used the support of his Indian banker allies to buy the defection of Suraj's general Mir Jafar, who he then installed as nawab.

Plunket, St Oliver (1629–1681)

Catholic primate of Ireland, and the last man to be martyred for Catholicism in England. Plunket was born in Meath and educated in Rome, where he was professor of theology from 1657. He left Rome and became archbishop of Armagh and primate of Ireland in 1669. In 1671 he went on a mission to the Hebrides. He was executed, along with 30 or more other victims, in the panic surrounding the fictitious Popish Plot reported by Titus **Oates**. Plunket's head is preserved at Drogheda and his body at Downside Abbey, Bath. Pope Paul VI canonized Plunket in 1976. His feast day is on 11 July.

Poitiers, Battle of

Battle of the **Hundred Years' War** held on 13 September 1326, when the English defeated the French. **Edward the Black Prince** (son of Edward III) was marching north with an army of 8,000 troops when he was intercepted near Poitiers by the French king, John II, who had 15,000 troops. Peace negotiations failed.

The first French attack by dismounted knights was broken up by English archers; a second attack was beaten off. With half the French troops dead or wounded, over 3,000 of those remaining fled. John's attack with his remaining men was defeated by a surprise assault by Edward's archers from the rear. King John, his son Philip, and 2,000 knights were taken prisoner, and about 3,000 French soldiers were killed.

poll tax

A tax levied on every individual, without reference to income or property.

Being simple to administer, it was among the earliest sorts of tax (introduced in England in 1379), but because of its indiscriminate nature (it is a regressive tax, in that it falls proportionately more heavily on poorer people) it has often proved unpopular.

- Poll tax was introduced in 1377 to help pay for the **Hundred Years' War**.
- The **Peasants' Revolt** of 1381 was sparked off by the oppressive poll tax of 1379.
- Poll tax was abolished in England in 1698.
- Margaret **Thatcher** introduced the community charge (nicknamed the poll tax) from 1989 to replace rates.
- The unpopularity of the community charge contributed to Thatcher's downfall and was replaced within four years by a council tax, based on property values and household size.

Poor Law

A system for poor relief, established by the Poor Relief Act of 1601. Each parish looked after its own poor, paid for by a parish tax. After the Royal Commission on the Poor Law of 1834, 'outdoor' relief for able-bodied paupers was abolished and replaced by **workhouses** run by unions of parishes. Conditions in such workhouses were designed to act as a deterrent for all but the genuinely destitute. Care of the poor was transferred to the Ministry of Health in 1918, but the Poor Law was in force until 1930.

Poplarism

An attempt in 1921 by the London borough of Poplar to force the richer boroughs to assist with poor relief in the East End. George Lansbury (1859–1940), later leader of the Labour Party, was imprisoned for supporting a rates strike, but a shared system was eventually introduced.

Powys, kingdom of

Ancient kingdom in Wales, bordering England in the east. It was frequently under threat from the English. Parts of Powys in the present English counties of Herefordshire, Worcestershire, and Shropshire were lost to the **Mercians** prior to the construction of **Offa's** Dyke in the late 8th

The name was restored for the present county of Powys, formed in 1974 from the counties of Breconshire, Montgomeryshire, and Radnorshire.

century. The rulers of Powys often fought those of neighbouring Gwynedd. The last ruler of Powys as an intact kingdom was Madog ap Maredudd. His successors ruled over a Powys divided into north and south.

press gang
Method used to recruit soldiers and sailors into the British armed forces in the 18th and early 19th centuries. In effect, it was a form of kidnapping carried out by the services or their agents, often with the aid of armed men. This was similar to the practice of 'shanghaiing' sailors for duty in the merchant marine, especially in the Far East.

Princes in the Tower
Popular name for King Edward V (1470–1483) and his younger brother Richard, Duke of York (1472–1483). They are said to have been murdered in the **Tower of London** by order of their uncle, the Duke of Gloucester, so that he could succeed to the throne as **Richard III**.

privatization
Selling or transferring state-owned or public assets and services (notably **nationalized** industries) to private investors. Supporters of privatization argue that the public benefits from greater efficiency thanks to the competitive market, and that it frees government resources for more appropriate uses. Opponents say that it transfers the country's assets from all the people to a controlling minority, that public utilities such as gas and water become private monopolies, and that a profit-making, state-owned company raises revenue for the government.

UK COMPANIES PRIVATIZED SINCE 1979

- British Telecom
- British National Oil Corporation
- British Airports Authority
- British Shipbuilders
- British Transport Docks Board
- National Freight Company
- Jaguar
- Water Supply
- British Rail
- British Gas Corporation
- British Airways
- British Aerospace
- British Steel
- British Water Board
- Enterprise Oil
- Rover Group
- Electricity and gas companies

Public Health Acts

Acts of Parliament that established a code of sanitary law. Edwin Chadwick's enquiry into *The Sanitary Condition of the Labouring Population* (1842) and the reports of the Health of Towns Commission (1844, 1845) had exposed the squalor and disease that existed, particularly in the industrial towns. The cholera epidemic of 1848 also increased concern.

- The 1848 Act set up a General Board of Health, which imposed local boards of health that oversaw street cleaning, refuse collection, water supplies, and sewerage.
- The 1872 Act created the Local Government Board to take over central responsibility for public health.
- The 1875 Act consolidated the previous acts and provided a complete code of sanitary law. It remained in force with little change for 60 years.

Puritan

From 1564, a member of the **Church of England** who wished to remove Roman Catholic rites from church services. The term also covers the separatists who withdrew from the church altogether. Puritans were convinced of human sinfulness and the wrath of God, and advocated plain living and hard work. They were increasingly identified with the parliamentary opposition under **James I** and **Charles I**. The Puritan emigrants who settled in New England in the 17th century, most of them Congregationalists and Presbyterians, had a profound, formative influence on American culture, political institutions, and education.

Puritan *Woodcut showing a Puritan family.*

Q–R

Quakers
Another name for the Society of **Friends**.

Queensberry, John Sholto Douglas, 8th Marquess of Queensberry (1844–1900)
British patron of boxing, who became marquess in 1858. In 1867 he gave his name to a new set of boxing rules. Devised by the pioneering British sports administrator John Chambers (1841–1883), the Queensberry Rules form the basis of today's boxing rules.

Douglas was father of Lord Alfred Douglas and disapproved of his friendship with Oscar Wilde. An insult from the Marquess of Queensberry led Wilde to sue for libel, a suit that ruined the playwright and led to his imprisonment.

Race Relations Acts
Acts of Parliament brought in to combat discrimination on the grounds of colour, race, nationality, or ethnic origin.

- The Race Relations Act 1965 set up the Race Relations Board to promote racial harmony, prevent discrimination, and deal with complaints. It made stirring up racial hatred or practising discrimination in a public place illegal.

- The Race Relations Act 1968 increased the powers of the Race Relations Board and made discrimination in housing and employment illegal. It also set up the Community Relations Commission.

- The Race Relations Act 1976 prohibited indirect as well as direct discrimination, for example in the provision of goods, services, facilities, employment, and accommodation, and in advertisements. It set up the Commission for Racial Equality to investigate discrimination.

Radical
Supporter of parliamentary reform before the **Reform Act** of 1832. From then on, the term became gradually interchangeable with **'Liberal'**. During

the 1860s the Radicals (led by Richard **Cobden**, John **Bright**, and J S Mill) campaigned for extension of the franchise, free trade, and *laissez-faire*, but after 1870, under the leadership of Joseph Chamberlain and Charles Dilke, they adopted a republican and semi-socialist programme. With the growth of socialism in the later 19th century, Radicalism ceased to exist as an organized movement.

Raffles, (Thomas) Stamford (1781–1826)

British colonial administrator, born in Jamaica. He served in the British **East India Company**, took part in the capture of Java from the Dutch in 1811, and while governor of Sumatra from 1818 to 1823 he was responsible for the acquisition and founding of Singapore in 1819. He was knighted in 1817.

Raglan, FitzRoy James Henry Somerset, 1st Baron of (1788–1855)

English general. He took part in the **Peninsular War** under **Wellington**, and lost his right arm at **Waterloo**. He commanded the British forces in the **Crimean War** from 1854, and ordered the charge at the Battle of **Balaclava**. The raglan sleeve, cut right up to the neckline with no shoulder seam, is named after him.

> ❝ Don't carry away that arm till I have taken off my ring. ❞
>
> **Lord Raglan**, attributed remark

Raleigh or Ralegh, Walter (c. 1552–1618)

English adventurer, writer and courtier to Queen **Elizabeth I**. He led a gold-seeking expedition to the Orinoco River in South America in 1595 (described in his *Discoverie of Guiana*). His aggressive actions against Spanish interests, including attacks on Spanish ports, brought him into conflict with the pacific **James I**. He was imprisoned for treason from 1603 to 1616, during which time he wrote his unfinished *History of the World*. He was executed on his return from an unsuccessful final expedition to South America. He is traditionally credited with introducing the potato to Europe and popularizing the use of tobacco.

> ❝ Fain would I climb, yet fear I to fall. ❞
>
> **Walter Raleigh**, written on a window-pane; underneath, Queen Elizabeth I wrote 'If thy heart fails thee, climb not at all'.

rationing

Restricted allowance of provisions or other supplies in time of war or shortage. Both Germany and Britain rationed food during **World War I**. During **World War II** food rationing was introduced in Britain in 1940. Each person was given a ration book of coupons. Bacon, butter, and sugar were restricted, followed by other goods, including sweets, petrol, clothing, soap, and furniture. In 1946, the world wheat shortage led to bread rationing. Food rationing finally ended in Britain in 1954. During the **Suez Crisis**, petrol rationing was reintroduced in Britain.

Rebecca Riots

Disturbances in southwest Wales from 1842 to 1844. They were a protest against **turnpike roads**, but were also a symptom of general unrest following the **Poor Law** Amendment Act of 1834, which made obtaining poor relief much harder. The rioters, many disguised as women, destroyed the tollhouses and gates. Each leader was known as 'Rebecca' and followers were 'her daughters'.

The rioters took their name from the biblical prophecy that the seed of Rebekah would 'possess the gate of those which hate them' (Genesis 24, 60).

Reform Acts

Acts of Parliament, also known as **Representation of the People Acts**, that extended voting rights and redistributed parliamentary seats.

- The 1832 Act abolished the **rotten borough**, redistributed county seats, and formed some new boroughs. The franchise was extended to male householders in property worth £10 a year or more in the boroughs and to owners of freehold property worth £2 a year, £10 copyholders, or £50 leaseholders in the counties.
- The 1867 Act redistributed seats from corrupt and small boroughs to the counties and large urban areas. It extended the franchise in boroughs to adult male heads of households, and in counties to males who owned, or held on long leases, land worth £5 a year, or who occupied land worth £12 on which they paid poor rates.
- The 1884 Act extended the franchise to male agricultural labourers.

Electoral reform: chronology

1822 Lord John Russell proposes a redistribution of seats. Whig Party espouses cause of reform.

1832 Reform Act involves redistribution of parliamentary seats from 'rotten boroughs' to urban constituencies. (Electorate 813,000 = 3% of population.)

1867 Reform Act extends voting rights. (Electorate 2,500,000 = 8% of population.)

1872 Ballot Act introduces secret ballots for elections.

1883 Corrupt and Illegal Practices Act sets limits on election expenses.

1884 Reform Act extends voting rights to male householders and ratepayers in the countryside. (Electorate 5,600,000 = 16% of population.)

1918 Representation of the People Act gives the vote to all men over 21 and all women ratepayers (or wives of ratepayers) over 30.

1928 Representation of the People (Equal Franchise) Act gives the vote to all women over 21.

1948 Representation of the People Act abolished the rights for more than one vote per person.

1969 Voting age reduced to 18.

1979 Constituencies established for direct election to European Parliament in Strasbourg.

1983 Number of parliamentary seats raised from 635 to 650.

1992 Number of parliamentary seats raised from 650 to 651.

1994 Number of UK seats in European parliament raised from 81 to 87.

1997 Number of parliamentary seats raised to 659.

Reformation

A movement in the 16th century to reform the Roman Catholic Church, which led to the establishment of Protestant churches. It was initiated by the German priest Martin Luther in 1517, and was anticipated in England by movements such as the **Lollards**. William **Tyndale's** translation of the New Testament with Luther's notes helped spread Luther's views to English-speakers.

Reform was helped when **Henry VIII** made England independent of the papacy, and the new views became prominent when the reformer Thomas **Cranmer** was made archbishop of **Canterbury** in 1533. Henry's daughter **Mary I** failed to restore papal supremacy, and when **Elizabeth I** succeeded her in 1558, Protestantism became firmly established.

Reith, John Charles Walsham, 1st Baron (1889–1971)

Scottish broadcasting pioneer who worked for the British Broadcasting Corporation (BBC). He was enormously influential in the early development of the BBC. As its first general manager (1922–27) and director general (1927–38), he established its high-minded principles of public-service broadcasting.

He held several ministerial posts in government during **World War II**, including minister of information in 1940, minister of transport in 1940, and minister of works in 1940–42. He was chair of the Colonial Development Corporation from 1950 to 1959. His publications include *Into the Wind* (1949).

Representation of the People Acts

Series of UK **acts of Parliament** from 1867 that extended voting rights, creating universal suffrage in 1928. The 1867 and 1884 acts are known as the second and third **Reform Acts**.

- The 1918 Act gave the vote to men over the age of 21 and women ratepayers (or wives of ratepayers) over the age of 30.
- The 1928 Act extended the vote to women over the age of 21.
- The 1948 Act abolished the right of anyone to have more than one vote.
- The 1969 Act reduced the minimum age of voting to 18.

Restoration

In English history, the period when the monarchy, in the person of **Charles II**, was re-established after the English **Civil War** and the fall of the Protectorate in 1660.

In literature, the term 'Restoration' is often applied generally to writers active at this period, most notably John Dryden, John Bunyan, and Samuel **Pepys**. 'Restoration comedy', popular drama played in the theatres newly reopened since **Cromwell's** time, was characterized by its bawdiness and wit.

Rhodes, Cecil John

(1853–1902)

UK-born South African politician, who was prime minister of Cape Colony from 1890 to 1896. Rhodes went to Natal in 1870. As head of De Beers

Rhodes *A caricature of the Imperialist Cecil Rhodes.*

Consolidated Mines and Goldfields of South Africa Ltd, he amassed a large fortune. He entered the Cape legislature in 1881, and was responsible for the annexation of Bechuanaland (now Botswana) in 1885. He formed the British South Africa Company in 1889, thus forming **Rhodesia** (now Zambia and Zimbabwe). He became prime minister of Rhodesia in 1890, but was forced to resign in 1896.

> 6 So little done, so much to do. 9
>
> **Cecil Rhodes** on the day he died

Rhodesia

In southern Africa, the former name of Zambia (Northern Rhodesia), which became independent in 1964, and Zimbabwe (Southern Rhodesia), which became independent in 1980 by the **Lancaster House Agreement**. Rhodesia was named after the politician Cecil **Rhodes**.

> 6 I don't believe in black majority rule ever in Rhodesia ... not in a thousand years. 9
>
> Rhodesian politician **Ian Smith**, speaking in 1976

Richard I, 'the Lion-Heart' (1157–1199)

Known in French as *Coeur-de-Lion*, Richard was king of England from 1189 to 1199. He spent all but six months of his reign abroad. He was the third son of Henry II, against whom he twice rebelled. In the third Crusade (1191–92) he won victories at Cyprus, Acre, and Arsuf (against Saladin), but failed to recover Jerusalem. While returning he was captured by the Duke of Austria, and was held prisoner until a large ransom was raised. He then returned briefly to England, where his brother **John** had been ruling in his stead. His later years were spent in warfare in France, where he was killed by a crossbow bolt in 1199. He left no heir.

Richard II or Richard of Bordeaux (1367–1400)

King of England from 1377, son of **Edward the Black Prince**. Richard succeeded his grandfather Edward III (1312–1377) when only ten, the government being in the hands of a council of regency. His fondness for favourites resulted in conflicts with Parliament, and in 1388 the baronial party, headed by the Duke of Gloucester, had many of his friends executed. Richard recovered control in 1389, and ruled moderately until 1397, when he had Gloucester murdered and assumed absolute power. Two years later, forced to abdicate in favour of his cousin Henry Bolingbroke (later **Henry IV**), he was jailed and probably assassinated.

> 6 My God! This is a wonderful land and a faithless one; for she has exiled, slain, destroyed, and ruined so many kings, so many rulers, so many great men, and she is always diseased and suffering from differences, quarrels, and hatred between her people. 9
>
> **Richard II**, in the Tower of London, September 1399

Richard III (1452–1485)

King of England from 1483. The son of Richard, Duke of York, he was created Duke of Gloucester by his brother Edward IV, and distinguished himself in the Wars of the **Roses**. On Edward's death in 1483, he became protector to his nephew Edward V, and soon secured the crown for himself on the plea that Edward IV's sons were illegitimate. He proved a capable ruler, but the suspicion that he had murdered Edward V and his brother (the **Princes in the Tower**) in 1483 undermined his popularity. In 1485 Henry, Earl of Richmond (later **Henry VII**), raised a rebellion, and Richard III was defeated and killed at **Bosworth**.

> 6 What prevaileth a handful of men to a whole nation? As for me, I assure you this day I will triumph by glorious victory or suffer death for immortal fame. 9
>
> **Richard III**, addressing his troops before the Battle of Bosworth

Riot Act

An **act of Parliament** passed in 1714 to suppress the **Jacobite** rebellions. If three or more persons assembled unlawfully to the disturbance of the public peace, a magistrate could read a proclamation ordering them to disperse ('reading the Riot Act'), after which they might be dispersed by force.

This was superseded by the Public Order Act of 1986, which was instituted in response to several inner-city riots in the early 1980s, and greatly extended police powers to control marches and demonstrations. Under the act a person is guilty of riot if in a crowd of 12 or more, threatening violence. The maximum sentence is ten years' imprisonment.

Roanoake

The first English settlement in North America, an island near Albermarle Sound, North Carolina. It was established by **Raleigh** in 1558 but only lasted ten months. A second colony was set up in 1587 by John White, whom Raleigh appointed as governor.

John White's granddaughter, born in 1587, was the first child born in America to English parents. She was called Virginia Dare.

Robert (I) the Bruce (1274–1329)

King of the Scots from 1306, successful guerrilla fighter, and grandson of Robert de Bruce (1210–1295). In 1307 he displayed his tactical skill in the Battle of Loudun Hill against the English under **Edward I**, and defeated the English again under Edward II at **Bannockburn** in 1314. Large English expeditions of 1322 and 1327 were beaten by Robert's 'scorched earth' policy. In 1328 the Treaty of Northampton recognized Scotland's independence and Robert the Bruce as king.

> ❲ They glory in their warhorses and equipment. For us the name of the Lord must be our hope of victory in battle. ❳
>
> **Robert the Bruce**, addressing his troops before the Battle of Bannockburn in 1314

Robin Hood

Legendary outlaw and champion of the poor against the rich, said to have lived in Sherwood Forest, Nottinghamshire, during the reign of **Richard I** (1189–99), with a band of followers known as his 'merry men'. Traditionally he is a nobleman who remained loyal to Richard and opposed King **John**. He appears in many popular ballads from the 13th century, and in William Langland's *Piers Plowman* in the late 14th century.

Many film versions of the legend have been made, including those of

1938, directed by Michael Curtiz and starring Errol Flynn, and 1991, directed by and starring Kevin Costner.

Rob Roy (1671–1734)

Nickname of Robert MacGregor, **Jacobite** outlaw of the Scottish Highlands. After losing his estates, he lived by cattle theft and extortion. Captured, he was sentenced to transportation but pardoned in 1727. He is a central character in Walter Scott's historical novel *Rob Roy* (1817). A film of *Rob Roy* was made in 1995, starring Liam Neeson.

Rodney, George Brydges, 1st Baron Rodney (1718–1792)

British admiral who spent many years in the West Indies. In 1762 he captured Martinique, St Lucia, and Grenada from the French. In 1780 he relieved Gibraltar by defeating a Spanish squadron off Cape St Vincent. In 1782 he crushed the French fleet under Count de Grasse off Dominica, for which he was raised to the peerage. He had become a baronet in 1764.

Roman Britain

Period in British history from 55 BC to the AD 400s. Caesar made two expeditions to Britain in 55–54 BC, but the actual conquest was not begun until AD 43. The province was garrisoned by three Roman legions based at Caerleon in South Wales, Chester, and York. During the reign of the emperor Domitian, the governer of the province, **Agricola**, campaigned in Scotland. After several unsuccessful attempts to conquer Scotland, the northern frontier was fixed between the Solway and the Tyne at **Hadrian's Wall**. During the 4th century Britain was raided by the Saxons, **Picts**, and Scots. The Roman armies were withdrawn in 407, but there were partial reoccupations until about 450.

- Colchester (Camulodunum), the location of the temple dedicated to the Divine Claudius, was the focus of the revolt of **Boudicca**.

- The spa at Bath was dedicated to the worship of Sulis Minerva, a combination of local and Roman deities.

- Roman roads still in use today include Watling Street from London to Wroxeter, the Fosse Way which runs through Cirencester, and Ermine Street from London to Lincoln and York.

- The Romans mined lead from the Mendips, in southwest England, and Derbyshire, and gold from Dolaucothi in southwest Wales.

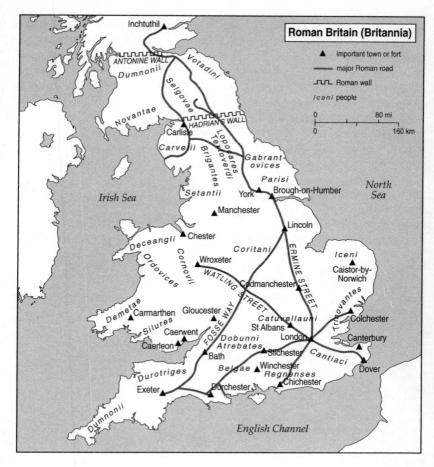

Roman Britain (Britannia)

▲ important town or fort
— major Roman road
⎍⎍ Roman wall
Iceni people

0   80 mi
0   160 km

Inchtuthil

ANTONINE WALL
Dumnonii
Votadini
Selgovae
Novantae
HADRIAN'S WALL
Carlisle
Carvetii
Lopocares
Textoverdi
Brigantes
Gabrant-
ovices
Parisi
Setantii
York   Brough-on-Humber
▲ Manchester
Lincoln
Deceangli
▲ Chester
Coritani
Cornovii
Wroxeter
Ordovices
WATLING STREET
Godmanchester
ERMINE STREET
Iceni
Caistor-by-
Norwich
Demetae
Carmarthen   Gloucester
Catuvellauni
Colchester
Silures
Caerwent
FOSSE WAY
St Albans
London
Trinovantes
Caerleon
Dobunni
Atrebates
Canterbury
Bath
Silchester
Cantiaci
Durotriges
Winchester
Belgae
Regnenses
Dover
Exeter   Dorchester
Chichester
Dumnonii

Irish Sea

North Sea

English Channel

Roses, Wars of the

Civil wars in England from 1455 to 1485 between the houses of **Lancaster** (whose symbol was a red rose) and **York** (whose symbol was a white rose). Lancaster and York both claimed the throne through descent from the sons of Edward III. As a result of **Henry VI**'s lapse into insanity in 1453, Richard, Duke of York, was installed as protector of the realm. Upon his recovery, Henry forced Richard to take up arms in self-defence.

The name 'Wars of the Roses' was given in the 19th century by the novelist Walter Scott. (**See** map on p. 170.)

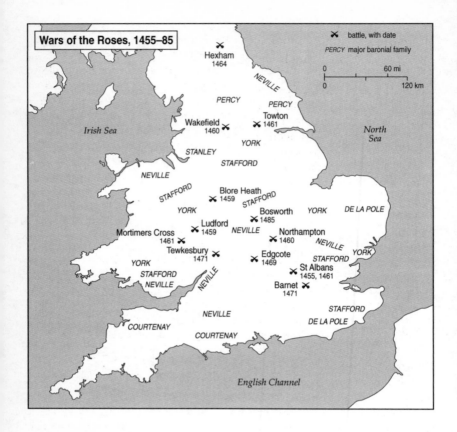

Wars of the Roses, 1455–85

✕ battle, with date
PERCY major baronial family

Hexham 1464

NEVILLE

PERCY   *PERCY*

Towton ✕ 1461

Wakefield ✕ 1460

Irish Sea

North Sea

YORK

STANLEY

STAFFORD

NEVILLE

STAFFORD   Blore Heath ✕ 1459 *STAFFORD*

YORK   Bosworth ✕ 1485   *YORK*   *DE LA POLE*

Mortimers Cross 1461 ✕   Ludford ✕ 1459   *NEVILLE*   Northampton ✕ 1460   *NEVILLE*   *YORK*

Tewkesbury ✕ 1471   Edgcote ✕ 1469   *STAFFORD*

YORK   St Albans 1455, 1461

STAFFORD

NEVILLE   *NEVILLE*   Barnet ✕ 1471

STAFFORD

NEVILLE   *DE LA POLE*

COURTENAY

COURTENAY

English Channel

rotten borough

English parliamentary constituency, before the Great **Reform Act** of 1832, that returned members to **Parliament** in spite of having small numbers of electors. Such a borough could easily be manipulated by those with sufficient money or influence.

Roundheads and Royalists

A Roundhead was a member of the Parliamentary party during the English **Civil War** of 1640–60, opposing the Royalist Cavaliers. The term Roundhead referred to the short hair then worn only by men of the lower classes. Men at the court of **Charles I** fashionably wore their hair in long ringlets, so the Parliamentarians chose to wear theirs short in contrast.

Many Parliamentarians were also **Puritans**, who thought they should live and dress simply and austerely.

Royalists were drawn from all classes, though their steadiest support came from the lesser gentry, and they embraced a wide range of religious opinions: Catholics and Arminians as well as moderate Anglicans and, after 1649, Presbyterians and Independents.

The Royalists were strongest in the northwest, and the Parliamentarians in the southeast; there were exceptions to this, such as Royalist Colchester and Parliamentarian Gloucester. The term 'Roundhead' is thought to have first been used in 1641, possibly by Queen Henrietta Maria.

Round Table conferences

Discussions on the future of India held in London in 1930–32 between representatives of British India, the Princely States, and the British government. The Indian princes agreed to join a united India (including Pakistan) at the first conference of 1930–31 but there was little progress in the second conference of 1931 as Mahatma Gandhi demanded a wider franchise. After the third conference in 1932, the British passed the Government of **India Act** in 1935.

Rowntree, Benjamin Seebohm (1871–1954)

English businessman and philanthropist. In 1899 he joined the family firm of confectioners, H I Rowntree in York. As chair of the firm from 1925 to 1941, he funded investigations into poverty in York and introduced pension plans and profit sharing for the benefit of his workers.

Three Rowntree Trusts, set up by Benjamin's father, Joseph, in 1904, fund research into housing and social care and support projects relating to social justice.

Royal Navy

The navy of Britain. **Alfred the Great** established a navy in the 9th century, and by the 13th century there was already an official 'keeper of the king's ships'. This office grew into the Navy Board, formed in 1546 to administer the 80-strong fleet of **Henry VIII**. The Navy Board administered the Navy until 1832, when the Board of Admiralty was instituted. The Admiralty was abolished in 1964 and replaced by the naval department of the Ministry of Defence.

- **Elizabeth I** transformed the Navy from a private fleet to a national defensive force.
- The navy gained the title 'Royal Navy' in the 1600s, during the reign of **Charles II**.
- The Royal Navy is third in world size, after the USA and Russia.
- The Royal Navy has been responsible for Britain's nuclear deterrence from 1969.

Royal Pavilion or Brighton Pavilion

Palace in Brighton, England, built in 1784 and bought in the early 19th century for the Prince Regent (the future **George IV**) who had it extensively rebuilt in a mix of classical and Indian styles. Queen **Victoria** was the last monarch to use it and it is now municipal property.

Rump, the

English parliament formed between December 1648 and November 1653 after Pride's purge of the **Long Parliament**, to ensure a majority in favour of trying **Charles I**. Cromwell replaced the Rump in 1653 with the **Barebones Parliament**, but it was reinstated after the Protectorate ended in 1659. Full membership of the Long Parliament was restored in 1660, and the Rump dissolved itself shortly afterwards. It was replaced by the Convention Parliament, which brought about the restoration of the monarchy.

S

Salisbury, Robert Arthur Talbot Gascoyne-Cecil, 3rd Marquess of Salisbury (1830–1903)

British **Conservative** politician. He entered the Commons in 1853 and succeeded to his title in 1868. As foreign secretary (1878–80), he took part in the Congress of Berlin, and as prime minister (1885–86, 1886–92, and 1895–1902), he gave his main attention to foreign policy, remaining also as foreign secretary for most of this time.

The 'Bob' in the expression 'Bob's your uncle' was Robert Gascoyne-Cecil, 3rd Marquess of Salisbury. As prime minister, he appointed his nephew, Arthur Balfour to a succession of posts.

---

6 English policy is to float lazily downstream, occasionally putting out a diplomatic boat-hook to avoid collisions. 9

Robert Gascoyne-Cecil, 3rd Marquess of Salisbury, during his time as foreign secretary

---

Salvation Army

Christian evangelical, social-service, and social-reform organization, which originated in 1865 in London, England, with the work of William Booth. At first called the Christian Revival Association, it was renamed the East London Christian Mission in 1870 and since 1878 has been known as the Salvation Army, now a worldwide organization. It has military titles for its officials, is renowned for its brass bands, and its weekly journal is the *War Cry*.

Scone

Site of the ancient Scone Palace (destroyed in 1559), near the village of New Scone, in Perth and Kinross, where many of the Scottish kings were crowned on the Stone of Destiny. The coronation stone was removed to

Westminster Abbey, London, by **Edward I** in 1297, but was returned to Scotland in 1996.

Scottish National Party (SNP)

Nationalist party advocating the separation of Scotland from the UK as an independent state within the **European Union**. It was formed in 1934 by the amalgamation of several early nationalist parties, and at first advocated only autonomy within the UK. It gained its first parliamentary victory in 1945 but did not make serious headway in parliament until the 1970s when it became an influential bloc at Westminster, and its support was crucial to James **Callaghan**'s Labour government.

It is now second only to the Labour Party in Scotland, having forced the Conservatives into third place.

The Stone of Destiny was removed without permission from Westminster Abbey by four students on Christmas Day 1950, and was kept at Arbroath Abbey until April 1951. Today the Stone of Destiny is on display at Edinburgh Castle.

Salvation Army *William Booth, founder of the Salvation Army.*

serfdom

The legal and economic status of peasants under **feudalism**. Serfs could not be sold like slaves, but they were not free to leave their master's estate without his permission. In England serfdom died out between the 14th and 17th centuries.

- Serfs worked the lord's land without pay for a number of days every week.

- Serfs performed extra labour at harvest time.

- Serfs were allowed to cultivate a portion of the lord's estate for their own benefit and paid a percentage of their produce to the lord every year.

- Serfs served their lords as soldiers in the event of conflict.

Settlement, Act of
A law passed in 1701 during the reign of **William III**, designed to ensure a Protestant succession to the throne. **Elizabeth II** still reigns under this act, which excluded the Roman Catholic descendants of **James II** in favour of the Protestant House of **Hanover**.

Seven Years' War
A war from 1756 to 1763, arising from the conflict between Britain and France, and between Austria and Prussia over colonial supremacy. (The French and Indian War in North America was also known as the Seven Years' War). Britain and Prussia defeated France, Austria, Spain, and Russia, and the war ended with the Treaty of Paris in 1763. Fighting against great odds, Prussia was eventually successful in becoming established as one of the great European powers.   Britain gained control of India, Spanish-ruled Florida (in exchange for Cuba), and many of France's colonies, including Canada.

Shaftesbury, Anthony Ashley Cooper, 7th Earl of Shaftesbury (1801–1885)
British **Tory** politician and reformer. He strongly supported the Ten Hours Act of 1847 and other **Factory Acts**, including the 1842 Act forbidding **child labour** and the employment of women in mines. He was also associated with the movement to provide free education for the poor and set up the Shaftesbury Homes to school homeless children. He became an earl in 1851.

> ❝ I cannot bear to leave the world with all the misery in it. ❞
>
> **Lord Shaftesbury**, aged 84, quoted in G W E Russell's
> *Collections and Recollections*

Shakespeare, William (1564–1616)
English dramatist and poet. Born in Stratford-upon-Avon, he was educated at the local grammar school. By 1592 Shakespeare was established in London as an actor and a dramatist, and from 1594 he was an important member of the Lord Chamberlain's Company of Actors. In 1598 the Company built the Globe Theatre; Shakespeare was a 'sharer' in the venture, entitled to a percentage of the profits. In 1603 the Company became the King's Men. By this time Shakespeare was the leading playwright of the

company and one of its business directors; he also continued to act. He retired to Stratford, where he died on 23 April 1616. His plays were written in blank verse with some prose, and he also wrote numerous sonnets.

- Shakespeare's lyric plays include *Romeo and Juliet* and *A Midsummer Night's Dream.*

- The comedies include *The Comedy of Errors, As You Like It,* and *Much Ado About Nothing.*

- The historical plays include *Henry VI* (in three parts), *Richard III,* and *Henry IV* (in two parts).

- The tragedies include *Hamlet, Othello, King Lear,* and *Macbeth.*

Shakesoeare *Title page of a 1623 Complete Works of Shakespeare.*

> ❝ All the world's a stage, / And all the men and women merely players: / They have their exits and their entrances; / And one man in his time plays many parts, / His acts being seven ages. ❞
>
> **William Shakespeare**, *As You Like It,* II. vii 139

Sheppard, Jack (1702–1724)
English criminal who became a popular hero by escaping four times from prison. Born in Stepney, in east London, he was apprenticed to a carpenter but turned to stealing. He was finally caught and hanged.

sheriff
In England and Wales, the crown's chief executive officer in a county for ceremonial purposes; in Scotland, the equivalent of the English county-court judge, but also dealing with criminal cases. In England, the office dates from before the **Norman Conquest**. The sheriff acts as returning

officer for parliamentary elections, and attends the judges on circuit.

The duties of keeping prisoners in safe custody, preparing panels of jurors for assizes, and

The word 'sheriff' comes from the Old English words scir meaning 'shire', and gerefa meaning 'reeve'.

executing writs, are supervised by the under-sheriff. The City of London has two sheriffs elected by members of the livery companies.

Simnel, Lambert (c. 1475–c. 1535)

English impostor, a carpenter's son who claimed to be Prince Edward, one of the **Princes in the Tower. Henry VII** discovered the plot and released the real Edward for one day to show him to the public. Simnel had a keen following and was crowned as Edward VI in Dublin in 1487. He came with forces to England to fight the royal army, and attacked it near Stoke-on-Trent on 16 June 1487. He was defeated and captured, but was contemptuously pardoned. He is then said to have worked in the king's kitchen.

Sinn Féin

Irish political party founded in 1905, whose aim is the creation of a united republican Ireland. The political force behind the rise of Irish nationalism from 1916 to 1921, Sinn Féin returned to prominence in the 1960s, when it split into 'Provisional' and 'Official' wings at the same time as the **Irish Republican Army** (IRA), with which it is closely associated. From the late 1970s 'Provisional' Sinn Féin assumed a more active political role; Gerry **Adams** became party president in 1978.

Sinn Féin participated in the multi-party negotiations (the Stormont Talks) and signed the agreement reached on Good Friday, 10 April 1998. The party gained 17.6% of votes in the June 1998 elections to the 108-seat Belfast assembly.

slave trade

The transportation of slaves from Africa to work in the New World, which began in the early 16th century. The need for slaves to work the British plantations in the Americas led to the development of the Atlantic triangle trade. By the late 17th century, when sugar plantations in the West Indies had become profitable, much of the slave trade was being organized by the British.

The Society for the Abolition of the Slave Trade was founded in 1787. After persistent campaigning, an **act of Parliament** in 1807 made it illegal for British ships to carry slaves or for the British colonies to import them. The Abolition Act of 1833 provided for slaves in British colonies to be freed and for their owners to be compensated.

British slaves were taken to Rome during the Roman occupation of Britain. Slaves from Ireland were imported to work in Bristol before the 11th century.

Social Democratic and Labour Party (SDLP)

Northern Ireland left-of-centre political party, aiming for Irish unification by non-violent means. Formed in 1970, the SDLP has adopted a constitutional, conciliatory role. Its leader, John **Hume**, played a key role in the negotiations that ended in the 1998 Good Friday Agreement on power-sharing. The SDLP secured 24 of the 108 seats in the new Northern Ireland Assembly, elected in June 1998. The party's deputy leader, Seamus Mallon, was voted deputy first minister (to Ulster Unionist David Trimble) by the first meeting of the Assembly.

Somme, Battle of the

Allied offensive in **World War I** during July–November 1916 on the River Somme in northern France, during which severe losses were suffered by both sides. It was planned by the Marshal of France, Joseph Joffre, and UK commander-in-chief Douglas **Haig**. The Allies lost over 600,000 soldiers and advanced 13 km/8 mi. The German offensive around St

---

It was the first battle in which tanks were used, though most of the Allied forces' 42 tanks broke down in the mud.

Quentin during March–April 1918 is sometimes called the Second Battle of the Somme.

South African Wars

Two wars between the British and the Dutch settlers (Boers) in South Africa, essentially over gold and diamond deposits in the Transvaal.

- *The War of 1881* started after the Boers in the Transvaal reasserted their independence, surrendered in 1877 in return for British support against the Africans. The British were defeated at Manjuba, and the Transvaal became independent.

- *The War of 1899–1902* also known as the *Boer War*, began after the Cape Colony prime minister, Cecil **Rhodes**, attempted to instigate a revolt among the *uitlanders* (non-Boer immigrants) against Kruger, the Transvaal president. The Boers invaded British territory, besieging Ladysmith, **Mafeking**, and Kimberley, but eventually conceded defeat by the Peace of Vereeniging.

❝ When is a war not a war? When it is carried on by methods of barbarism. ❞

Henry Campbell-Bannerman, British Liberal politician, condemning the Boer War in a speech in June 1901

South Sea Bubble
Financial crisis in Britain in 1720. The South Sea Company, founded in 1711, which had a monopoly of trade with South America, offered in 1719 to take over more than half the national debt in return for further concessions. Its 100 shares rapidly rose to 1,000, and an orgy of speculation followed. When the 'bubble' burst, thousands of investors were ruined.

The discovery that cabinet ministers had been guilty of corruption led to a political crisis. Robert Walpole became prime minister, protected the royal family and members of the government from scandal, and restored financial confidence.

Special Branch
Section of the British police originally established in 1883 to deal with Irish **Fenian** activists. All 42 police forces in Britain now have their own Special Branches. They act as the executive arm of MI5 (British intelligence) in its duty of preventing or investigating espionage, subversion, and sabotage; carry out duties at airports and seaports in respect of naturalization and immigration; and provide armed bodyguards for public figures.

Special Operations Executive (SOE)
British intelligence organization established in June 1940 to gather intelligence and carry out sabotage missions inside German-occupied Europe during **World War II**.

Some 11,000 agents were eventually employed, but screening was careless and a number of German agents infiltrated the organization, fatally damaging many operations before the agents were detected and removed.

Speenhamland system
Method of poor relief in England started by Berkshire magistrates in 1795, whereby wages were supplemented from the poor-rates. However, it encouraged the payment of low wages and was superseded by the 1834 **Poor Law**.

Spithead Mutiny
Mutiny of the Channel and North Sea fleets in April 1797, during the French Revolutionary Wars. The mutineers were making a stand about the appalling conditions on board ship. They won improved conditions and better pay and a royal pardon was granted. The success of this mutiny encouraged the outbreak of the more serious Nore mutiny the following month.

Stamford Bridge, Battle of
Battle on 25 September 1066 at Stamford Bridge, northeast of York, at which **Harold II** defeated and killed Harold Hardrada, King of Norway.

Harold was in the south with an army he had collected to meet the anticipated invasion by the Normans, and upon news of the Norse invasion immediately marched north. He confronted the Norse army at Stamford Bridge and a fierce battle ensued, in the course of which both the Norwegian king and Tostig, the English king's exiled brother, were killed.

> On meeting the Norse at Stamford Bridge, Harold offered the Norse king generous compensation if he retired or seven feet of earth for a grave if he stayed!

A few days later, news came that **William the Conqueror** had landed at Pevensey; Harold marched south and with a weary army fought the Battle of **Hastings**.

Stamp Act
UK **act of Parliament** in 1765 that sought to raise enough money from the American colonies to cover the cost of their defence. The act taxed (by requiring an official stamp) all publications and legal documents published in British colonies. Refusal to use the required tax stamps and a blockade of British merchant shipping in the colonies forced the repeal of the act. The Stamp Act Congress in October 1765 declared the act unconstitutional, with the slogan 'No taxation without representation', because the colonies were not represented in the British Parliament. The Stamp Act helped to precipitate the **American Revolution**.

Star Chamber

A civil and criminal court, named after the star-shaped ceiling decoration of the room in the Palace of Westminster, London, where its first meetings were held. Created in 1487 by **Henry VII**, the Star Chamber comprised some 20 or 30 judges. It was abolished in 1641 by the **Long Parliament**.

The Star Chamber became notorious under **Charles I** for judgements favourable to the king and to Archbishop **Laud**, such as the branding on both cheeks of William Prynne in 1637 for seditious libel. Under the **Thatcher** government of 1979–90 the term was revived for private ministerial meetings at which disputes between the Treasury and high-spending departments were resolved.

Statute of Westminster

Legislation of 1931 which gave the dominions of the British **Empire** complete autonomy in their conduct of external affairs. It made them self-governing states whose only allegiance was to the British crown.

Stephenson, George (1781–1848)

English engineer who built the first successful steam locomotive. He also invented a safety lamp independently of Humphrey Davy in 1815. He was appointed engineer of the Stockton and Darlington Railway, the world's first public railway, in 1821, and of the Liverpool and Manchester Railway in 1826. In 1829 he won a prize with his locomotive *Rocket.*

- Stephenson found that a slope of 1 in 200, common enough on roads, reduced the haulage power of a locomotive by 50%. It followed that railway gradients should be as low as possible.

- Stephenson advocated the use of malleable iron rails instead of cast iron.

- The gauge for the Stockton and Darlington Railway was set by Stephenson at 1.4 m/4 ft 8 in, which became the standard gauge for railways in most of the world.

- The Stockton and Darlington Railway was opened in 1825 by Stephenson's engine *Locomotion,* travelling at a top speed of 24 kph/15 mph.

- The *Rocket* weighed 4.2 tonnes, half the weight of *Locomotion.*

Stonehenge

Megalithic monument on Salisbury Plain, in Wiltshire, England. The site developed over various periods from a simple henge (earthwork circle and ditch), dating from about 3000 BC, to a complex stone structure, from about 2100 BC, which included a circle of 30 upright stones, their tops linked by lintel stones to form a continuous circle about 30 m/100 ft across.

Although Stonehenge is far older than **Druidism**, an annual Druid ceremony is held there at the summer solstice. At that time it is a spiritual focus for people with a nomadic way of life. However, on midsummers in the 1980s and 1990s, such 'travellers' were forcibly kept away by police.

- 'Stonehenge' is Old English for 'hanging stones'.
- Local sandstone, or sarsen, was used for the uprights, which measure 5.5 by 2 m/18 by 7 ft and weigh some 26 tonnes each.
- The bluestone used at Stonehenge came from Pembrokeshire, Wales, 217 km/347 mi away. It may have been transported by human labour, or have been deposited there by glaciers.
- Other prehistoric structures on Salisbury Plain include about four hundred round barrows.
- Stonehenge Down was purchased by public subscription in the 1920s. The view from Stonehenge was a gift to the nation, and is in the custody of English Heritage.

Stopes, Marie Charlotte Carmichael (1880–1958)
Scottish birth-control campaigner. Stopes studied botany at University College, London, and in Munich, Germany. Her field was research into fossil plants and primitive cycads. She taught at the University of Manchester from 1905 to 1911, the first woman to be appointed to the science staff there.

With her second husband H V Roe (1878–1949), she founded Britain's first birth-control clinic in London in 1921. In her best-seller *Married Love* (1918) she urged married women to enjoy sexual intercourse, a revolutionary view for the time. The Well Woman Centre in Marie Stopes House, London, commemorates her work.

Strafford, Thomas Wentworth, 1st Earl of Strafford (1593–1641)
English politician. He was originally an opponent of **Charles I**, but from 1628, when he became a baron, he was on the **Royalist** side. He ruled despotically as Lord Deputy of Ireland (1632–39), before he returned to England as Charles's chief adviser and received an earldom. He was impeached in 1640 by Parliament, abandoned by Charles as a scapegoat, and beheaded.

> ❝ Put not your trust in princes, nor in the sons of men: for in them there is no salvation. ❞

Thomas, Earl of Strafford, Biblical quote on discovering the king had signed his death warrant

Stuart or Stewart, House of

Royal family that inherited the Scottish throne in 1371 and the English throne in 1603. The house of Stuart ruled England until 1714, when Queen **Anne** died without heirs, and it was succeeded by the House of **Hanover**. The claimants to the British throne James Francis Edward Stuart (the 'Old Pretender', son of the deposed **James II** of England and VII of Scotland) and his son Charles Edward Stuart (the 'Young Pretender') both staged **Jacobite** rebellions in support of their claims, in 1715 and 1745 respectively.

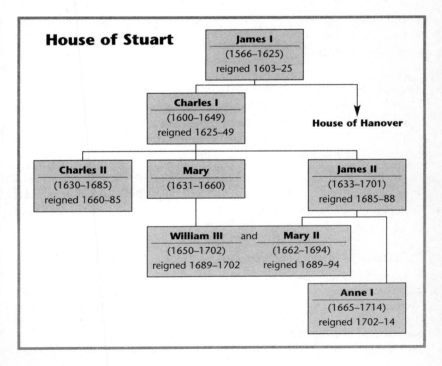

House of Stuart

James I
(1566–1625)
reigned 1603–25

Charles I
(1600–1649)
reigned 1625–49

House of Hanover

Charles II
(1630–1685)
reigned 1660–85

Mary
(1631–1660)

James II
(1633–1701)
reigned 1685–88

William III and **Mary II**
(1650–1702) (1662–1694)
reigned 1689–1702 reigned 1689–94

Anne I
(1665–1714)
reigned 1702–14

Succession, Acts of

Legislation of **Henry VIII** to establish the line of succession to the throne. The first act was passed in 1534, giving **Anne Boleyn's** children precedence over Princess Mary, after **Mary I**, Henry VIII's child by **Catherine of Aragón**. The king's subsequent marriages required further legislation, and in 1544 he was given the power to bequeath the throne by will, which he did, naming his children in the order of Edward, Mary, and finally Elizabeth. The Act of **Settlement** of 1701 established a Protestant succession.

Suez Crisis

Military confrontation from October to December 1956 following the nationalization of the Suez Canal by President Nasser of Egypt. In an attempt to reassert international control of the canal, Israel launched an attack, after which British and French troops landed.

At a London conference the Australian prime minister Robert Menzies was appointed to negotiate a settlement in Cairo. His mission was unsuccessful. In the end, widespread international censure forced the withdrawal of the British and French. The crisis resulted in the resignation of British prime minister Anthony **Eden**.

suffragette

A woman fighting for the right to vote. In the UK, women's suffrage bills were repeatedly introduced and defeated in Parliament between 1886 and 1911, and a militant campaign was launched in 1906 by Emmeline **Pankhurst** and her daughters. In 1918 women were granted limited franchise; in 1928 it was extended to all women over 21.

- The term 'suffragettes' was coined by a *Daily Mail* reporter.
- The suffragettes chained themselves to railings, heckled political meetings, refused to pay taxes, and in 1913 bombed the home of **Lloyd George**, then chancellor of the Exchequer.
- One woman, Emily Davison, threw herself under the king's horse at the Derby races in 1913 and was killed.
- Under the notorious 'Cat and Mouse Act' of 1913, suffragettes on hunger strike in prison could be repeatedly released to regain their health, and then rearrested.

Sunningdale Agreement

Pact of December 1973 between the UK and Irish governments, together with the Northern Ireland executive, drawn up in Sunningdale, England. It included provisions for a power-sharing executive in Northern Ireland. However, the executive lasted only five weeks before the UK government was defeated in a general election, and a general strike in May 1974 brought down the Northern Ireland government.

Supremacy, Acts of

Two UK **acts of Parliament**, in 1534 and 1559, that established **Henry VIII** and **Elizabeth I** respectively as head of the English church in place of the pope.

Swing Riots

Uprising of farm workers in southern and eastern England during 1830 and 1831. Farm labourers protested at the introduction of new threshing machines, which jeopardized their livelihood. They fired ricks, smashed the machines, and sent threatening letters to farmers. They invented a Captain Swing as their leader, and he became a figure of fear to the landed gentry. The riots were suppressed by the government, with 19 executions and almost 500 **transportations**.

T

Tamworth Manifesto

Sir Robert **Peel's** 1834 election address to his constituents in Tamworth. It was adopted as a blueprint for **Tory Party** philosophy, and is often considered to mark the point at which the Tory party became the **Conservative Party** of the later 19th and 20th centuries. Peel accepted the **Reform Act** of 1832 and the need for moderate reform to deal with genuine grievances, but radical proposals were to be rejected and any reform had to be balanced against the needs of the established interests of land, trade, and industry.

Telford, Thomas (1757–1834)

Scottish civil engineer who opened up northern Scotland by building roads and waterways. As official surveyor to the county of Shropshire, he built three bridges over the River Severn, and rebuilt many Roman roads to meet the need for faster travel. He constructed many aqueducts and canals, including the Caledonian Canal (1802–23), and erected the innovative Menai road suspension bridge

> In 1963 the new town of Telford, Shropshire, 32 km/20 mi northwest of Birmingham, was named after Thomas Telford.

between Wales and Anglesey (1819–26). In Scotland he constructed over 1,600 km/1,000 mi of road and 1,200 bridges, churches, and harbours.

Templars or Knights Templar or Order of Poor Knights of Christ and of the Temple of Solomon

Military religious order founded in Jerusalem around 1119–20 to protect pilgrims travelling to the Holy Land. Their international links allowed them to adapt to the 13th-century decline of the Crusades by becoming Europe's bankers. The Templars' independence, power, and wealth, rather than their alleged heresy, probably motivated Philip IV of France to suppress the order in 1307–14.

- The 'Temple of Solomon' in their full name refers to the site of their original headquarters in Jerusalem.
- The Templars lived under vows of poverty and chastity.
- The order comprised four ranks: servants, chaplains, sergeants, and knights, all of whom wore white surcoats with red crosses.
- In the 13th century there were as many as 20,000 Knights Templar.

Thatcher, Margaret Hilda, Baroness born **Roberts** (1925–)
British **Conservative** prime minister from 1979 to 1990. She was education minister from 1970 to 1974 and Conservative Party leader from 1975 to 1990.

In 1982 she sent British troops to the **Falklands War**. She confronted **trade-union** power during the miners' strike of 1984–85, **privatized** many public utilities, and reduced the influence of local government through such measures as the introduction of the community charge, or **poll tax**, in 1989. In 1990, splits in the cabinet over the issues of Europe and consensus government forced her resignation. She was created a life peer in 1992. An astute parliamentary tactician, she tolerated little disagreement, either from the opposition or from within her own party.

❖ To those waiting with bated breath for that favourite media catch-phrase, the U-turn, I have only one thing to say. You turn if you want to. The lady's not for turning. ❖

Margaret Thatcher, addressing the Conservative
Party Conference, 1980

Tintagel
Village resort on the coast of north Cornwall, southwest England. Legend has it that King **Arthur** was born and held court here. The castle ruins stand on Tintagel Head, a promontory 91 m/299 ft high on the Atlantic coast. It was a Norman stronghold from the mid-12th century, and the keep dates from the 13th century. Excavations have revealed evidence of a Celtic monastery on the site. It is thought that this may have existed from AD 350 to 850.

Titanic

British passenger liner, suppos- edly unsinkable, that struck an iceberg and sank off the Grand Banks of Newfoundland on its first voyage on the night of 14–15 April 1912. Estimates of the num- ber of lives lost, largely due to inadequate provision of lifeboats, vary between 1,503 and 1,517. In 1985 the *Titanic* was located by robot submarine 4 km/2.5 mi down in an ocean canyon, pre- served by the cold environment. In 1987 salvage operations began.

A series of six short slits was the only damage inflicted on the ship by the iceberg, and not, as has always been thought, a gaping 91 m/300 ft gash. The total area of openings was found to be only about 1.1 or 1.2 sq m/12 or 13 sq ft. High pressure forced the ocean through the holes, flooding the ship with about 39,000 tonnes of water before it finally went down.

Tolpuddle Martyrs

Six farm labourers from Tolpuddle, a village in Dorset, southwest England, who were **transported** to Australia in 1834 after being sentenced for 'administering unlawful oaths'. As a 'union', they had threatened to with- draw their labour unless their pay was guaranteed, and had been prepared to put this in writing. They were pardoned two years later, after nationwide agitation. They returned to England and all but one migrated to Canada.

> ❝ My Lord, if we have violated any law it was not done intentionally. We have injured no man's reputation, character, person or property. We were meeting together to preserve ourselves, our wives, and our children from utter degradation and starvation. ❞
>
> **George Loveless**, one of the Tolpuddle Martyrs, at their trial in March 1833

Tone, (Theobald) Wolfe (1763–1798)

Irish nationalist, prominent in the revolutionary society of the United Irishmen that aimed to overthrow English rule in Ireland. Disappointed with the progress of the group through nonradical means, he asked revolution- ary France for help in arming the resistance to English rule. Insurrection broke out in Ireland in 1798, but previous failed attempts at a French invasion of Ireland in 1796 and 1797 had reduced the enthusiasm of the French forces, and only small raids were made. Tone was captured in Donegal, and in his trial reaffirmed his hostility to England. Condemned to death, he slit his own throat in prison.

Tory Party

Forerunner of the British **Conservative Party**, from around 1680 until 1830. It was the party of the squire and parson, as opposed to the **Whigs** (supported by the trading classes and **nonconformists**).

The original Tories were Irish guerrillas who attacked the English, and the name was applied (at first insultingly) to royalists who opposed the **Exclusion Bill**. Although largely supporting the 1688 revolution, the Tories were suspected of **Jacobite** sympathies, and were kept from power between 1714 and 1760, but then held office almost continuously until 1830. The name is still applied colloquially to the Conservative Party.

Tower of London

A fortress on the bank of the River Thames, London. **William the Conqueror** established a camp here immediately after his coronation in 1066, and in 1078 Gundulf of Bec, bishop of Rochester, began building the White Tower on the site of British and Roman fortifications. It is probably the finest and best-preserved Norman keep in existence.

Today it is a barracks, an armoury, and a museum. In 1994 the crown jewels, traditionally kept in the keep, were moved to a specially designed showcase, the Jewel House.

Thomas **More,** Anne **Boleyn,** Catherine **Howard,** Lady Jane **Grey,** Earls **Essex** and **Strafford,** Archbishop **Laud,** and the Duke of Monmouth were among those imprisoned and executed at the Tower.

Tower of London Captivity of the Duke of Orleans in the Tower of London, about 1300.

Trades Union Congress (TUC)

Voluntary organization of trade unions, founded in 1868, in which delegates of affiliated unions meet each year to consider matters affecting their members. In 1997 there were 67 affiliated unions, with an aggregate membership of 6 million.

Around 30% of the employees in the UK belong to trade unions (25% in the private sector, and 60% in the public sector), compared with 14% in the USA and 8% in France.

trade union

Organization of workers that exists to promote and defend its members' interests, such as pay, working conditions, job security, and redundancy. As of May 1998, an employer must recognize a union if more than 40% of the workforce are members of it. Unions negotiate with employers. During an industrial dispute, an outside body such as the Advisory, Conciliation, and Arbitration Service (ACAS) may step in. Alternatively, trade-union members may take industrial action, such as going on strike.

> ❛ A company director who takes a pay rise of £50,000 when the rest of the workforce is getting a few hundred is not part of some 'general trend'. He is a greedy bastard. ❜
>
> **John Edmonds**, leader of the General Municipal Boilermakers union, addressing the TUC in Blackpool, 1998

Trade Unions in Britain: chronology

1799 The Combination Act outlaws organizations of workers combining for the purpose of improving conditions or raising wages.

1811 Luddite machine-breaking campaign against hosiers begins; it is ended by arrests and military action in 1812.

1818 Weavers and spinners form the General Union of Trades in Lancashire.

1824 The Combination Act allows trade unions to bargain peacefully over working hours and conditions.

1834 Six agricultural labourers from Tolpuddle, Dorset, are convicted of swearing illegal oaths and transported to Australia.

1851	The foundation of the Amalgamated Society of Engineers marks the beginning of the 'New Model Unionism' of skilled workers.
1868	The first Trades Union Congress (TUC) is held in Manchester.
1871	The Trade Union Act gives unions legal recognition.
1918–20	Widespread industrial unrest on return to a peacetime economy.
1926	A general strike is called by the TUC in support of the miners.
1930–34	Union membership falls as a result of economic recession.
1971	The Conservative government passes the Industrial Relations Act, limiting union powers.
1973–74	'Winter of Discontent'. Strikes bring about electoral defeat for the Conservative government. Labour introduces the 'social contract'.
1980	The Conservatives introduce the Employment Act, severely restricting the powers of unions to picket or enforce closed shop; this is extended in 1982.
1984	The miners' strike leads to widespread confrontation and divisions within the miners' union.
1984–90	The Conservative government continues to limit the powers of trade unions.
1998	The Labour government decides that employers have to recognize a union if at least 40% of the entire workforce votes in favour of union representation.

Trafalgar, Battle of

Victory of the British fleet, commanded by Admiral Horatio **Nelson**, over a combined French and Spanish fleet on 21 October 1805 during the **Napoleonic Wars**. Nelson was mortally wounded during the action. The victory laid the foundation for the supremacy of the British Navy throughout the 19th century.

- The battle is named after Cape Trafalgar, a headland in southwest Spain.
- The battle commenced at about 12 noon, and at 1.30 p.m. Nelson was mortally wounded by a musket-shot. By 3 p.m. the battle was over.
- Of the 33 French and Spanish ships, 15 were sunk; and of the 18 that escaped, 2 were wrecked on 24 October, and 4 taken by a British squadron on 3 November. The British lost none of its 27 ships.

transportation

Punishment of sending convicted persons to overseas territories to serve their sentences, introduced towards the end of the 17th century. It was abolished in 1857 after many thousands had been transported, mostly to Australia, but sentences of penal servitude continued in Western Australia until 1867.

Most convicts went into private service. Misbehaviour was punished by flogging, working in government chain gangs, usually on road building, or by confinement in a special penal settlement. Many convicts escaped to the bush, where some became bushrangers (bandits).

In all, about 137,000 male and 25,000 female convicts were transported to Australia.

Tudor dynasty

English dynasty (1485–1603), founded by **Henry VII**, who became king by overthrowing **Richard III** at the Battle of **Bosworth**. The last Tudor monarch was **Elizabeth I**. When she died childless, the throne passed to her cousin James VI of Scotland, who thus became **James I** of England and the first of the Stuart (Stewart) line.

• The Tudor Rose combines the red and white roses of **Lancaster** and **York**, brought together by the marriage of Henry VII and Elizabeth of York.

• The chief writers of Tudor times included playwrights Christopher Marlowe and William **Shakespeare**, and poets Sir Philip **Sidney** and Edmund Spenser.

• Tudor architecture is noted for its half-timbered houses, with multi-gabled roofs, and decorative brickwork; examples include Burghley House in Cambridgeshire and Longleat in Wiltshire.

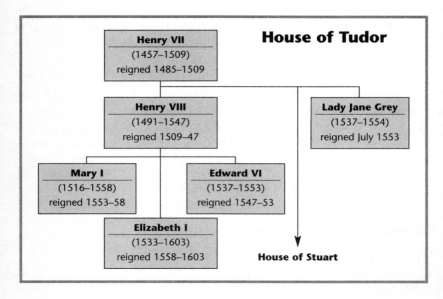

turnpike road

A road with a gate or barrier that prevents access until a toll has been paid. Turnpikes were common from the mid-16th to 19th centuries. In 1991, a plan for the first turnpike road to be built in the UK since the 18th century was announced: the privately funded Birmingham northern relief road, which is 50 km/31 mi long.

Turpin, Dick (Richard) (1705–1739)

English highwayman. The son of an innkeeper, he turned to highway robbery, cattle-thieving, and smuggling, and was hanged at York, England. Dick Turpin's legendary ride from London to York on his mare Black Bess is probably based on one of about 305 km/190 mi from Gad's Hill to York completed in 15 hours in 1676 by highwayman John Nevison (1639–1684).

Tyburn

A stream in London, England, near which (at the junction of the present Oxford Street and Edgware Road) Tyburn gallows stood from 1196 until 1783. After 1783 the place of execution was moved to **Newgate** prison. Among those executed at Tyburn were Perkin **Warbeck** and Jack **Sheppard** and, in the 16th and 17th centuries, many English Catholics. The Tyburn now flows underground.

Tyler, Wat (d. 1381)

English leader of the **Peasants' Revolt** of 1381. He was probably born in Kent or Essex, and may have served in the French wars. After taking Canterbury, he led the peasant army to London. **Richard II** met the rebels at Mile End and promised to redress their grievances, which included the imposition of a **poll tax**. At a further conference at Smithfield, London, Tyler was murdered.

> ❝ No man should be a serf, nor do homage or any manner of service to any lord, but should give fourpence rent for an acre of land, and ... no one should work for any man but his own will, and on terms of a regular covenant. ❞
>
> **Wat Tyler**, quoted in *Anonimalle Chronicle*

Tyndale, William (c. 1492–1536)

English translator of the Bible. The printing of his New Testament was begun in Cologne, Germany, in 1525 and, after he had been forced to flee, completed in Worms, a port on the River Rhine. Tyndale introduced some of the most familiar phrases to the English language, such as 'filthy lucre', and 'God forbid'. He was strangled and burned as a heretic at Vilvorde in Belgium.

U–V

Ulster Defence Association (UDA)

Northern Ireland Protestant paramilitary organization responsible for a number of sectarian killings. Fanatically loyalist, it established a paramilitary wing (the Ulster Freedom Fighters) to combat the **Irish Republican Army** (IRA) on its own terms and by its own methods. No political party has acknowledged any links with the UDA. In 1994, following a cessation of military activities by the IRA, the UDA, along with other Protestant paramilitary organizations, declared a ceasefire.

Ulster, kingdom of

A former kingdom and province in the north of Ireland, annexed by England in 1461. From Jacobean times it was a centre of English, and later Scottish, settlement on land confiscated from its owners. Ulster was divided in 1921 into Northern Ireland (the six counties Antrim, Armagh, Down, Fermanagh, Londonderry, and Tyrone) and the province of Ulster in the Irish Free State (counties Cavan, Donegal, and Monaghan).

underground

A rail service that runs underground. The London Underground, which opened in 1863 little more than a roofed-in trench, was the world's first. It is still the world's longest underground system, with over 400 km/250 mi of routes.

- The first underground trains were steam-powered.
- Glasgow also has an underground rail line.
- London's underground is nicknamed the 'tube'.
- Many large cities throughout the world have similar systems: Moscow's underground, the Metro, handles up to 6.5 million passengers a day.

Unilateral Declaration of Independence (UDI)

Un-negotiated severing of relations with a colonial power; especially the declaration made by Ian Smith's Rhodesian Front government on 11

November 1965, announcing the independence of **Rhodesia** (now Zimbabwe) from Britain.

Smith unilaterally declared Rhodesia an independent state, to resist sharing power with the black African majority. It was a move condemned by the United Nations and by the UK, who imposed sanctions (trade restrictions and an oil embargo). With the support of the UN, Britain imposed a naval blockade, but this was countered when South Africa broke sanctions. It was not until April 1980 that the Republic of Zimbabwe was proclaimed, after the **Lancaster House Agreement**.

Union, Acts of

The two acts of **Parliament** that formed the United Kingdom. The act of 1707 brought about the union of England and Scotland; that of 1801 united England and Ireland. The 1801 act was revoked in 1922, when the Irish Free State was set up.

The union flag is popularly called the Union Jack.

Victoria (1819–1901)

Queen of the United Kingdom from 1837 when she succeeded her uncle William IV, and Empress of India from 1877. In 1840 she married Prince Albert of Saxe-Coburg and Gotha. Her golden jubilee in 1887 and diamond jubilee in 1897 marked a waning of republican sentiment, which had developed with her withdrawal from public life on Albert's death in 1861. She and Albert had four sons and five daughters. After Albert's death she lived mainly in retirement. She died at Osborne House, her home in the Isle of Wight, and was buried at Windsor.

Victoria *Queen Victoria and her beloved Prince Albert, the Prince Consort, at Buckingham Palace in 1860.*

Victoria Cross

British decoration for conspicuous bravery in wartime, instituted by Queen **Victoria** in 1856.

It is bronze, with a 4 cm/1.5 in diameter, and has a crimson ribbon. Victoria Crosses are struck from the metal of guns captured from the Russians at Sevastopol during the **Crimean War**.

Viking invasion

The often forceful, but sometimes peaceful, settlement in Britain of Vikings, or Norsemen, the inhabitants of Scandinavia, in the period 800–1100.

A signal for the start of Viking raids on the British Isles was the sacking of the monastery of Lindisfarne in 793. Soon Viking rule was established in the Orkneys, Shetlands, Hebrides, and parts of north and western Scotland, in parts of Ireland, and increasingly in England (where the Vikings were known as 'Danes'). In England, the Vikings controlled most of the **Anglo-Saxon** kingdoms, an area known as **Danelaw**.

In Ireland they founded the cities of Dublin (841), Cork, and Limerick, but were halted by their defeat at the Battle of Clontarf in 1014.

- The Vikings plundered for gold and land.

- They had a sophisticated literary culture, with sagas and runic inscriptions, and an organized system of government with an assembly (*'thing'*).

- Greenland was visited by the Viking Eric the Red, and North America by his son Leif Ericsson, who named it 'Vinland'.

Wales, Prince of

A title conferred on the eldest son of the UK's sovereign. Prince Charles was invested as 21st Prince of Wales at Caernarfon in 1969 by his mother, **Elizabeth II**. The title was established in 1301 when **Edward I** conferred it on his eldest son Edward of Caernarfon along with the lands of the principality.

The earliest documented grantee was Edward II's grandson, **Edward the Black Prince**, with limitation 'to him and his heirs the kings of England'. Consequently, when a Prince of Wales succeeds to the throne, his title merges in the crown and requires a new creation for its separate existence.

Wales, Princes of (1301–)

1301	Edward (II)	**c. 1638**	Charles (II)
1343	Edward (the Black Prince)	**1688**	James Francis Edward (Old
1376	Richard (II)		Pretender)
1399	Henry of Monmouth (V)	**1714**	George Augustus (II)
1454	Edward of Westminster	**1729**	Frederick Lewis
1471	Edward of Westminster (V)	**1751**	George William Frederick (III)
1483	Edward	**1762**	George Augustus Frederick (IV)
1489	Arthur Tudor	**1841**	Albert Edward (Edward VII)
1504	Henry Tudor (VIII)	**1901**	George (V)
1610	Henry Stuart	**1910**	Edward (VII)
1616	Charles Stuart (I)	**1958**	Charles Philip Arthur George

Wallace, William (1272–1305)

Scottish nationalist who led a revolt against English rule in 1297, won a victory at Stirling, and assumed the title 'governor of Scotland'. **Edward I** defeated him at Falkirk in 1298, and Wallace was captured and executed.

Walpole, Robert, 1st Earl of Orford (1676–1745)

British Whig politician, the first 'prime minister'. As First Lord of the

Treasury and Chancellor of the Exchequer (1715–17 and 1721–42) he encouraged trade and tried to avoid foreign disputes until forced into the War of **Jenkins' Ear** with Spain in 1739. Opponents thought his foreign policies worked to the advantage of France. He held favour with George I and George II, struggling against **Jacobite** intrigues, and received an earldom when he eventually retired in 1742.

Walpole *Robert Walpole, before he became prime minister.*

> 6 My Lord Bath, you and I are now two as insignificant men as any in England. 9
>
> **Robert Walpole** to another peer on their promotion to the House of Lords

Walsingham, Francis (*c.* 1530–1590)

English politician and principal secretary of state to **Elizabeth I** from 1573 until his death. A staunch **Puritan**, he advocated a strong anti-Spanish foreign policy and controlled an efficient government spy network to identify and forestall Roman Catholic conspiracies against the queen. His exposure of the involvement of **Mary Queen of Scots** in such a plot persuaded Elizabeth to order her execution. Walsingham was knighted for his services in 1577.

War of 1812

The war between the USA and Britain caused by British interference with US merchant shipping as part of Britain's economic warfare against **Napoleonic** France. Tensions with the British in Canada led to plans for a US invasion but these were never realized and US success was limited to the capture of Detroit and a few notable naval victories. In 1814 British forces occupied Washington, DC, and burned the White House and the Capitol. A treaty signed in Ghent, Belgium, in December 1814 ended the conflict.

Warbeck, Perkin (c. 1474–1499)

Flemish pretender to the English throne. Claiming to be Richard, brother of Edward V, (see **Princes in the Tower**), he led a rising against **Henry VII** in 1497, and was hanged after attempting to escape from the **Tower of London.**

Warwick, Richard Neville, 1st or 16th Earl of Warwick (1428–1471)

English politician, called 'the Kingmaker'. During the Wars of the **Roses** he fought at first on the Yorkist side against the Lancastrians, and was largely responsible for placing Edward IV on the throne. Having quarrelled with him, Warwick restored **Henry VI** in 1470, but was defeated and killed by Edward at Barnet, Hertfordshire.

Waterloo, Battle of

Final battle of the **Napoleonic Wars** on 18 June 1815 in which a coalition force of British, Prussian, and Dutch troops under the Duke of **Wellington** defeated Napoleon near the village of Waterloo, 13 km/8 mi south of Brussels, Belgium. Wellington had 67,000 soldiers (of whom 24,000 were British, the remainder being German, Dutch, and Belgian) and Napoleon had 74,000. The French casualties numbered about 37,000; coalition casualties were similar including some 13,000 British troops.

> ❝I have got an infamous army, very weak and ill-equipped, and a very inexperienced staff. ❞
>
> **Arthur Wellesley**, 1st Duke of Wellington, in a letter dated 8 May 1815, just before the Battle of Waterloo

Watt, James (1736–1819)

Scottish engineer who developed the steam engine in the 1760s, making Thomas Newcomen's engine vastly more efficient by cooling the used steam in a condenser separate from the main cylinder. He eventually made a double-acting machine that supplied power with both directions of the piston and developed rotary motion. He also invented devices associated with the steam engine, artistic instruments, and a copying process, and devised the horsepower as a description of an engine's rate of working. The modern unit of power, the watt, is named after him.

Wellington, Arthur Wellesley, 1st Duke of Wellington (1769–1852)

Irish-born British soldier and Tory politician. As commander in the **Peninsular War**, he expelled the French from Spain in 1814. He defeated Napoleon Bonaparte at Quatre-Bras and **Waterloo** in 1815, and was a member of the Congress of Vienna. As prime minister (1828–30), he was forced to concede Roman Catholic emancipation.

- Wellington was born in Dublin.
- He became a national hero for his victories of 1808–14 in the Peninsular War and as general of the allied forces ranged against Napoleon.
- His London home was Apsley House, near Hyde Park.
- He is buried in St Paul's Cathedral by the side of **Nelson**.

Wesley, John (1703–1791)

English founder of Methodism. When the pulpits of the **Church of England** were closed to him and his followers, he took the gospel to the people. For 50 years he rode about the country on horseback, preaching daily, largely in the open air. His sermons became the doctrinal standard of the Wesleyan Methodist Church.

Wessex

A kingdom of the West Saxons in Britain, said to have been founded by Cerdic in about AD 500, covering Hampshire, Dorset, Wiltshire, Somerset, Devon, and the former county of Berkshire. In 829 Egbert established West Saxon supremacy over all England.

Whig Party

In the UK, the predecessor of the **Liberal Party.** The name was first used of rebel Covenanters and then of those who wished to exclude **James II**, as a Roman Catholic, from the English succession. The Whigs were in power continuously between 1714 and 1760. They pressed for industrial and commercial development, a vigorous foreign policy, and religious toleration. During the French Revolution, the Whigs demanded parliamentary reform in Britain, and after the passing of the **Reform Bill** in 1832 became known as Liberals.

Whittington, Dick (Richard) (c. 1358–1423)

English cloth merchant who was Mayor of London in 1397–98, 1406–07, and 1419–20. According to legend, he came to London as a poor boy with his cat when he heard that the streets were paved with gold and silver. His cat first appears in a play from 1605.

Wilberforce, William
(1759–1833)
English reformer who was instrumental in abolishing slavery in the British **Empire**. He entered **Parliament** in 1780; in 1807 his bill banning the **slave trade** from the West Indies was passed, and

Whittington *Dick Whittington, portrayed with his cat.*

in 1833, largely through his efforts, slavery was eradicated throughout the empire. He died shortly before the Slavery Abolition Act was passed.

❝ They charge me with fanaticism. If to be feelingly alive to the sufferings of my fellow-creatures is to be a fanatic, I am one of the most incurable fanatics ever permitted to be at large. ❞

William Wilberforce, speech in 1816

Wilkes, John (1727–1797)
British Radical politician, imprisoned for his political views. He was a Member of **Parliament** from 1757 to 1764 and from 1774. He championed parliamentary reform, religious tolerance, and independence of the United States of America.

Wilkes was born in Clerkenwell, London, and entered Parliament as a **Whig** in 1757. Outlawed in 1764 for his attacks on the Tory prime minister Bute in his paper *The North Briton*, he fled to France, and on his return in 1768 was imprisoned. He was four times elected MP for Middlesex, but the House of **Commons** refused to admit him and finally declared his opponent elected. This secured him strong working- and middle-class support, and in 1774 he was allowed to take his seat in Parliament.

William I, the Conqueror (c. 1027–1087)

King of England from 1066. He was the illegitimate son of Duke Robert the Devil and succeeded his father as Duke of Normandy in 1035. Claiming that his relative King **Edward the Confessor** had bequeathed him the English throne, William invaded England in 1066. He defeated **Harold II** at **Hastings**, Sussex, and became king of England.

William's coronation took place in Westminster Abbey on Christmas Day 1066. He completed the establishment of **feudalism** in England, compiling detailed records of land and property in the **Domesday Book**, and kept the barons firmly under control. He died in Rouen after a fall from his horse and is buried in Caen, France. He was succeeded by his son **William II**.

❝ A French bastard landing with an armed banditti and establishing himself King of England against the consent of the natives is, in plain terms, a very paltry, rascally original. ❞

Political writer **Thomas Paine** referring to William the Conqueror, *Common Sense*, 1776

William II, Rufus (c. 1056–1100)

King of England from 1087, the third son of **William the Conqueror**. He spent most of his reign attempting to capture Normandy from his brother Robert (II) Curthose, Duke of Normandy. His extortion of money led his barons to revolt and caused confrontation with Bishop Anselm. He was killed while hunting in the New Forest, Hampshire, and was succeeded by his brother **Henry I**.

William (III) of Orange (1650–1702)

King of Great Britain and Ireland from 1688, the son of William II of Orange and Mary, daughter of **Charles I**. He was offered the English crown by the parliamentary opposition to **James II**. He invaded England in 1688 and in 1689 became joint sovereign with his wife, **Mary II**. He spent much of his reign campaigning, first in Ireland, where he defeated James II at the Battle of the **Boyne** in 1690, and later against the French in Flanders. He died childless and was succeeded by Mary's sister, **Anne**.

- William was born in the Hague, in the Netherlands.

- When William was invited by both **Whig** and **Tory** leaders to take the crown from James, he landed with a small force at Torbay, Devon, on 5 November 1688.
- He was hated by Irish Catholics for spearheading the English reconquest of Ireland, but is still revered by Northern Irish Protestants for his key victory at the Boyne.

Wilson, (James) Harold (1916–1995)
Labour Party politician who was party leader from 1963 and prime minister in 1964–70 and in 1974–76. His premiership was dominated by the issue of UK admission to membership of the European Community (now the **European Union**), the social contract (unofficial agreement with the **trade unions**), and economic difficulties.

Wilson, born in Huddersfield, West Yorkshire, studied at Jesus College, Oxford, where he gained a first-class degree in philosophy, politics, and economics. During **World War II** he worked as a civil servant, and in 1945 stood for **Parliament** and won the marginal seat of Ormskirk. Assigned by Prime Minister Clement **Attlee** to a junior post in the ministry of works, he progressed to become president of the Board of Trade from1947 to 1951. He was knighted in 1976 and made a peer in 1983.

❝ A week is a long time in politics. ❞

Harold Wilson, an attributed remark

---

window tax
A tax on windows imposed in England in 1696, replacing the hearth tax. Scotland was exempt under terms of the Act of **Union** of 1707. Houses with fewer than seven (later eight) windows were exempted from 1792, but this led to windows being blocked up and new houses being built with fewer windows. It was abolished in 1851.

Windsor, House of
Official name of the British royal family since 1917, adopted in place of Saxe-Coburg-Gotha. Since 1960 those descendants of **Elizabeth II** not entitled to the prefix HRH (His/Her Royal Highness) have borne the surname **Mountbatten**-Windsor.

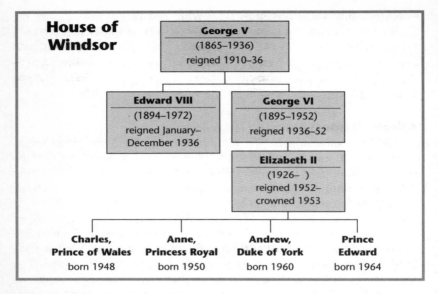

House of Windsor

George V
(1865–1936)
reigned 1910–36

Edward VIII
(1894–1972)
reigned January–
December 1936

George VI
(1895–1952)
reigned 1936–52

Elizabeth II
(1926–)
reigned 1952–
crowned 1953

Charles,
Prince of Wales
born 1948

Anne,
Princess Royal
born 1950

Andrew,
Duke of York
born 1960

Prince
Edward
born 1964

Wolfe, James (1727–1759)

An English soldier who served in Canada and commanded a victorious expedition against the French general Montcalm in Quebec on the Plains of Abraham, during which both commanders were killed. The victory of the British established their supremacy over Canada. Wolfe fought at the battles of Dettingen, Falkirk, and **Culloden**. With the outbreak of the **Seven Years' War**, he was posted to Canada and played a conspicuous part in the siege of the French stronghold of Louisburg in 1758.

Wollstonecraft, Mary (1759–1797)

British feminist associated with a group of radical intellectuals called the English Jacobins. Her book *A Vindication of the Rights of Woman* (1792) demanded equal educational opportunities for women. She married William Godwin in 1797 and died giving birth to a daughter, Mary (later Mary Shelley).

> ❝ The divine right of husbands, like the divine right of kings, may, it is hoped, in this enlightened age, be contested without danger. ❞
>
> **Mary Wollstonecraft** in *Vindication of the Rights of Woman* Chapter 3

Wolsey Thomas, Cardinal (c. 1475–1530)

English cleric and politician. In **Henry VIII**'s service from 1509, he became Archbishop of York in 1514, Cardinal and Lord Chancellor in 1515, and began the dissolution of the monasteries. His reluctance to further Henry's divorce from **Catherine of Aragón** led to his downfall in 1529. He was charged with high treason in 1530 but died before being tried.

workhouse

A former institution to house and maintain people unable to earn their own living. Groups of parishes in England combined to build workhouses for the poor, the aged, the disabled, and orphaned children from about 1815 until about 1930.

Sixteenth-century poor laws made parishes responsible for helping the poor within their boundaries. The 19th-century parish unions found workhouses more cost-effective. An **act of Parliament** of 1834 improved supervision of workhouses, where conditions were sometimes harsh, and a new welfare legislation in the early 20th century made them redundant.

World War I 1914–18

War between the Central European Powers (Germany, Austria-Hungary, and allies) on one side and the Triple Entente (Britain and the British **Empire**, France, and Russia) and their allies, including the USA (which entered in 1917), on the other side. An estimated 10 million people died and twice that number were wounded. The war was fought on the eastern and western fronts, in the Middle East, in Africa, and at sea.

By the early 20th century, the countries of Western Europe had reached a high level of material prosperity. However, competition for trade markets and imperial possessions worldwide had led to a growth of nationalistic sentiment. This nationalism created great political tension between the single-nation states such as France and Germany, and threatened the stability of multi-nation states such as Austria-Hungary.

The war was set in motion by the assassination in Sarajevo of the heir to the Austrian throne, Archduke Franz Ferdinand, by a Serbian nationalist in June 1914. When Austria declared war on Serbia on 28 July 1914, Russia mobilized along the German and Austrian frontier. Germany then declared war on Russia and France. On 4 August, Britain declared war on Germany.

An armistice was signed between Germany and the Allies at 5 a.m. on 11 November 1918, and fighting ceased on the Western Front at 11 a.m. the same day.

World War I: chronology

1914   June: Assassination of Archduke Franz Ferdinand of Austria, 28 June.

July: Germany offers Austria support in war against Serbia. Russia begins mobilization to defend Serbian ally.

August: Germany declares war on Russia. France mobilizes to assist Russian ally. Germany declares war on France and invades Belgium. Britain declares war on Germany, then on Austria. Dominions within the British Empire, including Australia, are automatically involved.

September: British and French troops halt German advance just short of Paris, and drive them back. First Battle of the Marne, and of the Aisne. Beginning of trench warfare.

October–November: First Battle of Ypres. Britain declares war on Turkey.

1915   April–May: Gallipoli offensive launched by British and dominion troops against Turkish forces. Second Battle of Ypres. First use of poison gas by Germans. Italy joins war against Austria.

1916   February: German offensive against Verdun begins, with huge losses for small territorial gain.

May: Naval Battle of Jutland between British and German imperial fleets ends inconclusively.

July–November: First Battle of the Somme, a sustained Anglo-French offensive which wins little territory and costs a huge number of lives.

September: Early tanks are used by British on Western Front.

1917   February: Germany declares unrestricted submarine warfare. Russian Revolution begins and tsarist rule is overthrown.

March–April: Germans retreat to Siegfried Line (Arras–Soissons) on the Western Front.

April–May: USA enters the war against Germany.

July–November: Third Ypres offensive including Battle of Passchendaele.

September: Germans occupy Riga.

December: Jerusalem taken by British forces under Allenby.

1918   January: US President Woodrow Wilson proclaims 'Fourteen Points' as a basis for peace settlement.

March: Treaty of Brest-Litovsk with Central Powers ends Russian participation in the war. Second Battle of the Somme begins with German spring offensive.

July–August: Allied counter-offensive, including tank attack at Amiens, drives Germans back to the Siegfried Line.

September: Germany calls for an armistice.

October: Armistice offered on the basis of the 'Fourteen Points'.

November: Austria-Hungary signs armistice with Allies. Germany agrees armistice. Fighting on Western Front stops.

1919   January: Peace conference opens at Versailles.

May: Demands are presented to Germany.

June: Germany signs peace treaty at Versailles, followed by other Central Powers.

World War II 1939–45

War between Germany, Italy, and Japan (the Axis powers) on one side, and Britain, the **Commonwealth**, France, the USA, the USSR, and China (the Allied powers) on the other. An estimated 55 million lives were lost (20 million of them citizens of the USSR and 6 million Jews killed in the Holocaust), and 60 million people in Europe were displaced because of bombing raids. The war was fought in the Atlantic and Pacific theatres. In May 1945 Germany surrendered but Japan fought on until August, when the USA dropped atomic bombs on Hiroshima and Nagasaki.

Under Adolf Hitler, Germany embarked on a programme of aggressive expansionism from which it could not withdraw. Britain and France declared war on Germany on 3 September 1939, two days after German forces had invaded Poland. In the following months (the 'phoney' war) little fighting took place until April 1940 when the Germans invaded Denmark and Norway. By the end of May, Germany had invaded Holland, Belgium, and France, and over 338,000 Allied troops had to be evacuated from **Dunkirk** to England. Following the German aerial bombardment of British cities known as the **Blitz**, the RAF averted a planned invasion of Britain in the Battle of **Britain**.

The major turning point for the Allies was victory in the Battle of El **Alamein** (October–November 1942). The Allies launched the successful **D-day** invasion of Normandy on 6 June 1944 under the command of US General Eisenhower. By spring 1945, the Allied advances from west and the east had joined. All German forces in northwest Germany, Holland, and Denmark surrendered to Field Marshal **Montgomery** on 5 May, and Germany's final capitulation came into effect at midnight on 8–9 May.

World War II: chronology

1939   September: German invasion of Poland; Britain and France declare war on Germany.

1940   April: Germany occupies Denmark, Norway, the Netherlands, Belgium, and Luxembourg.

       May–June: Evacuation of Allied troops from Dunkirk to England.

       June: Italy declares war on Britain and France; the Germans enter Paris.

       July–October: Battle of Britain between British and German air forces.

       September: Japanese invasion of French Indochina.

1941   April: Germany occupies Greece and Yugoslavia.

       June: Germany invades the USSR; Finland declares war on the USSR.

       December: The Germans come within 40 km/25 mi of Moscow, with Leningrad (now St Petersburg) under siege. Japan bombs Pearl Harbor, Hawaii, and declares war on the USA and Britain. Germany and Italy declare war on the USA.

1942	January: Japanese conquest of the Philippines.
	June: Naval battle of Midway, the turning point of the Pacific War.
	August: German attack on Stalingrad (now Volgograd), USSR.
	October–November: Battle of El Alamein in North Africa.
	November: Soviet counteroffensive on Stalingrad.
1943	May: End of Axis resistance in North Africa.
	August: Beginning of the campaign against the Japanese in Burma (now Myanmar).
	September: Italy surrenders to the Allies.
	October: Italy declares war on Germany.
	November: The US Navy defeats the Japanese in the Battle of Guadalcanal.
	November–December: The Allied leaders meet at the Tehran Conference.
1944	January: Allied landing in Nazi-occupied Italy: Battle of Anzio.
	March: End of the German U-boat campaign in the Atlantic.
	6 June: D-day: Allied landings in Nazi-occupied and heavily defended Normandy.
	September: Battle of Arnhem on the Rhine; Soviet armistice with Finland.
	December: German counteroffensive, Battle of the Bulge.
1945	February: The Soviets reach the German border; Yalta conference; Allied bombing campaign over Germany (Dresden destroyed); the US reconquest of the Philippines is completed; the Americans land on Iwo Jima, south of Japan.
	April: Hitler commits suicide; Mussolini is captured by Italian partisans and shot.
	May: Germany surrenders to the Allies.
	July: The Potsdam Conference issues an Allied ultimatum to Japan.
	August: Atom bombs are dropped by the USA on Hiroshima and Nagasaki; Japan surrenders.

Wycliffe, John (c. 1320–1384)

English religious reformer. Allying himself with the party of John of Gaunt, which was opposed to ecclesiastical influence at court, Wycliffe attacked abuses in the church, maintaining that the Bible rather than the church was the supreme authority. He criticized such fundamental doctrines as priestly absolution, confession, and indulgences, and set disciples to work on the first translation of the Bible into English. He wrote many popular tracts in English (rather than Latin). His followers were known as **Lollards**.

York, House of

English dynasty founded by Richard, Duke of York (1411–1460). Richard claimed the throne through his descent from Lionel, Duke of Clarence (1338–1368), third son of Edward III, whereas the reigning monarch, **Henry VI** of the rival House of **Lancaster**, was descended from the fourth son, John of Gaunt. The argument was fought out in the Wars of the **Roses**.

Richard was killed at the Battle of Wakefield in 1460, but the following year his son became King Edward IV. Edward was succeeded by his son Edward V (one of the **Princes in the Tower**) and then by his brother **Richard III**, with whose death at the Battle of **Bosworth** the line ended. The Lancastrian victor in that battle was crowned **Henry VII**, and consolidated his claim by marrying Edward IV's eldest daughter, Elizabeth, thus founding the House of **Tudor**.

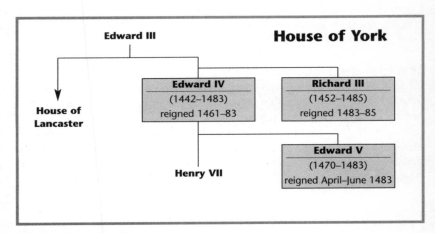

Young Pretender

The nickname of **Charles Edward Stuart**, claimant to the Scottish and English thrones.

Ypres, Battles of

Three major battles in **World War I** between German and Allied forces near Ypres, a Belgian town in western Flanders, 40 km/25 mi south of Ostend. Neither side made much progress in any of the battles, despite heavy casualties, but the third battle in particular (also known as **Passchendaele**) in July–November 1917 stands out as an enormous waste of life for little return. The Menin Gate (1927) in western Flanders is a memorial to British soldiers lost in these battles.

Zinoviev Letter

Forged letter dated 25 October 1924 allegedly from Grigoriy Zinoviev, chairman of Comintern, inciting British communists to rebellion. It was printed in the British press just before the general election, and drew an official protest from the Foreign Office to the Soviet Union. In 1966 it was proved to be a forgery perpetrated by a group of White Russian émigrés with the aim of damaging the **Labour Party**. Although Labour lost the 1924 election, the letter probably made little difference.

Appendix

Chronology of British and Irish History from 55 BC to AD 1999

Owing to the breadth of subject matter and length of time scale, this is a necessarily selective

55 BC	First Roman expedition to Britain.
AD 43	Roman invasion of Britain.
c. AD 50	Foundation of Londinium (London) and Verulamium (St Alban's).
122	Start of construction of Hadrian's Wall across northern England.
late 2nd century	Early Christian communities probably established in Britain.
402	Last issue of Roman coins to be found in Britain.
450–600	Expansion of area settled by Germanic peoples in England.
601	Augustine enthroned as first archbishop of Canterbury.
625–40	Period when first English coins issued.
late 7th century	*Book of Durrow*, the earliest surviving decorated English book.
698–721	Lindisfarne Gospels.
793–95	First recorded Viking raids on Britain.
830s	Norse settlement in Ireland; Norse town foundation included Dublin.
843	Formation of Scotland when King Kenneth MacAlpin of the Scots becomes king of Pictland.
865	Arrival in England of the 'great army', which started Viking settlement in England.
893	*Anglo-Saxon Chronicle* started.
973	Coronation of King Edgar of Wessex, symbolizing completion of Wessex conquest of England.
991	Danish victory at the Battle of Maldon, leading to King Ethelred's first payment of Danegeld.
1017	King Canute reorganizes England as four earldoms.
1039–63	Reign of Gruffydd ap Llywelyn of Gwynedd and Powys.
1066	Norman invasion of England, led by William the Conqueror.
1085	William the Conqueror orders the compilation of Doomsday Book.
1139–53	Civil war in England during Stephen's reign.
1170	Murder of Thomas à Becket.
1215	King John accepts Magna Carta; followed by civil war.
c. 1250	Song 'Sumer is icumen in' first written down.
1258	Welsh rulers acknowledges Llewelyn ap Gruffydd of Gwynedd as 'Prince of Wales'.
1264–65	Civil war in England.
1265	Simon de Montfort holds parliament in England.
1276	English invasion of Wales.
1284	Statute of Wales issued, providing for English government in Wales.
1296	English invasion of Scotland.
1306	Robert the Bruce crowned king of Scotland.
1314	Scots defeat English at Battle of Bannockburn.

Chronology of British and Irish History from 55 BC to AD 1999 (continued)

1337 Start of Hundred Years' War between England and France.

1366 Statutes of Kilkenny legislating relations in Ireland between English and Irish.

1400 Death of Geoffrey Chaucer, leaving his *Canterbury Tales* unfinished.

1415 English defeat French in Battle of Agincourt.

1449–53 French retake English-ruled territory in France apart from Calais.

1455 Battle of St Albans, marking start of the Wars of the Roses between supporters of King Henry VI (Lancastrians) and the Dukes of York and supporters (Yorkists).

1476 William Caxton establishes printing press in Westminster.

1485 Invasion of Henry Tudor, who kills Richard III at Battle of Bosworth and becomes King Henry VII, founding the Tudor dynasty.

1534 Act of Supremacy confirms Henry VIII in powers formerly exercised by the pope in England.

1539–40 Larger religious houses in England dissolved.

1549 First English prayer book introduced.

1559 In Scotland, John Knox attacks idols, marking start of Scottish Reformation.

1578–80 Sir Francis Drake circumnavigates the globe.

1587 Execution of Mary, Queen of Scots, by order of Queen Elizabeth I of England.

1588 Spanish Armada sent against England.

1590 First known production of plays by William Shakespeare.

1600 Foundation of the East India Company.

1603 Union of Crowns: James VI of Scotland succeeds Queen Elizabeth I as ruler of England.

1605 Gunpowder Plot: Guy Fawkes captured while preparing explosion for opening of parliament.

1607 First successful English settlement on American mainland at Jamestown, Virginia.

1642–46 First Civil War.

1648 Second Civil War.

1649 Execution of Charles I; republican government established.

1653–58 Protectorate of Oliver Cromwell.

1660 Restoration of monarchy, with Charles II as king.

1666 Great Plague and Fire of London.

1675 Greenwich Observatory founded 1665–1666.

1688 'Glorious Revolution': flight of Catholic James II; accession of Protestants William III and Mary II.

1690 Battle of the Boyne: William III defeats Irish and French army.

1701 Act of Succession settles succession to English throne on Electress Sophia of Hanover and her descendants.

1707 Union of Scotland and England.

1715, 1745 Jacobite Rebellions.

1756–63 Seven Years' War, ending with the Treaty of Paris.

1768–71 James Cook's first voyage of discovery.

1776 American Declaration of Independence from Britain.

1801 Union of Britain and Ireland.

1805 Battle of Trafalgar: Royal Navy defeats French and Spanish fleets.

1815 Battle of Waterloo: Britain and allies defeat French.

1825 Opening of the Stockton and Darlington Railway.

1840 Introduction of penny postage.

1845–46 Great Famine in Ireland.

Chronology of British and Irish History from 55 BC to AD 1999 (*continued*)

1854–56	Crimean War: Britain and France fight Russia.
1882	Married Women's Property Act.
1899–1902	South African War.
1901	Guglielmo Marconi transmitted wireless message from Poldhu, Cornwall, to Newfoundland.
1911	Parliament Act reduces power of Lords. Ernest Rutherford identifies nuclear atom.
1914–18	World War I
1916	Easter Rising in Dublin.
1921	Partition of Ireland with separate governments in the north and the Irish Free State.
1922	Foundation of the British Broadcasting Company (Corporation from 1927).
1924	First Labour government, with Ramsay MacDonald as prime minister.
1926	General Strike. John Logie Baird demonstrates television.
1931	Formation of coalition National Government, with Ramsay MacDonald as prime minister.
1936	Abdication crisis: Edward VIII abdicates.
1939	Following German invasion of Poland, Britain declares war on Germany (World War II).
1940–45	Churchill appointed prime minister of coalition government; British withdrawal from Dunkirk; Battle of Britain. Howard Florey develops penicillin for medical use.
1947	Britain grants independence to India, Pakistan, and Burma.
1953	Francis Crick and James Watson announce double-helix structure of DNA.

1956	Suez crisis. Nuclear power station at Calder Hall opened.
1964	Creation of the Welsh Office.
1965	Rhodesia makes Unilateral Declaration of Independence from Britain.
1969	Outbreak of 'the troubles' in Northern Ireland. Open University founded.
1973	Britain joins the European Economic Community.
1974	Britain establishes direct rule of Northern Ireland.
1978	First test-tube baby born.
1979	Margaret Thatcher elected first female prime minister.
1982	Falklands War.
1984–85	Miners' strike.
1992	Church of England votes to allow ordination of women to the priesthood.
1994	Paramilitary organizations declare ceasefire in Northern Ireland. Privatization of British coal mines. Channel Tunnel opens.
1996	Northern Ireland ceasefire collapses. Geneticists at the Roslin Institute in Edinburgh, Scotland, clone an adult sheep, named Dolly.
1997	Victory of Labour Party in general election; Tony Blair becomes prime minister. Death in a car accident in Paris of Diana, Princess of Wales. Multiparty talks on Northern Ireland begin. Paramilitary ceasefire resumed.
1997	Following referenda in Wales and Scotland, the government announces plans for a Welsh Assembly and a Scottish Parliament.
1998	Ireland, Britain, and political parties in Northern Ireland reach peace

Chronology of British and Irish History from 55 BC to AD 1999 (*continued*)

agreement over Northern Ireland involving the devolution of a wide range of powers to a Northern Ireland Assembly.

1999 Welsh Assembly and Scottish Parliament elections; both bodies sit for the first time, with responsibilities covering a wide range of domestic affairs.

Conciliatory statements from both sides of the Northern Ireland peace process result in the creation of cross-community government in Belfast. New Northern Ireland executive meet for the first time as powers are devolved to the province from the British Government.

Sovereigns of England and the United Kingdom from 899

Reign	Name	Relationship
West Saxon Kings		
899–924	Edward the Elder	son of Alfred the Great
924–39	Athelstan	son of Edward the Elder
939–46	Edmund	half-brother of Athelstan
946–55	Edred	brother of Edmund
955–59	Edwy	son of Edmund
959–75	Edgar	brother of Edwy
975–78	Edward the Martyr	son of Edgar
978–1016	Ethelred (II) the Unready	son of Edgar
1016	Edmund (II) Ironside	son of Ethelred (II) the Unready
Danish Kings		
1016–35	Canute	son of Sweyn I of Denmark
1035–40	Harold I	son of Canute
1040–42	Hardicanute	son of Canute
West Saxon Kings (restored)		
1042–66	Edward the Confessor	son of Ethelred (II) the Unready
1066	Harold II	son of Godwin (father-in-law of Edward the Confessor)
Norman Kings		
1066–87	William I	illegitimate son of Duke Robert the Devil
1087–1100	William II	son of William I
1100–35	Henry I	son of William I
1135–54	Stephen	grandson of William II
House of Plantagenet		
1154–89	Henry II	son of Matilda (daughter of Henry I)
1189–99	Richard I	son of Henry II
1199–1216	John	son of Henry II
1216–72	Henry III	son of John

Sovereigns of England and the United Kingdom from 899 (*continued*)

Reign	Name	Relationship
1272–1307	Edward I	son of Henry III
1307–27	Edward II	son of Edward I
1327–77	Edward III	son of Edward II
1377–99	Richard II	son of Edward the Black Prince (son of Edward III)

House of Lancaster

1399–1413	Henry IV	son of John of Gaunt (son of Edward III)
1413–22	Henry V	son of Henry IV
1422–61, 1470–71	Henry VI	son of Henry V

House of York

1461–70, 1471–83	Edward IV	son of Richard, Duke of York (great-grandson of Edward III)
1483	Edward V	son of Edward IV
1483–85	Richard III	brother of Edward IV

House of Tudor

1485–1509	Henry VII	son of Edmund Tudor, Earl of Richmond
1509–47	Henry VIII	son of Henry VII
1547–53	Edward VI	son of Henry VIII
1553–58	Mary I	daughter of Henry VIII
1558–1603	Elizabeth I	daughter of Henry VIII

House of Stuart

1603–25	James I	great-grandson of Margaret (daughter of Henry VII)
1625–49	Charles I	son of James I
1649–60	the Commonwealth	

House of Stuart (restored)

1660–85	Charles II	son of Charles I
1685–88	James II	son of Charles I
1689–1702	William III and Mary II	son of Mary; daughter of James II
1702–14	Anne	daughter of James II

House of Hanover

1714–27	George I	son of Sophia (granddaughter of James I)
1727–60	George II	son of George I
1760–1820	George III	son of Frederick (son of George II)
1820–30	George IV (regent 1811–20)	son of George III
1830–37	William IV	son of George III
1837–1901	Victoria	daughter of Edward (son of George III)

Sovereigns of England and the United Kingdom from 899 (*continued*)

Reign	Name	Relationship
House of Saxe-Coburg		
1901–10	Edward VII	son of Victoria
House of Windsor		
1910–36	George V	son of Edward VII
1936	Edward VIII	son of George V
1936–52	George VI	son of George V
1952–	Elizabeth II	daughter of George VI

Scottish Monarchs 1005–1603

This table covers the period from the unification of Scotland to the union of the crowns of Scotland and England.

Reign	Name	Reign	Name
Celtic Kings		*English Domination*	
1005–34	Malcolm II	1292–96	John Baliol
1034–40	Duncan I	1296–1306	annexed to England
1040–57	Macbeth	*House of Bruce*	
1057–93	Malcolm III Canmore	1306–29	Robert I the Bruce
1093–94	Donald III Donalbane	1329–71	David II
1094	Duncan II		
1094–97	Donald III (restored)	*House of Stuart*	
1097–1107	Edgar	1371–90	Robert II
1107–24	Alexander I	1390–1406	Robert III
1124–53	David I	1406–37	James I
1153–65	Malcolm IV	1437–60	James II
1165–1214	William the Lion	1460–88	James III
1214–49	Alexander II	1488–1513	James IV
1249–86	Alexander III	1513–42	James V
1286–90	Margaret of Norway	1542–67	Mary
		1567–1625	James VI[1]

1 After the union of crowns in 1603, he became James I of England.

Succession List of the Archbishops of Canterbury

Date elected	Name	Date elected	Name	Date elected	Name
601	Augustine	655	Deusdedit	740	Cuthbert
604	Laurentius	668	Theodore	761	Bregowine
619	Mellitus	693	Berthwald	765	Jaenbert
624	Justus	731	Tatwine	793	Ethelhard
627	Honorius	735	Nothelm	805	Wulfred

Succession List of the Archbishops of Canterbury (continued)

Date elected	Name	Date elected	Name	Date elected	Name
832	Feologeld	1333	John de Stratford	1805	Charles Manners-
833	Ceolnoth	1349	Thomas		Sutton
870	Ethelred		Bradwardine	1828	William Howley
890	Plegmund	1349	Simon Islip	1848	John Bird Sumner
914	Athelm	1366	Simon Langham	1862	Charles Thomas
923	Wulfhelm	1368	William Whittlesey		Longley
942	Oda	1375	Simon Sudbury	1868	Archibald
959	Aelfsige	1381	William Courtenay		Campbell Tait
959	Brithelm	1396	Thomas Arundel	1883	Edward White
960	Dunstan	1398	Roger Walden		Benson
c. 988	Ethelgar	1399	Thomas Arundel[1]	1896	Frederick Temple
990	Sigeric	1414	Henry Chichele	1903	Randall Thomas
995	Aelfric	1443	John Stafford		Davidson
1005	Alphege	1452	John Kempe	1928	William Cosmo
1013	Lyfing	1454	Thomas Bourchier		Gordon Lang
1020	Ethelnoth	1486	John Morton	1942	William Temple
1038	Eadsige	1501	Henry Deane	1945	Geoffrey Francis
1051	Robert of	1503	William Warham		Fisher
	Jumieges	1533	Thomas Cranmer	1961	Arthur Michael
1052	Stigand	1556	Reginald Pole		Ramsey
1070	Lanfranc	1559	Matthew Parker	1974	Frederick Donald
1093	Anselm	1576	Edmund Grindal		Coggan
1114	Ralph d'Escures	1583	John Whitgift	1980	Robert Alexander
1123	William de Corbeil	1604	Richard Bancroft		Kennedy Runcie
1139	Theobald	1611	George Abbot	1991	George Leonard
1162	Thomas à Becket	1633	William Laud		Carey
1174	Richard (of Dover)	1660	William Juxon	1928	William Cosmo
1184	Baldwin	1663	Gilbert Sheldon		Gordon Lang
1193	Hubert Walter	1678	William Sancroft	1942	William Temple
1207	Stephen Langton	1691	John Tillotson	1945	Geoffrey Francis
1229	Richard le Grant	1695	Thomas Tenison		Fisher
1234	Edmund of	1716	William Wake	1961	Arthur Michael
	Abingdon	1737	John Potter		Ramsey
1245	Boniface of Savoy	1747	Thomas Herring	1974	Frederick Donald
1273	Robert Kilwardby	1757	Matthew Hutton		Coggan
1279	John Peckham	1758	Thomas Secker	1980	Robert Alexander
1294	Robert Winchelsey	1768	Frederick		Kennedy Runcie
1313	Walter Reynolds		Cornwallis	1991	George Leonard
1328	Simon Meopham	1783	John Moore		Carey

[1] Restored.

The British Commonwealth

Association of 54 countries and their dependencies, the majority of which once formed part of the British Empire and are now independent sovereign states. The Commonwealth has no charter or constitution. Date established: 1931. Founding members: Anguilla, Australia, Bermuda, British Antarctic Territory, British Virgin Islands, Canada, Cayman Islands, Channel Islands, Cook Islands, Falkland Islands, Falkland Islands Dependency, Gibraltar, Isle of Man, Montserrat, New Zealand, Niue, Norfolk Island, Pitcairn Islands, Tokelau, Turks and Caicos Islands, St Helena, UK. Address: Commonwealth Secretariat, Marlborough House, Pall Mall, London SW1 5HX, UK; phone: (020) 7839 3411; fax: (020) 7930 0827; e-mail: info@commonwealth.int. Web site: www.thecommonwealth.org/

Country	Capital	Date joined	Area in sq km/ sq mi	Constitutional status
In Africa				
Botswana	Gaborone	1966	582,000/224,710	sovereign republic
British Indian Ocean	Victoria	1965	60/23	British dependent territory
Cameroon	Yaoundé	1995	475,440/183,567	emergent democratic republic
Gambia	Banjul	1965	10,700/4,131	sovereign republic
Ghana	Accra	1957	238,300/92,007	sovereign republic
Kenya	Nairobi	1963	582,600/224,941	sovereign republic
Lesotho	Maseru	1966	30,400/11,737	sovereign constitutional monarchy
Malawi	Zomba	1964	118,000/45,559	sovereign republic
Mauritius	Port Louis	1968	2,000/772	sovereign republic
Mozambique	Maputo	1995	799,380/308,640	emergent democracy
Namibia	Windhoek	1990	824,000/318,146	sovereign republic
Nigeria	Lagos	1960[1]	924,000/356,756	sovereign republic
St Helena	Jamestown	1931	100/38	British dependent territory[2]
Seychelles	Victoria	1976	450/173	sovereign republic
Sierra Leone	Freetown	1961[3]	73,000/28,185	sovereign republic
South Africa	Pretoria	1910[4]	1,221,000/471,428	sovereign republic
Swaziland	Mbabane	1968	17,400/6,718	sovereign republic
Tanzania	Dodoma	1961	945,000/364,864	sovereign republic
Uganda	Kampala	1962	236,900/91,467	sovereign republic
Zambia	Lusaka	1964	752,600/290,578	sovereign republic
Zimbabwe	Harare	1980	390,300/150,694	sovereign republic
In the Americas				
Anguilla	The Valley	1931	155/59	British dependent territory[2]
Antigua and Barbuda	St John's	1981	400/154	sovereign constitutional monarchy[5]
Bahamas	Nassau	1973	13,900/5,366	sovereign constitutional monarchy[5]
Barbados	Bridgetown	1966	400/154	sovereign constitutional monarchy[5]
Belize	Belmopan	1982	23,000/8,880	sovereign constitutional monarchy[5]
Bermuda	Hamilton	1931	54/20	British dependent territory[2]
British Virgin Islands	Road Town	1931	153/59	British dependent territory[2]

The British Commonwealth (continued)

Country	Capital	Date joined	Area in sq km/ sq mi	Constitutional status
Canada	Ottawa	1931	9,958,400/3,844,93	sovereign constitutional monarchy[5]
Cayman Islands	Georgetown	1931	300/115	British dependent territory[2]
Dominica	Roseau	1978	700/270	sovereign republic
Falkland Islands	Port Stanley	1931	12,100/4,671	British dependent territory[2]
Grenada	St George's	1974	300/115	sovereign constitutional monarchy[5]
Guyana	Georgetown	1966	215,000/83,011	sovereign republic
Jamaica	Kingston	1962	11,400/4,401	sovereign constitutional monarchy[5]
Montserrat	Plymouth	1931	100/38	British dependent territory[2]
St Christopher–Nevis	Basseterre	1983	300/115	sovereign constitutional monarchy[5]
St Lucia	Castries	1979	600/231	sovereign constitutional monarchy[5]
St Vincent and the Grenadines	Kingstown	1979	400/154	sovereign constitutional monarchy[5]
Trinidad and Tobago	Port of Spain	1962	5,100/1,969	sovereign republic
Turks and Caicos Islands	Grand Turk	1931	400/154	British dependent territory[2]
In the Antarctic				
Australian Antarctic Territory	uninhabited	1936	5,403,000/2,086,098	Australian external territory[2]
British Antarctic Territory	uninhabited	1931	390,000/150,579	British dependent territory[2]
Falkland Islands Dependencies	uninhabited	1931	1,600/617	British dependent territories[2]
Ross Dependency	uninhabited	1931	453,000/174,903	New Zealand associated territory[2]
In Asia				
Bangladesh	Dhaka	1972	144,000/55,598	sovereign republic
Brunei	Bandar Seri Begawan	1984	5,800/2,239	sovereign monarchy
India	Delhi	1947	3,166,800/1,222,701	sovereign republic
Malaysia	Kuala Lumpur	1957	329,800/127,335	sovereign constitutional monarchy
Maldives	Malé	1982	300/115	sovereign republic
Pakistan	Islamabad	1947[6]	803,900/310,385	sovereign republic
Singapore	Singapore	1965	600/231	sovereign republic
Sri Lanka	Colombo	1948	66,000/25,482	sovereign republic
In Australasia and the Pacific				
Australia	Canberra	1931	7,682,300/2,966,136	sovereign constitutional monarchy[5]
Cook Islands	Avarua	1931	300/115	New Zealand associated territory[2]

The British Commonwealth (continued)

Country	Capital	Date joined	Area in sq km/ sq mi	Constitutional status
Fiji Islands	Suva	1970[7]	18,274/7,056	sovereign republic
Norfolk Island	Kingston	1931	34/13	Australian external territory[2]
Kiribati	Tawawa	1979	700/270	sovereign republic
Nauru	Yaren	1968	21/8	sovereign republic
New Zealand	Wellington	1931	268,000/103,474	sovereign constitutional monarchy[5]
Niue	Alofi	1931	300/115	New Zealand associated territory[2]
Papua New Guinea	Port Moresby	1975	462,800/178,687	sovereign constitutional monarchy[5]
Pitcairn Islands	Adamstown	1931	5/2	British dependent territory[2]
Solomon Islands	Honiara	1978	27,600/10,656	sovereign constitutional monarchy[5]
Tokelau	Nukunonu	1931	10/3.8	New Zealand associated territory[2]
Tonga	Nuku'alofa	1970	700/270	sovereign monarchy
Tuvalu	Funafuti	1978	24/9	sovereign constitutional monarchy[5]
Vanuatu	Villa	1980	15,000/5,791	sovereign republic
Western Samoa	Apia	1970	2,800/1,081	sovereign republic
In Europe				
Channel Islands		1931	200/77	UK crown dependencies[2]
Guernsey	St Peter Port			
Jersey	St Helier			
Cyprus	Nicosia	1961	9,000/3,474	sovereign republic
Gibraltar	Gibraltar	1931	6/2	British dependent territory[2]
Malta	Valletta	1964	300/115	sovereign republic
Isle of Man	Douglas	1931	600/231	UK crown dependency[2]
United Kingdom	London	1931	244,100/94,247	sovereign constitutional monarchy[5]
England	London			
Northern Ireland	Belfast			
Scotland	Edinburgh			
Wales	Cardiff			
Total			**34,310,000/ 13,247,091**	

[1] Suspended 1995; rejoined 1999. [2] Dependencies of full sovereign Commonwealth members. [3] Suspended 1997. [4] Withdrew from membership 1961 and readmitted 1994. [5] Queen Elizabeth II constitutional monarch and head of state. [6] Left 1972 and rejoined 1989. [7] Left 1987 and rejoined 1997.